The Corporate Warriors

The Corporate Warriors

DOUGLAS K. RAMSEY

Houghton Mifflin Company

BOSTON

1987

Library of Congress Cataloging-in-Publication Data

Ramsey, Douglas K.
The corporate warriors.

Bibliography: p.
1. Competition — United States — Case studies.
2. Competition, International — Case studies.
3. Strategic planning — Case studies.   I. Title.
HD 41.R27   1987   338.8'3'0973   86-20954
ISBN 0-395-35487-0

Printed in the United States of America

P   10   9   8   7   6   5   4   3   2   1

For family and friends,
who put up with me
and the book these
past three years.

*War is a simple art: its essence
lies in its accomplishment.*
— Napoleon Bonaparte

Acknowledgments

To the dozens of chief executive officers and businessmen I've interviewed over the years; their names are too many to mention, but they all contributed, some wittingly, some not, to this author's perception of the right way — and the wrong way — to wage corporate war. To Gwen Edelman, my literary agent, for encouraging me to write *The Corporate Warriors* in the first place. To Nan Talese and Signe Warner at Houghton Mifflin for not losing faith in the project despite all the delays. To two of the most capable business reporters I know, for their help in researching this book: Cynthia Rigg on the People Express story and David Neustadt on General Motors. And finally, to Sun Tzu, the Chinese philosopher who, twenty-five hundred years after writing *The Art of War*, provided the spark for this book!

SPECIAL ACKNOWLEDGMENT

WILLIAM BURGER

Particular credit for *The Corporate Warriors* goes to Bill Burger, who collaborated with me from the start on this project. His commitment to its completion and success was unwavering. Bill, a writer at *Newsweek*, conducted many of the interviews for the chapters on Ted Turner, MCI, *Penthouse*, and Coca-Cola, and his insightful reporting helped bring added riches to those tales of corporate warfare.

Contents

Introduction

"WAR IS CAPITALISM with the gloves off." With that terse comment, the protagonist in Tom Stoppard's 1976 play, *Travesties*, provided an apt metaphor for business. Parallels between war and business have been drawn before, but never more frequently than in the lexicon of modern management. The corporate battlefield has become the site of takeover attacks and market penetration, price wars and sales skirmishes, poison pills and merger maneuvers. The language of war is now an established part of the corporate vernacular. But beyond the surface similarities are lessons for today's business executive in military strategy.

In short, business resembles nothing so much as war itself. For every major takeover battle, there are losing as well as winning sides; a territory may be a market share or one particular industry, and the competitor is the enemy. A company's success — even its survival — therefore depends on an amalgam of offensive and defensive strategies: frontal assaults, surprise attacks, propaganda (read advertising), intelligence gathering (market research), organization, and administration. These are just some of the elements on which war, military and corporate, is calculated, planned, and waged. It is on the strength of these elements, too, that commanders on the battleground or in the boardroom rise or fall, triumph or are vanquished.

The great military strategists and philosophers have said it all before, some of them centuries ago. There are crucial lessons for the executive in the writings of the great war thinkers, from Sun Tzu and Niccolò Machiavelli to Karl von Clausewitz and Ferdinand Foch. Blitzkrieg or scorched earth, encirclement or preemptive attack, strategic withdrawal or fortification: the prescriptions vary, but the theories and strategies, tested in military combat, are as applicable to the wars on Madison Avenue, Wall Street, and Main Street as they were to feudal China, Italy's city states, or the two world wars in this century.

For companies and for armies, the ultimate goal of conflict is the same — victory, in the marketplace or on the battlefield. As Clausewitz defined it, there are really two kinds of war, "one to overthrow the enemy, the other to gain land." Most corporate battles are of the second type, since few executives aim to destroy their competitors altogether. The goal is to "gain land" by winning new customers and securing larger shares of a given market. "Complete subjugation of the enemy," Clausewitz added, "is not essential in every case." The same is true in business.

The genesis of this book is traceable to my three-year stint as Far East correspondent for *The Economist*, the weekly magazine that my British colleagues insisted on calling a newspaper. Time after time, I was struck by the ability of Japanese businessmen up and down the corporate ladder to quote from Sun Tzu's *The Art of War*. Later, as business editor of *Newsweek* magazine, in conversations with American and European chief executives I ran across occasional references to Karl von Clausewitz's *On War*, published in the early 1800s, to explain strategies pursued by their corporations in the late 1900s. *On War*, which remains the most prominent single contribution to the shape of modern military strategy in Europe and the United States, sat prominently on the bookshelf of at least one executive interviewed by a researcher for this book. Along with the works of dozens of other philosophers and military commanders, these tomes argued the pre-eminence of strategy long before "strategic planning" became a buzz word in American M.B.A. programs.

The basic concept of war strategy varies little from one philosopher to the next. "There have existed in all times, fundamental principles on which depend good results in warfare," wrote Swiss philosopher Henri de Jomini. "These principles are unchanging, independent of the kind of weapons, historical place or time." Modern military science generally recognizes nine "principles" of strategy that are equally applicable to corporate conflict.

1. Maneuver: the need for flexibility, keeping options open to deploy troops, expand manufacturing, cut prices, and so on;
2. Objective: clearly defining the goal of combat, targeting where the company should be at the end of it;
3. Offense: attacking the enemy or competitor;
4. Surprise: Clausewitz called it "the foundation of all military undertakings";
5. Economy of force: mobilizing the fewest resources and personnel necessary to achieve the objective;
6. Mass: "Concentrate your strength" is the way Sun Tzu put it;
7. Unity of command: clear lines of authority extending from the commanding — or chief executive — officer;
8. Simplicity: what military officers summarize with the acronym KISS: *Keep It Simple, Stupid!*;
9. Security: maintaining secrecy and loyalty inside the military or corporate unit.

All nine principles recur throughout this book. Don Burr, the founder of People Express, demonstrated his strength of maneuver when his airline adopted a new route strategy to cope with the flight controllers' strike that threatened to kill the three-month-old airline in its infancy. Bob Guccione, the publisher of *Penthouse*, underscored the importance of mass in withholding London copies of his magazine until a full-scale attack on *Playboy* was possible with a U.S. edition. And without the security surrounding Coca-Cola's top-secret "Project Harvard," the launching of Diet Coke would probably not have gone as smoothly as it did.

Leadership is also crucial. Without it, Marshal Foch stated firmly, "No battle and no victory is possible." There is no single formula or character to define good leadership in the corporate context, but the executives profiled in the following pages are indisputably considered "leaders" by corporate America. That doesn't mean, however, that they are cut from the same mold.

Roger Smith is as low-key and self-effacing as Ted Turner and Guccione are brash, autocratic, and unconventional. The strategy and tactics that allowed Burr to build People Express in a matter of months would probably not have worked for MCI's Bill McGowan in his decade-long cat-and-mouse challenge to AT&T. Still, the executives examined here share some traits. All are strong, hands-on managers, in one case, to a fault: Burr may have ultimately lost his company, People Express, because he breached Foch's edict that "many fine generals try to keep an eye on too many things [and] end in impotence." All had their own visions for the companies they were building, or *re*building, in the case of General Motors and Coca-Cola. All got personally involved in mapping the strategies that were crucial to victory on the corporate battlefield. And all were blessed with what Foch called "the will to conquer . . . and a supreme resolve which the commander must, if need be, impart to the soldier's soul."

The corporate warriors you will meet also share a willingness, even eagerness, to take risks. "Great successes in war," wrote Karl von Moltke, "are not achieved without great risks." Time after time the bosses of MCI, *Penthouse*, People Express, and Turner Broadcasting bet their companies in order to make significant gains in the marketplace; time after time their companies emerged stronger and more powerful. Without strong leadership they may have foundered; without taking the risks none would have succeeded as spectacularly in the free market as each eventually did. These chief executives also share something that Winston Churchill defined as "legerdemain." "There is required for the composition of a great commander not only massive common sense and reasoning power," Churchill wrote in *The World Crisis 1915,* "not only imagination, but also an element of legerdemain, an original and sinister touch, which leaves the enemy puzzled as well as beaten."

Alliances also play a key role in corporate combat. As Bob Guccione proved by linking up with the highly respectable Times Mirror Publishing Company, a well-placed ally could lay the groundwork for a magazine invasion that *Penthouse* would have been unable to mount on its own. And MCI's linkup with

IBM would set the stage for competition with AT&T for the rest of the century. Corporations must know when and where to strike such alliances, and how to keep their allies from switching allegiances later in the game.

The battles recounted in the following pages focus on corporate and marketing strategy rather than the power struggles that typify takeover battles and management squabbles. *The Corporate Warriors* is about the struggle among companies for control of markets. In today's marketplace, however, it is not always clear which company is the aggressor, which the defender. Strategic lines are blurred. For most of the 1970s, Pepsi-Cola mounted a devastating and effective attack on Coca-Cola's market. When Coke finally woke up to the "Pepsi Challenge" and revised its strategy to meet that challenge, it went on the offensive. The strategy that let Pepsi lure new drinkers would not have worked for Coca-Cola when it wanted to get them back. Both companies were implementing offensive as well as defensive strategies at one and the same time — an almost perfect reflection of the competitive marketplace.

But is business really war? There are obviously limits to the personal damage acceptable in a business context. In war, death becomes an acceptable price to pay for victory. In business, companies may go bankrupt, but the individuals who suffer defeat are free to go to work for someone else. Defense may be an objective in itself for businesses, but it is considered tactical by most combat strategists, leading inevitably to an assumption of the offense. There is also a more stringent code of ethics in business, although the code is, admittedly, not always observed. In short, not every tactic that is acceptable in war is permissible in business. But within reason, the metaphor works, and provides basic training for business executives interested in obtaining the competitive edge shared by most of the successful strategists in corporate America.

Had I written a seventh chapter for this book, it would have been titled "Strategy vs. Tactics." At times it is difficult to see the forest from the trees, the bigger picture from the individual manager's direct "line of sight." Few of the leaders described sat down one day and mapped out a detailed strategy. Corporate leadership is an exercise in continual planning, frequent shifts in tactics, and periodic review of the direction and execution of strategic policies — and not by just one man. The French politician Talleyrand once insisted that "war is much too serious a thing to be left to military men." By the same token, business is much too serious a thing to be left to chief executive officers. The problem in condensing corporate history and strategy into a few dozen pages of narrative is that decisions arrived at by tens or hundreds of people must be attributed either to the amorphous "corporation" or the leader of that entity. As far as possible, I have attempted to distill — admittedly in hindsight — the essence of each company's strategic thinking, looking at it through the eyes of the man (in these cases, all happen to be male) in charge, the chief executive officer.

There are plenty of case studies in corporate conflict. Primarily, I have tried to be contemporary, focusing on market face-offs that are likely to persist into the 1990s and beyond. One key battle in that time frame is AT&T vs. IBM, as the deregulated telephone company moves into computers and the computer giant pushes into telecommunications. But as of this writing, neither company had defined and executed strategy to the extent that an outsider could assess which of them is likely to carry the day; that book remains to be written. A second cull of corporate candidates was for examples in industries that, for one reason or another, capture the interest and imagination of readers. That triage left a dozen or so prime examples of major, ongoing corporate battles, among them the cases recounted in this book as well as a handful of others: Miller vs. Anheuser-Busch in beer; Burger King vs. McDonald's in fast-food retailing, and so on. Most of them, interestingly, put down their roots in the last twenty years, for instance, People Express and Turner Broadcasting in the 1980s and *Penthouse* and MCI in the 1970s. It is ultimately the drama of each corporate battle and the presence of strong protagonists to "personify" each story that became a deciding factor in the battles chosen.

The quotations from military thinkers are included for a reason: to signal important changes in strategic thinking that reflect the wisdom derived from the writings of a Clausewitz or a Sun

Tzu. I have made no attempt to attribute specific lessons of military strategy to the decisions of companies and executives. True, several of the key players openly pay homage to the influence of military service in shaping the way they do business (Ted Turner), or to careful study of writings on military strategy. But it is doubtful that any of them thought about wartime analogies when it came to betting their companies — or their own careers — on a major strategic decision.

If the quotes on military strategy provide signposts, then the case studies represent a road map for corporate strategy — in this case, six corporate strategies — and the responses of the competition. The most important lesson in all six chapters is the same: the necessity to think and act strategically, or as Clausewitz put it, to fix "the point where, the time when, and the numerical force with which the battle is to be fought." That, in a nutshell, is the challenge facing all managers in modern business.

The Corporate Warriors

CHAPTER I

Captain Outrageous

TED TURNER VS. THE NETWORKS

"WE'RE ON a pirate ship at sea!" Ted Turner was emphatic, gesturing dramatically to the advertising salesmen sitting in no particular order around the room. Turner himself commanded attention: his salt-and-pepper hair and close-cropped mustache set off a leathery complexion that seemed five or ten years older than the trim and muscular body of the sportsman, who was still several months away from his fortieth birthday. Like Turner, most of the salesmen were clad in civvies — boots or sneakers, jeans, short-sleeved shirts. Most were setting foot on the grounds of Hope, Turner's five-thousand-acre plantation in South Carolina, for the first time. They were raw recruits, hand picked to spearhead a drive for national advertisers to buy time on his tiny Atlanta TV station, which was beginning to distribute its programming to stations around the country via satellite.

It was early in the summer of 1978, and the stations Turner had in his sights were in the cable industry. For years rural communities around the country had relied on cable systems to receive broadcast signals in areas not easily reached by over-the-air broadcasting. In the late 1970s, cable held out the promise of allowing TV viewers a much wider spectrum of programming. Cable could provide thirty, fifty, even a hundred

I

channels, and crystal-clear reception. Cable systems would "pass on" to viewers the signal of existing over-the-air stations, but the channel capacity meant that other suppliers of programs could obtain equal access to viewers hooked up to cable. As more and more cities around the country authorized the building of cable systems, Turner foresaw that cable could become a medium to reach millions of viewers nationwide.

Turner was not a cable system operator. He owned a small UHF station in Atlanta, WTCG, channel 17, which had such a weak signal that it couldn't always be seen even in Atlanta. But after winning the right to televise Atlanta Braves baseball games to the hometown over his channel, he had started sending the same broadcasts by cable to other stations around the South. It didn't take long before he realized that cable operators were hungry for new programming to put on their unused cable channels. If Turner could supply the channel 17 programs to stations outside the Atlanta area, he could cover his programming costs by charging cable operators for the service, and then make a profit by selling advertising.

Until now, Turner told his recruits, the three big broadcasting networks, ABC, CBS, and NBC, could count on booking billions of dollars in advertising every year because there was virtually no competition for their national TV dollars. But with the advent of national cable television, he exclaimed, stalking the room like a beast, the dawn of a new age in TV broadcasting would provide a golden opportunity to take some of that market away from the networks. Turner wouldn't let go of his pirate ship metaphor. "I'm your captain," he told the salesmen, still pacing the large living room that opened onto acres of sun-drenched green. "We're going to go out and raid all the other ships on the ocean. We want their advertising and we're going to get it."

It wasn't uncommon for Turner to cast himself in the role of the pirate captain. A keen yachtsman, he had won the America's Cup as captain of the *Courageous*, earning for himself a nickname that was as pertinent to his ambitions in the broadcasting industry as it was to his pursuits on the high seas, Captain Outrageous. Outrageously, he talked openly of beating the giant TV networks at their own game. Even admitting that he couldn't match their spending dollar for dollar on programming or building up a rival network, Turner believed that he could eventually challenge them. To do so, he would have to pick and choose his targets, settling for small victories, guerrilla-style.

Ted Turner also had the temperament of a guerrilla. To some, he was obnoxious, a bully. To others, he was a rascal, a gambler. Above all, he was combative, a survivor. Turner was expelled twice from Brown University, the second time for repeatedly breaching dormitory rules concerning women in the rooms.

In guerrilla warfare, small units acting independently play the principal role.

— Mao Ze-dong

Turner left Brown for good in 1960 to work for his father, Ed, a Mississippi native and salesman who had built up a small but flourishing billboard business in Atlanta. Three years later, Ed Turner committed suicide, barely days after arranging to sell the family business, Turner Outdoor Advertising. Ted had pretty much decided to make a career in the family business, and his future was threatened. Not surprisingly, he was vicious in his determination to stop the deal from going through. He refused to hand over the billboard leases that were part of the sale. He also threatened to burn the company's records, build competing billboards, and starve out his new competition, in the market and in the courts. He never had to live up to his threats. The would-be owners of Turner Outdoor Advertising dropped the deal in exchange for stock in the Turner billboard company — now *Ted* Turner's company, run by a twenty-four-year-old with no college degree and precious little business experience.

Profits from the billboards fueled Turner's push into an industry that had preoccupied him since childhood, broadcasting. Five years after taking control of Turner Outdoor Advertising, he bought an ailing AM radio station in Chattanooga and quickly added two more stations to his stable. But radio had never been his real ambition. He really wanted to own a TV station, but one of those typically cost five to ten times what he could pay. But in 1969, while still holding on to his radio outlets,

Turner found an affordable TV station: UHF (Ultra High Frequency) WJRJ, in Atlanta. Of the five stations serving Atlanta, channel 17 was the smallest. The other four were VHF (Very High Frequency) stations; in the 1960s, most TV sets were equipped to receive only the stronger VHF signal. So for Turner, it was a gamble. Channel 17, the only TV station he could afford, was the only one up for sale.

In January 1970 Turner paid $2.5 million for channel 17, changed its call letters to WTCG, and merged his billboard and TV holdings, becoming the controlling shareholder and renaming the entity Turner Communications. For the first time, Ted Turner was serving notice that he had ambitions to build his father's company into something much greater than a billboard advertising business. Just how great, Turner himself didn't know. Initially he wanted to expand the station's franchise in the Atlanta market, but he was already looking farther afield, to a regional network of stations throughout the South.

To that end, in early 1970 Turner asked his board of directors to approve the purchase of another UHF station, this one in Charlotte, North Carolina. The board refused. They were nervous because the networks had shied away from the weaker UHF signal, keeping most viewers in the habit of VHF viewing. Unperturbed, Turner dipped into his pocket and bought the Charlotte station on his own. He wouldn't forget the snub by his board of directors. He was used to running the company by fiat, and some of the holdover directors from the days when his father ran the company would eventually find themselves dropped from the board. Ted Turner was going to bet his company more than once, and he wasn't going to brook further opposition from within his own ranks.

By 1972 Turner had pulled off a major coup in the Atlanta market, outbidding his rivals for the rights to televise Atlanta Braves games to the hometown fans the following year. For the first time, Atlantans had to tune their sets to channel 17 on the UHF dial. And for the first time, local advertisers discovered the TV station that some considered a plaything for the youthful billboard operator. The Braves were also a draw in other parts of the South, and Turner began relaying his broadcast signal to other areas hooked up to cable. By 1975 nearly 400,000 cabled homes in parts of Georgia, Florida, Alabama, South Carolina, and Tennessee could watch the channel. Gradually non-cable stations joined in, and Turner created the Atlanta Braves Network, a loose collection of thirty-two TV stations throughout the Southeast, which bought local rights to use Turner's baseball broadcasts.

Turning channel 17 into a regional network was expensive. The UHF signal was hardly strong enough to cover the Atlanta market. To get it to other parts of the Southeast, it had to be relayed by telephone lines; in turn, cable stations would pass on the signal to subscribers over cable, and non-cable stations rebroadcast it over the air. All told, by 1975 transmission costs were running half a million dollars annually, making the business only marginally profitable. Turner knew he had to find a way to reduce the costs of distributing the Braves games around the Southeast. He also knew that if he was successful, channel 17 might be able to sign up cable systems in other parts of the country, especially in areas not served by a local major-league baseball franchise.

Turner saw the answer to his problem 22,300 miles above the earth. RCA had launched a revolutionary satellite, Satcom-1, which was equipped with transponders able to pick up and then re-send TV signals anywhere in the United States. One of America's media giants, Time Inc., was the first to book space on the satellite, embarking on a completely new technology to distribute movie programming to cable operators under the Home Box Office (HBO) banner. All they had to do was invest in satellite receiving dishes, "pull down" the HBO signal from Satcom-1, and send it along cables to their subscribers, who would pay extra for the exclusive service. Turner was amazed by the simplicity of the new technology. HBO was effectively creating a national TV network from scratch, and there was nothing to stop others with similar foresight from doing the same. The monopoly held by the three big broadcast networks, Turner told himself, was crumbling even more quickly than he had hoped.

Turner contacted RCA. For roughly $1 million a year, he was

told, he could lease one of Satcom-1's two dozen transponders and have channel 17's signal beamed down all over the United States. Since he was already paying a little over half that amount to send WTCG and the Atlanta Braves games around the Southeast alone by way of AT&T phone lines, the cost seemed minor, provided that Turner could sign up cable systems in other parts of the country to carry his Atlanta channel. Since most cable systems had unused channels available and were trying to provide a greater diversity of programming for their subscribers, Turner figured that the market was ready for a "national" cable service, carrying not just baseball games, but other fare as well, including news and movies.

Less than three months after contacting RCA, Turner applied to the Federal Communications Commission (FCC) in Washington to create a company to send the channel 17 signal up to a transponder Turner leased on Satcom-1. There were roadblocks ahead. The FCC had ruled that a broadcaster couldn't send a TV signal directly to a satellite. It had to be done through an independent contractor, called a common carrier in the industry. The objective was to prevent individual companies from having complete control over the origination, transmission, and ultimate showing of TV programming. Much as the major networks were limited to owning no more than seven TV stations at any one time, the FCC wanted to keep any single programmer from controlling new sources of programming.

The FCC also restricted cable systems in their choice of which independent TV stations that originated outside the local market they could carry. Under the rule, cable systems could select their quota of two or three nonlocal independent stations only from the nearest cities. Dubbed the leapfrogging rule, the regulation was designed to prevent the emergence of "super" stations, which would beam their signals to markets anywhere in the country, in short, just the sort of TV creature Turner had in mind for channel 17.

Fortunately for Turner, deregulation was soon to become the new catchword in Washington. In December 1976 the FCC lifted the leapfrogging rule. The same month, the agency granted a common-carrier license to Ed Taylor, a former Western Union executive who had helped Turner get into the satellite business. Taylor was now rewarded with a contract from Turner Communications to act as the common carrier between channel 17 and Turner's transponder on Satcom-1. The FCC also reduced the minimum size required for receiving dishes with which the cable operators received the broadcast signal from the satellite. New technology and cutting the dish size from thirty to fifteen feet in diameter also reduced the cost to cable stations by about 50 percent. With that, Turner knew he was in business: many cable stations had been reluctant to carry programming from outside their own local area because of the capital costs involved in satellite reception. Since cost was no longer a major obstacle, the cable operator could, by acquiring one satellite dish, pull down other programs transmitted over the same satellite as Turner's.

The new technology allowed Turner's Atlanta station to somersault into the ranks of national TV. On the evening of December 17, 1976, Turner began beaming channel 17's programming across the United States. Very few homes could actually pick up the "SuperStation" that evening. It would take time for cable operators to install their dishes and pass along the signal to local cable subscribers. But for Ted Turner it was one of the most critical turning points in television history. In an instant, a small Atlanta TV station was, in principle, available anywhere in the United States. Just like ABC or NBC or CBS. For the first time, Turner firmly believed, the networks were no longer invincible. The oligopoly in place since the dawn of TV broadcasting would never again be the same.

Two years after his SuperStation began its slow but steady push into cable homes around the country with channel 17's standard fare, Ted Turner became obsessed with news. Strong news departments were the hallmark of the major TV networks, lending a sense of purpose, credibility, and public service. Turner wasn't a news "junkie" and knew that news programming could never be a major moneymaker. But for any TV magnate with national aspirations, news programming was essential. He had toyed with the idea of creating an evening news program in Atlanta to go up against the main network newscasts, but without the financial resources to challenge the networks on their own ground, the effort was bound to flop. Instead, his thoughts turned to a strategy that was at once more expensive but less risky, and to Reese Schonfeld, a career news executive.

Schonfeld had first met Ted Turner in Washington four years earlier, in the fall of 1974. Schonfeld had made a name for himself producing programs that competed with the major TV networks. He set up a venture for United Press International called UPI Television News, which supplied mainly international news coverage to stations that didn't have the means to "cover" the world themselves. He also created a short-lived TV venture financed by beer magnate Joseph Coors to produce public-interest programming. At the time of his first meeting with Turner, Schonfeld was setting up the Independent Television News Association (ITNA), an early pioneer of satellite transmission to distribute TV news items to independent stations across the country. He had been asked by a mutual friend to brief the owner of channel 17 on the impact of satellite technology on TV distribution. Three years later, in late 1977, Schonfeld met Turner again, this time trying to sell ITNA's news service for use on the SuperStation. Turner wasn't buying, but the idea stuck.

Schonfeld had written off the SuperStation as a client when, twelve months later, he got a call from Turner and accepted Turner's offer to fly him down to Atlanta from New York. Turner wanted to meet again in person to discuss the possibility of starting something much grander than ITNA: a cable news channel that would cover the news on a live basis all day long, every day.

When Schonfeld arrived to meet Turner for only the third time, Turner's Atlanta headquarters had grown from a nondescript, two-story brick building on West Peachtree to include a large, decrepit white-frame house next door. Employees had named it the haunted house, and Schonfeld could see why. Partly because of the shabby state of Turner's existing premises, Schonfeld proposed that he headquarter the cable news channel in Washington, where the channel would have to maintain a substantial news-gathering operation anyway. "No," Turner insisted. "I want it in Atlanta, even if it costs me a couple million more. This is my home." As it was, Schonfeld had arrived in Atlanta armed with a preliminary budget indicating that it would cost approximately $14 million to launch the project. Turner didn't seem fazed by the sums, which surprised Schonfeld. He had presented virtually the same proposal to Time Inc.'s HBO subsidiary, which decided to hold off entering the news business because of the costs involved. But here, the Atlanta entrepreneur and broadcaster was effectively dismissing cost as an issue.

In fact, Turner was well aware that start-up costs for a cable news channel could bankrupt his company. Cable operator subscribers would be vital. If enough of them signed up for what Turner had christened CNN, Cable News Network, he'd be able to borrow enough money to launch the project. So on December 5 Turner made his pitch at the 1978 Western Cable Show in Anaheim, California. In a meeting with the board of directors of the National Cable Television Association (NCTA), Turner said he would need to sign up enough cable operators to place CNN in 7.5 million homes, over half of all cable homes. In return he would supply the service free of charge to the operators. The practice was virtually unheard of at the time. For his part, Turner figured that with a base of 7.5 million homes, he could make up his costs through advertising revenues.

Turner's proposal was bold, but the response was not, partly because it seemed too good to be true. Most of the big cable operators were unwilling to count on Turner to supply a quality service for nothing. It was one thing, they figured, for Turner to use satellite technology to supply them with the channel 17 diet of sports programs and reruns of 1960s sitcoms. But news programming was another issue. The big TV networks spent hundreds of millions on their thirty-minute evening news shows, while Turner was talking about providing the same quality twenty-four hours a day. Turner's reluctance to put serious news on his Atlanta station, even if it was for strictly financial reasons, raised serious questions about his personal commitment to news programming.

By the time the Western Cable Show disbanded, Turner had

lined up only 400,000 homes, nowhere near the figure he needed to make a go of CNN. Arriving back in Atlanta, Turner picked up the phone to call Schonfeld and break the bad news. "We'll do it some other time," he said optimistically. Schonfeld was disappointed, uncertain whether Turner was giving up on the project. In time, he would learn that Turner wasn't a quitter.

Despite the setback Turner was becoming an undisputed power in the infant cable industry. His SuperStation was reaching into nearly 3 million cable homes, only one in five of all cable homes in the United States but nearly triple the number a year earlier. Above all, advertising sales were starting to pick up, and the SuperStation depended exclusively on ads to make a profit. Beginning in the summer of 1978, Turner had begun beefing up his sales force, adding offices in New York and Chicago, followed later by Los Angeles and Detroit. By selling channel 17 as a national station to advertisers outside the Atlanta area, Turner figured he could start raising ad rates for all advertisers on his SuperStation. But progress was slow. National advertisers were reluctant to buy time on a national medium that didn't even register in the all-important Nielsen ratings. Local Atlanta advertisers also began to gripe at Turner's obvious attempt to ratchet upward his rates for thirty-second spots on channel 17.

Worried about undermining the local revenues that would continue to be necessary while the SuperStation was making its mark nationally, Turner had to find a way out of the bind. The solution turned out to be simple, if untested. Channel 17 would "split" its TV signal, sending different commercials up to Satcom-1 for the national market. Ed Taylor, Turner's common carrier, continued to pick up the signal in Douglasville, Georgia, about twenty-five miles west of Atlanta, "uplinking" it from there to the satellite. But now, instead of picking up the signal that went out from WTCG's broadcast tower, Taylor picked up a concentrated microwave signal beamed straight to Douglasville. All the programming was the same; only the commercials would be different. So the TV signal Taylor sent to Satcom-1 to be pulled down by local cable operators would contain advertising of broad national appeal, while Atlanta advertisers could continue to buy time on channel 17 to reach local viewers only.

Turner knew the risk involved in splitting the signal. With no Nielsen ratings for the SuperStation, national advertisers might refuse to sign up without at least the guarantee of reaching the Atlanta market. But in short order it was clear that advertisers weren't insisting on ratings in the traditional sense. Toyota, the sole auto advertiser for Turner's Atlanta Braves games on channel 17, immediately signed up for the national feed. Nestlé and Kellogg followed suit. In less than a year, Turner had signed up seventy-five national accounts for the SuperStation, most of them under multiyear contracts that ran as long as five years. That first year, ad revenues jumped by more than $5 million. Turner was beginning to amass the cash flow he'd need to expand his presence in TV, and to add a basketball team, the Atlanta Hawks, to his empire.

Turner was in a position to resurrect plans for a cable news network, and a severe personal blow pushed him into action. On May 6, 1979, Atlanta Braves general manager Bill Lucas, the only black running a major-league ball club and a close friend of Turner's, died of a heart attack. (Turner later appointed Lucas's widow to his company's board of directors.) Significantly, Lucas, only forty-three, was less than three years older than Turner, whom Lucas's death seemed to catalyze. Within forty-eight hours Turner called Reese Schonfeld about the news project they'd left on the shelf six months earlier. "Nobody lives forever," Turner began. "Let's do it." Years later, Turner couldn't recall the conversation, but he acknowledged that the death of his friend may have played a part in his decision to give CNN the green light.

The day of Lucas's funeral, Schonfeld met with Turner at his office at Fulton County Stadium, home of the Braves. Turner promised Schonfeld complete editorial control over CNN and authorized him to start pulling a staff together immediately. He also told him not to worry about the business side. SuperStation ad sales were expanding and the sales force was in a good position to go after many of the same advertisers to air commercials on CNN. This time, Turner told Schonfeld, he wouldn't let naysayers in the industry deter him. At a Las Vegas industry convention in June, Turner wouldn't be looking for advance sign-ups; he would simply tell cable operators that CNN would be on the air a year later, and those who didn't sign up for the service would be sorry.

Turner knew he had to do more than talk tough. He needed to project the appearance of being as strong as his rhetoric; if he didn't, others in the industry would conclude that he was promising more than he could deliver. A lot of the skepticism centered on his ability, or inability, to sustain a quality news network over the long haul, so he needed Reese Schonfeld badly. Schonfeld had a proven track record in TV news, and he could also draw top names from the news business itself to give CNN the credibility that Turner still lacked. CNN would also need an on-camera "star" for the announcement in Las Vegas, and Schonfeld immediately called Richard Leibner in New York. Leibner was the consummate agent. As chairman of N. S. Bienstock, Leibner, more than any other agent, was responsible for sending TV news salaries into the stratosphere; he represented most of the top talent at CBS, among them Dan Rather. Few network or local executives would fill slots without first checking Leibner's client roster. Schonfeld made it clear that Turner needed a big name, and he needed one immediately. That narrowed the list, because few of Leibner's clients could get out quickly from contracts, and even fewer were unemployed. There was one exception: Daniel Schorr.

Dan Schorr had been out of network television for nearly three years, and the sixty-two-year-old veteran CBS correspondent hadn't expected to go back into daily TV news. Network executives shunned the man who, in 1976, had become embroiled in a controversy over his role in the publication of a confidential congressional study on past CIA abuses. While suspended at CBS, Schorr also criticized the network for its kid-gloves handling of Richard Nixon's resignation. Schorr charged it was a quid pro quo for future concessions from the FCC, which regulates the broadcast industry. The correspondent's renegade behavior attracted enormous media attention, and despite his reputation as one of Washington's best TV newsmen, Schorr was widely seen as too hot to handle by any of the networks. CBS agreed to a generous severance package, on the condition that Schorr stay off TV through 1978, which he did. Meanwhile, he kept busy in other media. He wrote a book, *Clearing the Air*, about his experiences at CBS, he wrote a syndicated newspaper column, and he broadcast regular radio commentaries on National Public Radio. Then in 1979, freed of his commitment to CBS, Schorr began doing commentaries for Reese Schonfeld's Independent Network News three times a week.

Keeping busy and working a lot of the time out of his Georgetown home in Washington, Schorr was surprised on May 18, a Friday, by a call from his long-time agent, Leibner.

"Do ya know who Ted Turner is?" the agent asked.

"Sure," Schorr shot back. "*Time* had a piece on him just a few weeks back."

In fact, Turner regularly cropped up in the TV industry's bible, *Broadcasting*, the Mouth of the South relentlessly talking up the future of cable TV. But like most newsmen, Schorr had never taken Turner seriously. No one at the networks did.

"Well," Leibner continued, "he's planning to start an all-news channel on cable TV, and he's interested in talking to you about it."

Schorr paused. "Should I be interested?"

"I think it's worth looking into," Leibner replied. "He seems pretty serious about it and he's talking about putting up a lot of money."

"What does he want out of me?" Schorr asked.

Leibner replied that Turner wanted Schorr to be his chief correspondent in Washington. After a flurry of calls between Leibner and Turner, and then Leibner and Schorr, the former CBS correspondent agreed to fly, over the weekend, to Las Vegas from Los Angeles, where he was set to give a speech on Sunday. Turner would pick up the tab, and they'd have plenty of time to talk before a scheduled press conference Turner wanted to hold at four in the afternoon. Turner was secure that Schorr would accept his offer. In his own mind, the TV magnate was irrevocably committed to the news channel. If Schorr balked, Turner would announce the new service anyway. He wouldn't turn back. It had become a rule of law with Turner after CNN was first shot down: never turn back. When it came to new ventures, Turner Broadcasting had to lead. The cable industry would inevitably follow.

Because Schonfeld and Schorr essentially worked for the same organization, ITNA, Schonfeld entered the picture only after Schorr agreed to meet Turner in Las Vegas. He called Schorr directly and told him that he, Schonfeld, would be running CNN. Schorr was relieved, but still uncertain about signing on with someone as mercurial as Ted Turner. Schonfeld said he wanted to see Schorr before Turner got to him on Monday, so they agreed to fly from New York to Los Angeles together. For several hours on the plane and later at the Beverly Hilton, where Schorr was staying, the two newsmen talked about Turner and his vision of a news channel that never went off the air. Schonfeld dissipated some of Schorr's concerns that the concept was even viable, then offered Schorr the job Turner wanted him for, Washington bureau chief.

Schorr said no. "I don't consider myself a very good administrator," he told Schonfeld. "And there's nothing I hate more than signing other people's expense accounts."

"All right," Schonfeld conceded. "We'll call you chief correspondent."

Again Schorr backed away. "Really, Reese, I don't like the 'chief' term at all. If it's all the same to you, just call me senior correspondent."

Schorr was beginning to feel the lure of the CNN assignment, but he was also worried about committing himself to making a success of the organization itself. He was interested in a relatively flexible assignment that would allow him to report and do his own commentaries, without taking responsibility for either the Washington bureau or any other part of the CNN organization. The brouhaha at CBS had hurt Schorr's image among network TV executives, and if CNN failed, Schorr felt, he didn't want his reputation tarnished with the public as well.

The next morning Schorr left L.A. to meet the man who might soon be his new boss. Just before ten on Monday morning, Schorr rode an elevator up to Ted Turner's suite at the Las

Vegas Hilton. Schonfeld was already there. So was Terence McGuirk, a trusted aide still in his twenties who had already worked for Turner for seven years. McGuirk was affable; Schorr had a harder time figuring out Turner. At first glance he was everything Schorr had expected: crass, boisterous, full of himself. In Schorr's experience, even at CBS, network executives tended to be overly courteous, refined, very businesslike. Turner had none of those traits. Can this man, Schorr thought to himself, really hold his own in the TV news business? Schorr decided not to answer the question. Instead, he focused on the substance of Turner's history in news.

"You're on the record as anti-news," Schorr charged. "You put news on at three in the morning in Atlanta. Your anchorman once read the news with a picture of Walter Cronkite over his face. And now you're telling me you want to do serious news?"

Turner was unrepentant. He knew he needed Schorr, but he wasn't about to apologize. "What I do on that channel has nothing to do with this," he replied. "That's there, this is here. Cable News Network will be a serious news operation. We're going first class."

At least his concerns had been aired, Schorr thought, and Schonfeld seemed convinced that Turner meant business and had the financial backing to deliver on his promise. In short order, he got down to what Turner wanted out of him. "There are a few things I need to know," Schorr continued. "First, do you expect me to read commercials on the air?"

"No," Turner answered flatly.

"What about mentioning sponsors of programs or teasing commercials?"

Again Turner replied with an emphatic no and continued, "Listen. Let's make this easy. You go with Terry and you two write a contract that satisfies you. You put whatever you want in there and you've got it. How does that sound?"

Surprised at the speed with which Turner was willing to make a decision that would have taken months at any of the big networks, Schorr was impressed. "I can hardly argue with that."

By three that afternoon, Schorr and McGuirk had hammered out a one-page agreement that would suffice until both sides'

lawyers and Schorr's agent could add the finishing touches. The
document contained a clause allowing Schorr to refuse any assignment that in any way conflicted with his personal standards
or ethics. Schorr had nothing to object to. Turner was handing
him editorial carte blanche with a salary 10 percent higher than
his top pay at CBS. He would also receive a retainer of half his
future salary for the year or so leading up to CNN's launch date
while continuing to earn a living from his newspaper column
and radio commentaries.

Turner read the contract once, nodded his approval, and
headed off to his four o'clock press conference with Schorr,
Schonfeld, and McGuirk in tow.

Approaching the conference room where a couple of dozen
members of the trade press were gathering, the importance of
the occasion began to sink in. "Okay," Schorr muttered audibly,
"here I go, gambling a lifelong reputation."

Without breaking stride, Turner turned to his new senior
correspondent. "You're gambling a reputation," he said, a trace
of bravado in his voice. "I'm gambling $100 million!"

CNN was certainly a gamble. Turner was convinced that the
twenty-four-hour news operation was feasible and would provide a platform from which to challenge the networks that dominated the American news business. Ever the guerrilla, Turner
was targeting a single, albeit significant, area of programming
for the networks, and he was doing it from a position of
strength. Almost by definition, a round-the-clock news channel
could always have an edge on the networks, whose primary
function was to deliver prime-time entertainment programming.
For years news executives had tried to expand the nightly news
from thirty to sixty minutes, to no avail. Local affiliates counted
on the rest of prime-time access to air their own local news as
well as syndicated entertainment shows, all of which accounted
for a major portion of their advertising revenues. By contrast, affiliates don't get a cut of revenues for network news programs,
so it was never in their interest to see the broadcasts expanded
beyond thirty minutes. Now Turner would have twenty-four
hours a day to explore the issues, talk with newsmakers, provide

live coverage of breaking news stories — the works. He was putting his house in order. With the SuperStation, he would make money. With CNN, he stood to gain something far more essential in his long-run battle for a premier position in American broadcasting: respectability.

Turner knew that the vital center of each major network was its news operation. Now he was ready to strike, and he expected his CNN announcement to come as a surprise to executives at all three networks. In fact, it was more than that, "a shock," one CBS insider remembered. There had been rumors around for months that Turner wanted to get into the news business, but was he really going to spend tens of millions of dollars on an operation that would never shut down? By network standards, they figured, Turner could hardly run the operation *two* hours a day, much less twenty-four, on the budget he seemed to be forecasting. And why were Reese Schonfeld and Daniel Schorr getting involved with a crackpot Southern entrepreneur with delusions of grandeur? The questions went unanswered.

> *The hostile main army in the field is a false objective, and the real objectives are the vital centers.*
>
> — General William Mitchell

CBS's imposing headquarters on Sixth Avenue in Manhattan had a nickname, Black Rock. The ebony-colored, stone and tinted glass skyscraper seemed an unlikely target for Turner. Like the building itself, CBS appeared impenetrable. Officially CBS welcomed the presence of an all-day, all-night news channel. But inside the network, as well as inside ABC and NBC headquarters down Sixth Avenue in either direction, Turner's planned venture was dismissed out of hand — either it wouldn't get off the ground or, if it did, CNN wouldn't last for long. The programming would fall short of network standards and fail to attract viewers, or the venture would collapse when Turner ran out of money.

To show the networks and the public that his operation was more than just a small Atlanta station, Ted Turner decided to restructure his whole organization to take into account the fact that it was more than just a small Atlanta station. In August 1979 he renamed it the Turner Broadcasting System, used the company's acronym for new call letters, and channel 17 became WTBS. Since 1974 Turner had sold off the radio stations and billboard units that once fueled the company's growth. Most of the proceeds went to shareholders in return for their shares in the parent company, further consolidating Ted Turner's standing as the single largest shareholder. Combined with a steady policy of buying back shares from smaller investors in yearly tender offers, the repurchases allowed Turner to boost his holdings in the company to 87 percent. With CNN in the works, Turner wanted to escape even the slightest interference from the board of directors or edgy shareholders who would be afraid of the losses that were bound to pile up before CNN turned the corner into profitability.

Only days after Turner announced his company's new name, the entire organization was in jeopardy. TBS employees were left wondering whether there would be any company at all. Hurricane-strength winds and forty-foot waves turned the annual 605-mile Fastnet race off England's southern coast into a nightmare; some thirty yachts were abandoned or sunk and eighteen men drowned. Turner, sailing his sixty-one-foot *Tenacious* with a twenty-man crew that included his eldest son, Teddy, was reported missing. The wire services began barraging Turner's office in Atlanta with requests for biographical information as they began working up obituaries. For most of a day, Turner's secretary, Dee Woods, was on the line to officials in Plymouth, the finish line for the Fastnet race, but no one could tell her anything. Then the phone rang, and Turner's voice came through loud and clear, and curiously casual after the tempest. "Dee?" he asked in his usual drawl. "This is Ted. How are ya?" Not only had Turner and the *Tenacious* finished the race, they had won it, finishing so quickly that some observers had missed the winner completely in the pandemonium.

When Turner won the America's Cup in 1977 aboard the *Courageous*, after failing to reach the finals in 1974, it was a tribute to his tenacity. After Fastnet, Turner seemed both tenacious and courageous. Above all, though, he was obsessed with winning, even against the odds. If any of his business rivals doubted Ted Turner's ability to persevere and prevail before the Fastnet race, his victory should have erased most of those doubts.

The Fastnet race was also a curious reminder to the folks back in Atlanta that, to a large extent, WTBS and the forthcoming CNN were creatures of Ted Turner. Almost no one believed that they could survive, much less prosper, without him. The force of Turner's renegade personality and unbridled ambition as much as anything else would make, or break, the assault on the networks. "Lead, follow, or get out of the way," Turner was fond of saying. Ultimately Turner's leadership more than his money would determine the fate of TBS. At Fastnet, Turner not only proved he could pull through, he again proved, as he had in 1977, that he could beat the competition. It was a crucial moment for the whole Turner organization. For those brief, scary hours during the Fastnet race, the employees had tasted the vulnerability of working in an organization dominated by one man. But they had also sampled the euphoria of winning — vicariously, admittedly, but winning nonetheless. Victory in their battle with the big TV networks seemed possible. What Turner had done off the southern English coast, he and his crew could do in TV-land.

The awe and praise that characterized the publicity surrounding Turner in the wake of Fastnet may have made it easier to proceed with one of the most critical phases in the CNN project, hiring top-flight people to staff the news channel. Reese Schonfeld began recruiting the six hundred to seven hundred people required to get CNN on the air. If network executives were confident that Turner couldn't challenge their supremacy in news, they wouldn't be for long. At first they didn't worry about defections from network news divisions. Schorr, after all, had been persona non grata at the networks since severing his links with CBS. And when Schonfeld hired a deputy to take on the administrative chores at CNN, he picked Burt Reinhardt, another veteran of non-network news, who had worked with Fox Movietone News, UPI Television News, and most recently, Paramount Pictures. These choices convinced network executives that Turner would have a hard time recruiting top talent in TV. But soon Ted Turner was rumored to be dangling lucrative contracts in front of key personnel. He was out to buy — some said "steal" — the best people he could get away from the networks.

Turner knew he couldn't put CNN on a par with the network organizations without an insider's knowledge of TV news. He had also been astonished at the publicity and critical acclaim surrounding Dan Schorr's "defection" to CNN, with newspaper reviewers almost over-

> *Know thy enemy; your victory will never be endangered.*
> — Sun Tzu

night vesting a surprising amount of confidence in CNN's editorial product. So right from the start, he and Schonfeld began a concerted effort to raid the networks of quality people. The task wasn't easy because the top people were reticent to ditch guaranteed jobs and tenure for uncertain benefits in a start-up venture that Ted Turner could torpedo at the first sign of big losses. All Turner could offer was involvement in an unprecedented undertaking in TV news. Most of the network executives he approached said no; a few said yes.

First on board was Jim Kitchell, the original director of the *Huntley-Brinkley Report* and a veteran of twenty-nine years at NBC. Kitchell became CNN's head of operations. Then came Sam Zelman, who had been at CBS for twenty years. Zelman had been a bureau chief in Saigon, a producer at *60 Minutes*, executive producer of the network's 1968 election coverage, and the head of news for CBS's five "O and O's," its owned and operated stations in New York, Los Angeles, Philadelphia, Chicago, and Boston. At CNN Zelman would be in charge of hiring the anchors and bureau correspondents to determine the news channel's on-air "personality." In time Zelman raided the ranks of ABC News for some of his top talent. ABC's Washington bureau chief, George Watson, agreed to assume the same job at CNN, and three veteran ABC correspondents, Don Farmer, Bernard Shaw, and Bill Zimmerman, made the switch, too. They were all looking for more "air" time, the exposure that could be counted in seconds and minutes because nightly newscasts were limited to twenty-two minutes. The correspondents were also tempted by the chance to get in on the ground floor of the first-ever all-news TV channel.

On the corporate side, two CBS alumni came on board. One was Robert Wussler, a former president of CBS Television and CBS Sports. Wussler was fired by the network in 1978, although he continued to work as a CBS consultant. He had a reputation for being a no-nonsense, somewhat nasty broadcasting executive who got things done. Like Turner, he was temperamental, so most insiders gave him six months before a falling-out with the boss. The other CBS veteran was Ed Turner, no relation to Ted. He had produced the *CBS Morning News* in the mid seventies, then quit the network to head up Metromedia's news division.

The team that Turner put together had an impressive list of credentials. The raids on network personnel hadn't deprived ABC, CBS, or NBC of any key personnel, but Turner had the people he wanted, renegades. And most of them were motivated the way Turner wanted them to be motivated. Having been passed over, pushed aside, or simply fired by a network, they were out to "show" their former employers. The consensus among their former network colleagues was that no one could air "network"-quality news twenty-four hours a day. Turner's maverick newsmen knew that CNN was a gamble, but the payoff would be sweet if the new channel could break up the networks' grip on TV news. The pioneers wouldn't necessarily make more money at CNN, although several got nominal pay increases from their network assignments. The real payoff would be the psychic reward.

If the hiring phase seemed to be proceeding without a hitch, the technological build-up hit a major one. On December 6, NASA launched a rocket carrying a new TV satellite into space. Like Satcom-1, which it was supposed to replace eventually, Satcom-3 was owned by RCA, and Turner had reserved a twenty-four-hour transponder on the new "bird" for CNN. That night Jim Kitchell called a special NASA phone number, listened to the countdown and clockwork launch, and went to bed convinced that CNN's final technical obstacle was behind it. Within seventy-two hours, the obstacle was back, larger than ever. The bird was lost in space.

Ted Turner first heard the news from Terry McGuirk. He'd just arrived in his hotel suite in Anaheim for the Western Cable Show. "There's still a chance they may find it," McGuirk speculated. "But it doesn't look good." CNN, scheduled to go on the air in just six months and twenty-one days, had no satellite. Satcom-3 had vanished from NASA's tracking screens, Turner confirmed to reporters, but CNN would go on the air anyway, even if it meant broadcasting from a different satellite. He kept up the pretense of confidence for nearly forty-eight hours. Privately, Ted Turner was worried. The reverse threatened to kill CNN in its infancy.

Worry turned to anger. In February RCA called a meeting of Satcom-3 leaseholders. The company offered all of them space on another satellite, Comstar D-2. Turner knew that CNN couldn't beam down from the Comstar bird. Most cable operators used only one receiving dish, and it was pointed at the main satellite, Satcom-1, used by such cable programmers as HBO. To receive CNN from Comstar, cable systems would have to buy new dishes just to receive the news channel, and Turner was convinced that none of them would be willing to foot the extra bill. In short, CNN had to be available on Satcom-1 or it couldn't make it. Yet, according to RCA, there were no empty transponders on the existing cable satellite. McGuirk, who represented Turner at the meeting, bristled, because he knew for a fact that there were two vacant transponders on Satcom-1. He got through to Turner in Nassau, where his boss had just finished a race from Miami.

"Ted, you've got to get up here right away," McGuirk insisted. "RCA doesn't want to give us a space on Satcom-1. They're talking about putting us on Comstar."

"Set up a meeting for Tuesday morning," Turner ordered.

He didn't have to say more. McGuirk knew Turner was angry. In short order, the folks at RCA would know it, too.

With CNN's very existence at stake, Turner knew he had to resort to the same sort of tactics he had used to prevent the sale of his father's billboard business. He would have to threaten anything and everything short of divine retribution in an effort to cajole RCA into reconsidering its position. It was common knowledge that RCA was reluctant to allocate an available Satcom-1 transponder to CNN, and in the absence of a prior legal commitment, RCA might well stand firm in its re-

> *Maneuvers ... are threats. He who appears most threatening wins.*
>
> — Ardant du Picq

fusal. Turner knew that the only way he could reverse RCA's position was to make it more expensive for the company to stick to its guns than to meet his demands.

In RCA's law library high above New York's Rockefeller Plaza, Turner and McGuirk sat down with RCA general counsel Andrew Ingles and a platoon of other RCA executives and lawyers. The mood was as dark as the stained panels on the walls. Ingles opened the meeting, assuring Turner that he could put CNN on the air in June 1980, four months later, but that Satcom-1 was all booked up, so it would have to be over the limited Comstar D-2.

Worried that RCA might be trying to kill off a potential competitor for its NBC subsidiary, Turner erupted. "I'm going to sue your ass, buddy."

The expletive had its desired effect; the RCA executives were stunned.

Turner went on. "I've spent $35 million already, and I'll be damned if I'm going to let a punk like you stick me on some God-forsaken Comstar satellite. You know damn well that no cable system in the country has a dish pointed at that thing. I have got to be on Satcom, and that's where you're going to put me. Because if you don't, I'll haul you into court and tear you apart." Out of his chair now, stalking the room while wagging his finger at the RCA people, Turner vowed to fight them to the end. "I may lose this whole thing, but I'll bleed you guys to death. Your chairman had better know what you're telling me here today, because if he doesn't, you're going to be out of a job." Turner was getting personal; having threatened their jobs, he had to threaten RCA itself. "I'll make so much trouble for you that your stock's going to go through the floor."

"Mr. Turner," Andy Ingles began. Dazed and taken aback by Turner's vehemence and decibel level, the RCA executive said he'd see what he could do. Turner had guessed right. The decision to put CNN on Comstar had not been made by the board of directors. It was clear that trouble was brewing, and Ingles needed to cover himself. If RCA wanted to get into a costly legal fight with Turner, so be it. But he didn't want to make that decision.

Back in Atlanta, McGuirk went through all the papers in the RCA file. He came across a 1976 contract with RCA that gave Turner a right of first refusal for an RCA transponder as partial payment for RCA's purchase of a large earth station north of Atlanta owned by Turner. Turner's lawyers promptly notified RCA that they wanted to exercise that option for a transponder on Satcom-1. The case wasn't open-and-shut, but RCA executives knew that it would give Turner an edge in court. In early March they called a truce, signing a judicial consent order that forced RCA to give Turner a Satcom-1 transponder for 180 days, starting June 1, 1980. CNN was back in business. Turner never blinked in his showdown with RCA.

That didn't mean he wouldn't back down if the project's future was on the line. That became apparent in a dispute that soon flared up between Turner and Bristol-Myers. Turner had been talking with the big pharmaceutical company for months about a $25 million advance commitment to sponsor medical news on CNN over ten years. But barely an hour before the two sides were supposed to announce their deal to a press conference at a cable convention in Anaheim, the talks broke down. Bristol had made its final offer, and Turner rejected the price Bristol was willing to pay for commercials as too low. Exasperated, the pharmaceutical executives walked out, leaving Turner to call off the press conference — and explain why. Bristol-Myers vice president Marvin Koslow had to all intents and purposes called Turner's bluff.

Turner turned to CNN's chief advertising salesman, Gerald Hogan. "Should we go along with them on this one?"

Hogan bristled. "I'm not sure it's worth it."

"I know," Turner said, "but we've got to do it. We need this deal. We'll try to make up for it later. Let's get them back in here."

Hogan took the elevator to the lobby; the Bristol-Myers team was getting ready to leave. "Let's go back up there," he said. "I think we've got a deal."

Back in the negotiating room, Turner and Koslow shook hands. There was no time to write a contract. The two men signed a blank piece of paper, then trekked down to the conference room where reporters were waiting. Waving the dummy contract in the air, Turner proudly announced the deal. Turner had met his match in Koslow. It was a strategic retreat. CNN needed something to show it meant business, and now the news channel had its first advertiser.

But to get CNN on the air, Ted Turner needed more than ad contracts. He needed as much as $30 million, and possibly more, if advertising sales didn't take off immediately. Some of the money could be squeezed from the cash flow of his profitable SuperStation. But Turner intended to foot most of the CNN start-up bill with $20 million from the anticipated sale of his TV station in Charlotte. Westinghouse, through its cable-and-communications subsidiary, Group W, agreed to buy the Charlotte outlet in the spring of 1979, but nearly a year after the original deal, the transaction was in limbo. A coalition of minority groups was challenging the station's license, telling the FCC that Turner's station was not complying with minority hiring regulations. Talks between Turner and the FCC dragged on for months, and Westinghouse insisted that the deal was off until the licensing problem was resolved. Finally, on April 9, Turner arrived in Charlotte with Henry Aaron, the former Atlanta Braves star who had broken Babe Ruth's record for career home runs. Turner asked Aaron to come because the ex-ballplayer had high visibility among local minority groups, and he could help sell leaders of the minority coalition on a compromise to push the sale through. The tactic worked, but not until Turner agreed to a list of substantial concessions. In exchange, the group agreed to drop its opposition to the license renewal. A few weeks later, the FCC approved the sale, and Turner had the $20 million seed money he needed to start CNN.

The initial financing was in place, but Turner was still having trouble signing up cable systems to carry the service. The previous autumn he had emphatically claimed that CNN would be going into 3.5 million cabled homes by June 1, a respectable audience for the advertisers he was pitching. By April, however, cable systems representing only 1.2 million homes were under contract to CNN, with barely eight weeks to go before its scheduled debut. He couldn't attract customers by threatening, his maneuver in other situations. His salespeople were beginning to sense a lack of confidence on the part of potential advertisers that CNN could meet its original goal, and a few advertisers that *had* bought time on CNN in advance were beginning to review their commitments. Turner's response was to keep promising that CNN would meet its 3.5 million–home goal.

In a memo to the advertising sales staff, the head of advertising for Turner Broadcasting, Don Lachowski, spoke for Turner. "Our position has to be that CNN will *average* 3.5 million homes between June 1 and December 31, 1980," Lachowski stated. "[We] will have four million CNN households by the end of the year, so we should have no problem in meeting the 3.5 million average for the seven months — or come so close that it won't be a problem with the advertisers."

Turner was toughing it out, bluffing again. He had no idea whether CNN could sign up four million homes by the end of the year. In fact, it looked unlikely. Many existing cable systems carried only twelve channels, all of them booked up with local network and independent channels, basic cable networks such as Turner's own SuperStation, and pay channels such as HBO. For these systems, operators couldn't take CNN even if they wanted to. Those that *could* open up a channel for CNN, moreover, wanted to see the news network operating first. Finally, and perhaps most important, CNN wasn't cheap. Originally Turner had proposed to provide the service free of charge, to entice new cable operators to CNN. But when it became clear that he would be unable to get CNN into enough homes fast enough to attract the big ad dollars that would be his main source of revenue, he relented. Cable systems that already were carrying WTBS would have to pay fifteen cents per subscriber per month for CNN, those that weren't, twenty cents. If a cable system charged its subscribers a monthly fee for CNN beyond the "basic" monthly cable fee, CNN would in turn charge the cable organization more for the service. The end result was a system to guarantee Turner a cut out of every subscriber's cable fee.

By the last week of May, CNN's news team was doing dry-run rehearsals that Turner taped and brought with him as a sales and promotional tool to the 1980 National Cable Television Association annual meeting in Dallas. On the eve of CNN's launch, he had just under two million homes under contract to carry the service. He also had eleven advertisers, but all the advertisers together had committed only $1.15 million for the remaining seven months of 1980. According to Turner's own estimate, that would cover only half of CNN's operating expenses for a *single month*. The losses would be huge, and the $20 million Turner earned from the sale of his TV station in Charlotte would barely last the first year. Turner knew he could raise loans by pledging more of the company's assets, but CNN needed a major boost in ad revenues, which would now depend on the untested product itself, the all-day news channel that some network executives and trade journalists had taken derisively to calling in advance Chicken Noodle News.

Three huge yellow-and-white-striped tents covered the lawn in front of Turner's new headquarters. It was the first Sunday in June, and hundreds of invited guests mingled, helping themselves to the platters of paté, boiled shrimp, and barbecued tenderloin. Dressed in a worn blue blazer and rumpled gray slacks, Ted Turner worked the crowd as other CNN staffers treated small groups of guests to a tour of the sleek facility. At 5:30, the tours ended, and Turner officially introduced the CNN team. At 6:00, the cameras focused on CNN's anchor team.

"Good evening, I'm Dave Walker."

"And I'm Lois Hart. Now here's the news."

So it began. "We're gonna stay on until the end of the world," Turner had said earlier, with typical hyperbole. "And when that day comes, we'll cover it, play 'Nearer My God to Thee,' and sign off."

They led the news that day with an update on the Vernon Jordan shooting in Indiana, then cut to a commercial for Bristol-Myers's Maalox Plus. Then came a second commercial, for Nestea, which was promptly interrupted by the news department to go back to Fort Wayne for live coverage of President Carter's arrival for a visit with the hospitalized Jordan.

There it was: *live* coverage, the type of news reporting that was impossible in print and almost never done by the big broadcasting networks. To a large extent, the networks *couldn't* do what CNN was embarking on. Although they ran their news departments all day, every day, the networks were confined in the number of hours of programming they could produce and air each day — early morning programs, occasional news "breaks" during the day, a thirty-minute evening newscast, and for some, late-night programming. The networks, Turner knew, were masters of digesting the news. They had the money and the time to preproduce news programs, going live only for major news stories like the attempted assassination of Ronald Reagan, space shots, and the like. Turner saw that ability to digest the news as negative: the networks would screen the news through a filter of bias, a liberal, Eastern bias. The great strength of CNN, he agreed from the start with Reese Schonfeld, would be that viewers could get more of their news free of any network bias. Their programming, by definition, would provide viewers with a more immediate, less sanitized view of all the day's news. It would also allow CNN to explore in greater depth issues that were too complex or too touchy or too lengthy to be handled effectively in the shorter network newscasts.

That first summer Schonfeld pulled out all the stops to maximize CNN's ability to go live on a breaking story. The cable channel provided credible, gavel-to-gavel coverage of the 1980 Democratic and Republican conventions, competing with the best political reporting teams at CBS, NBC, and ABC. Schonfeld also took every chance he could to latch on to a story and provide running coverage throughout the day. In September a Titan missile exploded in Arkansas, tossing its nuclear warhead several hundred feet away into a cow pasture. CNN rented a flatbed truck to get an earth station to the scene so correspon-

dent James Allen Miklaszewski could broadcast live every fifteen or thirty minutes. Even after the air force denied that the
missile had been armed, CNN stuck with the story, giving
viewers a play-by-play account of the air force's efforts to deal
with the warhead. When air force officials tried to obstruct reporters' view of the site, CNN rented a cherrypicker to lift a
cameraman fifty feet above the ground, giving him a clear shot.
The broadcast networks would handle the story in ninety seconds or so on the evening news; CNN could keep viewers tuned
in, telling the running tale as it unfolded. It was an early, telling
sign that Turner's news channel could provide serious, in-depth
coverage and turn the liability of its high cost into an asset.

If Turner was convinced that he could capitalize on that asset,
his main banker wasn't. Worried at the size of CNN's losses,
First Chicago decided to call in Turner's $12 million line of
credit. Turner would have to find new financing quickly if he
wanted to keep CNN on the air. During the summer of 1980,
Turner had turned to a leading consultant in the cable industry,
Bill Daniels, for a cash fix. Daniels had something of a reputation as a Mr. Fix-It in the cable business. Based in Denver, he
invested heavily in cable systems in the Southwest and frequently put together deals for other investors and cable companies. From the start, Daniels was taken with the notion of an
all-news channel. He felt it would be a major step forward for
the cable industry that, up until then, was identified with reruns
of old network sitcoms. Daniels was personally prepared to invest $5 million in CNN and had commitments from associates
for another $5 million. The package he worked out included an
additional $10 million from several banks, secured with deben-
tures and warrants on Turner stock. Before the deal could be
concluded, the banks got wind of First Chicago's decision to pull
its line of credit to TBS, and they followed suit. CNN was less
than six months old and had already won plaudits for the quality of its programming, but to informed outsiders it appeared to
be a high-cost operation that would have a tough time ever
breaking even. That, in turn, convinced bankers that CNN
would become an indefinite drain on TBS's SuperStation earnings. And since Turner was losing money as well, year in and

year out, on his two sports franchises, TBS appeared to be, in a word, overextended.

Turner had to bite the bullet. By November he himself was making the rounds of the big banks, looking for a creditor to replace First Chicago. He was repeatedly urged to raise money by issuing new stock in Turner Broadcasting and *then* come back to the banks for loans. After years of buying back stock from other shareholders, Turner was adamant that he wouldn't solve his financial problems by diluting his control of the firm. But he knew his back was against the wall. Finally, as he had with Bristol-Myers, he opted for a tactical retreat. The company filed a registration statement with the Securities and Exchange Commission (SEC) to issue one million new shares, reducing Turner's personal stake in the company from 87 to 79 percent. With that, Turner began negotiating in earnest with a group of banks led by Citicorp Industrial Credit to replace First Chicago.

Suddenly, Turner slipped. Appearing on *Donahue*, a popular Chicago morning talk show syndicated to stations around the country, Turner, never very adept at thinking before he spoke, speculated that his company would begin turning a profit in 1982. Whether that was true or not, Turner had been expressly warned by his lawyers and investment bankers that he was forbidden to even speculate on future performance according to the SEC's "quiet period" rules prior to a stock flotation. The gaffe was compounded two weeks later when Turner Broadcasting announced that it expected to post a hefty $6.5 million pretax *loss* in the first quarter of 1981. A much bigger loss than anyone had been expecting, it made Turner's rosy forecast on the *Donahue* show appear either overly optimistic or, in the worst case, downright misleading.

For once Turner's reckless disregard for convention backfired. His investment bankers warned Turner that the flap had severely hurt TBS's standing with big institutional investors. The stock issue would be a rough one, they concluded, and might not even net TBS half the $14.5 million cash demanded by his creditors-in-waiting. Late in April, only weeks after making it, Turner withdrew the stock offering and turned to the banks for a deal on whatever terms they required. The consortium led by Citicorp and Manufacturers Hanover Trust agreed to extend a $50 million line of credit, but Turner would have to pay dearly for the loan, with interest payments pegged at three full percentage points above the prime rate — double the premium they had been asking under the old arrangement. Turner was also forced to pledge all his personal, as well as corporate, assets to secure the loan.

It was a clear defeat, and Turner resented the terms imposed on him. But at least he had the money to maneuver. He would need that money soon. Ted Turner was about to get a competitor.

The big TV networks were gunning for Turner. Publicly they dismissed his challenge in TV news. But as it became clear that CNN was capable of putting out a strong editorial product, network executives questioned Turner's financial ability to keep CNN on the air despite the burgeoning losses. Network executives had spread the word on Wall Street that Turner couldn't turn a profit on CNN for years, ultimately convincing lenders like First Chicago that CNN would (a) collapse or (b) have to be sold to an outside bidder with deeper pockets. "CNN will make it," one network advertising executive forecast in an interview with *Business Week* magazine. "But the people who will make it are those who buy Turner out."

With the networks overtly threatening to undermine him by invading the cable industry themselves, Turner decided that he couldn't avoid an outright display of the conflict that was now inevitable. Addressing nearly a thousand industry insiders at the 1980 Western Cable Show in Anaheim in December, Turner vehemently attacked the enemy. "Two of the three

> *A general cannot avoid a battle when the enemy is resolved upon it at all hazards.*
> — Niccolò Machiavelli

networks are here, trying to get you to affiliate with them even though their public stance in Washington and to the business press is anti-cable," he told his early-morning audience. "They're here because they're beaten. That's the reason they're here and that's the *only* reason." He reserved special ridicule for CBS, which was throwing a big black-tie dinner the same week aboard the *Queen Mary* to launch CBS Cable, a culture and arts network. "Where the hell were they when you needed them?" Turner asked his sympathetic listeners, all of them aware that for several years CBS had dismissed the potential of cable and, on more than one occasion, had sworn that it would never supply programming to the systems that would compete with the fare it supplied to its over-the-air network affiliates. Turner also slammed the networks' entertainment departments for serving up a "diet of disasters, scandal, and sleazy sex." His attack was meant to draw attention to the more upbeat, clean-cut "family" fare on his SuperStation.

Turner wasn't finished. Several months after the Anaheim convention, on May 11, he announced to a packed news conference in Washington, D.C., that CNN was suing the networks and key White House officials, including President Ronald Reagan, to win access to the White House TV pool. For years the networks had cooperated in covering the White House by selecting a camera crew belonging to one of the three networks to shoot the action and share the footage with the other networks and news organizations, including CNN. But CNN was not allowed to be a full member of the pool. The networks uniformly opposed CNN's entry as a fourth member.

At his Washington press conference, Turner spelled out the challenge that until now seemed almost quixotic. "For the last fifteen years ABC, CBS, and NBC have . . . enjoyed a monopoly over this market," he said, referring to TV news in general. "Our efforts to break this monopoly outside the legal process have been fruitless, and now we are forced to take this action both for the good of the news business and for the good of the American people." Turner went on to use the briefing to show part of a quasi documentary called *Television: The Moral Battleground*, produced by TBS. The eighty-minute videotape was highly critical of the networks' daytime and prime-time programming. "They are totally irresponsible," Turner intoned. "Consciously or unconsciously, they are tearing this nation down — or tearing it apart." Turner was attempting to assume the high moral ground in his battle with the networks and he didn't care how he did it.

Network executives promptly dismissed Turner's invective as the rantings of a two-bit entrepreneur who was playing out of his league. They were also not above pointing out that Turner's own SuperStation was spending a lot of its original production money on daytime as well as prime-time soap operas with little redeeming value. Still, Turner had thrown down the gauntlet, and press coverage surrounding his lawsuit brought the debate over network programming standards and practices into wider currency and greater popular scrutiny. Turner had managed to turn a spotlight on the networks, forcing them to defend themselves. Once again, Turner's threats were working. The guerrilla was keeping his enemy off guard.

At least one network, ABC, was beginning to see that Ted Turner was right. He had proved there was a role for twenty-four-hour news on cable television, and unless one of the big networks got involved soon, it might be too late to enter the business. So a little more than a year after CNN went on the air, ABC and Westinghouse's Group W, which owned a number of major cable systems around the country, announced that they were teaming up to launch an all-news cable service. The Satellite News Channel (SNC) was to be essentially a "headline" service, airing capsule news summaries and three complete news reports each hour, similar to the format used by all-news radio stations. SNC would debut in the spring, to be followed by a second, more comprehensive service, similar to CNN's, in late 1982. Although ABC wouldn't confirm the numbers, industry insiders figured that the two broadcasting giants were willing to invest at least $40 million to launch SNC.

The decision by ABC and Westinghouse to challenge Turner was, in part, a by-product of CNN's success. Despite early problems signing up cable systems, CNN ended 1980, as promised, with more than four million subscribers. And the ranks of CNN advertisers jumped from seventeen to some seventy companies. But the entry of a well-heeled rival was expected to slow CNN's progress to profitability, and shareholders began bailing out. After the ABC/Group W announcement, Turner's stock fell from $17 a share to $13.50 in the over-the-counter market. A few days later, Turner stock was trading at $11, and the value of Ted Turner's personal holdings in the company had plummeted by more than 35 percent. Fortunately, the credit line from Citicorp and Manufacturers Hanover had been signed, sealed, and delivered two months earlier; otherwise the company's dramatically lessened value would probably have destroyed the deal.

Turner didn't spend much time licking his wounds, or counting his paper losses. The morning after, he summoned Schonfeld, his chief financial officer, Bill Bevins, and chief engineer, Gene Wright, to his office. "I want to do another news channel, and get it up on the satellite before SNC," he told his colleagues. "It's our best chance — hell, maybe our *only* chance — to beat these guys. We've got to be out there first." Turner had known for more than a month that ABC and Group W were talking abut a news channel, and two weeks before the official announcement he had heard that the deal was done. Now he wanted CNN to create the same kind of headline service as the Satellite News Channel was supposed to be. The second channel would be expensive, but CNN could piggyback a lot of the costs on the existing operation. And the cost of not creating a new channel was prohibitive. CNN could survive against a single headline service, but not against the competing full-service news channel ABC was planning. If Turner let that happen, the market would be saturated, and CNN's ad revenues would probably fall by 50 percent. Turner had always felt there was room for only one CNN. If there were two full-fledged services, neither could project a profit in the foreseeable future.

The idea of a second news channel wasn't totally new. Turner and Schonfeld had previously discussed creating a service to supply frequent, brief recaps of the news, much like an all-news radio station. It could be a strong complement to CNN's more in-depth programming, and most of the new cable systems going into operation around the country had plenty of channel space to allocate. But only Turner and Schonfeld were sold on the strategy of pre-empting SNC by putting a competing channel on the air, and doing it faster than ABC and Westinghouse could get their act together. Turner was convinced that if he made life difficult enough for SNC, its parents would pull out.

After all, they had moved into the field only to stop *him*, not out of any long-term commitment to the cable industry.

Bevins argued that the new service would be too expensive and could break the company, and the ad staff concurred. They were having a hard enough time pitching advertisers on CNN without fragmenting the market even further. Despite those objections, Turner decided to proceed with CNN-Two. But before he could do so, he had to clear the proposed expansion with the company's creditors. Three days after the first brainstorming session in Atlanta, he met a representative of Citicorp. The banker assured Turner that his bankers were committed to CNN's survival and had no quarrel with the aggressive strategy Turner was outlining for him. In fact, Turner's bankers didn't have much choice. Unless CNN retaliated quickly and strongly, the presence of a long-term competitor in cable news would raise major doubts about Turner's ability to make payments on the outstanding loans.

The creditors behind him, Turner had one last call to make, this one to threaten a prolonged fight if his adversary didn't back down. It was to Daniel Ritchie, Group W's chairman and a key architect of the SNC venture. Turner tried to talk Ritchie into dropping the plan, which, he warned, could be suicidal to both companies. Ritchie politely declined, convinced that the combined resources of ABC and Westinghouse would allow SNC to triumph eventually in a war of attrition that Turner didn't have enough cash to survive.

Less than two weeks after the SNC announcement, Turner held a press conference in Boston's Copley Plaza Hotel. He announced that CNN-Two would go on the air January 1, 1982, several months before SNC. Compared to CNN, Turner told reporters, the new service would be a "compact, hard-news service catering to viewers who want a quicker, more concise summary of the day's events." Turner drew a bead on the ABC-Westinghouse venture as he cited a statement by Roone Arledge, the president of ABC News. Arledge was on record as saying that ABC's *World News Tonight* would keep its best stories for itself and not release them to SNC. "So you can see," Turner concluded, "what you're going to be getting from them is a second-rate, horseshit operation." Turner didn't mince words.

After ensuring that CNN's headline service would get a head start over SNC, Turner was eager to secure another tactical advantage — in the number of homes his new service could reach. ABC and Westinghouse had decided to transmit SNC over a transponder on Westar-4, a new satellite that wouldn't even be launched until the spring. Even then, it wasn't considered a standard satellite for cable operators. Most systems weren't equipped to receive signals from Westar-4, and it would take years before cable operators would buy the extra receiving equipment to pull down the SNC signal. Turner had leased space on another Westar satellite, but he knew that if CNN-Two were to take off, it would have to be available on the Satcom-1 that carried CNN and other major cable networks.

Turner had been talking with Warner Communications for more than a year about a vacant transponder they owned on the satellite. He was interested in it as a backup for CNN, but at more than $1 million a year, the price was too high for a transponder that might never be used. Now, with time of the essence and the banks behind him, Turner approached Warner's new cable joint venture with American Express, Warner Amex Cable Communications, ready to make a deal.

Warner Amex had its own reason to come to terms with Turner. Group W was one of its principal competitors and stood to enhance its reputation as a cable operator if the venture with ABC succeeded. Warner itself didn't want to get into the programming business, so it offered Turner a different type of deal. Warner Amex would put CNN-Two on its Satcom-1 transponder in exchange for the exclusive right to sell all commercial time on *both* CNN services for the next two years. The payoff would be a hefty commission for Warner Amex on all advertising sales. It was a steep price to pay, but Turner was certain that getting CNN-Two on the standard cable bird would give him a leg up on SNC. The deal would also serve notice on Turner's rivals that he had no intention of sitting back and allowing SNC to make inroads into CNN's market.

While Turner saw the new service as a strike at SNC, he also wanted to use it to make inroads into the markets of the three big broadcasters. He decided to offer CNN-Two to over-the-air stations. For a price, they could use up to four hours a day of the programming as if it were their own. Independent stations, Turner believed, might use the service for their regular national newscasts. And network affiliates could use the programming overnight, when network news departments virtually shut down. Any station that signed on for CNN-Two, moreover, would have to agree to supply local news footage at cost to Turner Broadcasting, providing both CNN channels with greater access to news events around the country in much the same way as the big networks could rely on their affiliates for local coverage on a breaking story. By the following June, more than fifty stations had purchased the CNN-Two service, including independent and network affiliates in seven of the Top Ten markets. Turner had hoped for more sign-ups, but network executives were impressed that he had been able to recruit as many stations as he did.

It wasn't the first time network executives had to sit up and take notice. CNN's ad revenues had quadrupled in 1981 to just under $16 million, and after eighteen months of operation the news channel was going into more than eleven million homes. Still, Turner was vulnerable where the larger media groups weren't — in the wallet. For all of 1981, TBS lost more than $13 million on less than $100 million in revenues. TBS carried a negative net worth on its books, and stock market officials were threatening to delist the Turner stock from over-the-counter trading. Turner was also fighting a unionization drive at his Atlanta headquarters. If he lost the battle, higher wages could put CNN out of business overnight.

ABC was counting on its solid financial position to outflank Turner in its cable-come-lately strategy. Its partner, Westinghouse, owned dozens of cable systems that were automatic clients for SNC. And to get the channel in as many other homes as possible, ABC and

In war, numbers alone confer no advantage.

—Sun Tzu

Westinghouse decided to *pay* cable operators to carry SNC. The maneuver — similar to the one that had turned Getty Oil's ESPN into the largest cable network in the country — changed

the economics of cable for Turner, too. When it began broadcasting in late June, SNC had 2.6 million subscribers, double
the number signed up for CNN-Two. Turner would now have
to give away the new service even to cable systems that didn't
buy CNN itself. And as ABC had forecast, cable operators
began urging Turner to reduce his fees for the basic CNN service, which had accounted for about half of all revenues for the
news channel, with the other half covered by commercials. The
pressure was intense at an industry convention in Las Vegas in
May 1982, but Turner refused to give in. He was willing to give
CNN-Two to anyone who would carry it, but he wouldn't reduce fees for CNN. Instead, Turner lobbied heavily on his "insider" role in the cable industry. He stressed that TBS was
committed to cable for the long haul, unlike, he implied, ABC
and Westinghouse. His not-so-subtle message was blazoned
across a billboard outside the Las Vegas convention hotel: "I
was cable before cable was cool."

Turner was convinced that ABC and Westinghouse wouldn't
persevere with SNC unless it became profitable quickly. The
companies were reportedly willing to pump $40 million into the
venture, but SNC could well lose money after twelve months of
operation, as CNN had in the early days. Turner knew that internal pressure from ABC and Westinghouse stockholders
would be tremendous if losses began piling up, cutting into dividends. "ABC and Westinghouse are public companies and they
can't afford to stick with disaster," Turner told an interviewer.
"Just look at their record in television. They're in the business
of canceling things that don't succeed quickly." Turner, who
controlled his own company, couldn't be accused of pulling the
plug too quickly, at least not at CNN.

In fact, with less than a month to go before SNC went on the
air, a programming decision from Turner threatened to undermine morale at the network. Reese Schonfeld had become unhappy with a key program in CNN's prime-time lineup, Sandy
Freeman's interview program. The 10:00 P.M. time slot was crucial to CNN's overall ratings, and Schonfeld felt that Freeman's
hour-long show was turning off viewers. So in late spring, as
Freeman's contract came up for renewal, Schonfeld proposed

that the interviewer be dropped. To Schonfeld's relief, Turner agreed. A few weeks later, however, Turner called Schonfeld into his office and told him that Freeman's contract *would* be renewed. Schonfeld suspected that Turner had worked out some deal with Freeman's agent, despite Turner's frequent promises that he wouldn't interfere on the editorial side of CNN, which was to be Schonfeld's domain. When Turner refused to reconsider his decision to keep Freeman, Schonfeld resigned.

The loss of Schonfeld was an important internal blow. Much of the news organization at CNN had been hired by the veteran newsman. Schonfeld was also seen as an important buffer between the rank and file and Ted Turner himself. Schonfeld's resignation also raised the specter of Turner's getting more involved in the editorial process. At the same time, Schonfeld was no longer considered by cable operators and advertisers to be essential to the success of the operation. His hand-picked number two, Burt Reinhardt, would assume his duties. And unlike the early days, when a lot of CNN's editorial integrity hinged on Schonfeld's credentials, the operation was now respectable in its own right. Schonfeld had effectively made himself redundant. CNN could get along without him, and Turner knew it. There were no mass resignations, no pullouts by advertisers following Schonfeld's departure.

The ongoing battle with ABC in cable news, meanwhile, set Ted Turner to thinking about a longer-run strategy. Until now, the plan had been to compete, guerrillalike, in specific segments of the market for advertising dollars, with WTBS for entertainment, CNN for news. But it was clear from ABC's venture into cable that the network enjoyed the one thing Turner didn't have — unlimited funds. Yet if he was going to assume the major role in communications, he would need the clout that only the top three networks enjoyed. To attain it, he would have to acquire one of the networks. Since Turner didn't have the means to finance an outright takeover, his only option would be to sell his own company to one of the networks for stock, and use his leverage as a major shareholder to gain control.

Thus began a plot to take over CBS. Late in the summer of

1981, his number two on the business side, Bob Wussler, a former CBS employee, arranged a secret meeting between Turner and CBS chairman Thomas Wyman. On the table was a proposal to sell TBS for $150 million to the broadcasting giant. The meeting at Atlanta's Hartsfield International Airport led to further discussions in New York, but the deal fell through. Ted Turner wanted CBS stock, not cash. He wanted a say in running the number one TV network. Wyman refused. The transaction would have made Turner the biggest individual shareholder in CBS, even larger than its founder and Wyman's predecessor as chief executive officer, William Paley.

For the most part, Turner kept his ambitions to himself, until June 1982. Then he went public, brashly promising something he quite possibly couldn't deliver. In speeches to groups in both Chicago and New York, the cable magnate said that he planned to take over one of the three major networks *within the next eighteen months!* Network executives laughed off the boast. Untempered in his now-public challenge to the networks, Turner threatened to file an antitrust complaint against ABC over its joint venture with Westinghouse, which, Turner charged, "should be broken into little pieces."

Aware that none of the networks would cave in easily to his ambitions, Turner sent another jolt through their ranks. He began talking about setting up a fourth network if he failed in his bid to acquire one of the existing broadcasters. Other media companies had toyed with the idea before, concluding that it would be too hard to crack the existing oligopoly, but Turner had already proved he could succeed where others hadn't. And for Turner there was little downside risk in threatening to build a fourth network. The very *talk* of it would force CBS, among others, to take him seriously and conceivably resume in earnest the merger talks that had begun in Atlanta.

Turner's concept of a fourth network was ingenious. It would feed programming by satellite to stations around the country, even those affiliated with the Big Three networks. The stations could then pick and choose which programs to air in prime time among the offerings of their own networks as well as Turner's. If it worked, the concept would strike a devastating blow to the networks' monopoly over the prime-time programming of their affiliates and drastically undercut network advertising revenues. Turner himself couldn't afford to develop the programming, so he took the idea to Hollywood. At a meeting he arranged on September 14 at the Beverly Hills Hotel, Turner met with production executives from Paramount, Universal, and several other major studios and TV production companies, all of which supplied prime-time programming to the networks. For years, in fact, the studios had griped about not getting a big enough share of the profits earned by the networks on their prime-time offerings. The studios were also powerless to decide when and if a program should be canceled. ABC, CBS, and NBC held all the cards, and the real profits for the studios came only from the sale of syndication rights. Turner was proposing to give the studios more control over their programming and a bigger stake in the profits from first-run shows. His fourth network would turn over one night a week to a different studio to fill as each saw best. The studios would therefore have the power to renew or cancel their own shows, and Turner would hand them a substantial chunk of the advertising proceeds. In exchange, the studios would foot the bill for developing new shows, traditionally the role of the big networks. In short, the studios would take the risk of financing development and production in return for a faster and larger payback.

The studio executives didn't buy it. With the average weekly production cost of a one-hour prime-time show running at nearly $750,000, most studios were happy to leave the financing to the networks. The production companies were also worried about being shut out of ABC, CBS, and NBC if they hooked up with Turner on a fourth network that was, at best, a risky proposition, given Turner's track record. Thanks, they told Turner, but no thanks.

If network executives in New York were relieved at Turner's failure to get Hollywood to go along with him, the relief was short-lived. Turner was pulling off modest but well-publicized coups against network programmers. Earlier in the year, WTBS had signed the first non-network TV contract with the NCAA, to broadcast nineteen college football games. Turner also outbid the networks for the big Georgetown-Virginia basketball game, then turned around and resold the SuperStation telecast to broadcast stations around the country, many of them network affiliates. In August 1982, when a football strike appeared likely, Turner struck a deal with the NFL Players Association to carry a series of all-star games; sixty-nine of the ninety-five television stations that carried the first struck game were network affiliates. CBS had been reduced to airing small-time college games and Canadian football before yanking them because of low ratings. Little by little, Ted Turner was making his presence felt at the networks. He was still perceived as more gadfly than real rival, but for Turner, ever the maverick, the small victories lent a stature usually reserved for much more powerful media groups.

CNN Headline News (née CNN-Two) was now available on more than one hundred over-the-air TV stations nationwide, many of them network affiliates. The networks did little more than dismiss Turner as an upstart, but ironically, they began reacting to ABC and *its* challenge to Turner. Barely days after SNC went on the air, NBC created *NBC News Overnight*, designed to take away some of the overnight audience for whom CNN had become a staple viewing diet. CBS entered the fray in October with *Nightwatch*. ABC expanded *Nightline* and created a short-lived but serious interview show called *The Last Word*. The networks, under the National Association of Broadcasters banner, also joined the lobbying fight to force cable systems to pay higher copyright fees for reruns aired on networks such as Turner's SuperStation. It was evident that the networks no longer took the competition lightly. They were worried that Turner was making permanent inroads into markets that they should have been developing all along. He was forcing them to react, to commit resources to new programming that might not turn out to be economical in the long run. The networks were scrambling for a response to Turner.

The most concrete response, of course, was SNC and its giveaway strategy to win over cable systems. It was threatening Turner's position by limiting the subscription rates he could charge for his two news channels. The Atlanta TV tycoon decided to attack ABC and its SNC partner in court. Westinghouse had bought the TelePrompTer cable system that served upper Manhattan in 1981, right after TelePrompTer agreed to carry CNN as a basic service. After the acquisition, Westinghouse pulled out of the deal with CNN, asserting that there were no available channels on the TelePrompTer system. What's more, CNN was denied access to *any* of the two hundred cable systems owned by Westinghouse. The Manhattan system, Turner decided, would be a test case. So when TelePrompTer began airing SNC in late 1982, Turner filed suit.

ABC and Westinghouse promptly countersued. "If anything," Group W chairman Daniel Ritchie stated, "we have bent over backwards to compete fairly with Turner in all of his services in the face of his intimidation and highly questionable practices." Ritchie's countersuit charged that TBS had threatened cable operators with harassment, lawsuits, adverse publicity, withholding of WTBS, and challenges to their franchise licenses if the operators chose to carry SNC instead of one of the two CNN services. The fight over who would supply news programming to cable operators was deteriorating into what many analysts feared would be a protracted, costly legal battle that could eventually kill off *both* suppliers. If it did, the same insiders believed, ABC or another of the big networks would probably step in to fill the void with a twenty-four-hour news service operated out of the same news department that supplied regular network newscasts.

More than ever, Turner was realizing that he was vulnerable. To withstand the competition, he needed more financial backing. And where better to turn than to one of ABC's rivals? Turner asked for a meeting with CBS chairman Wyman again, this time in mid February, over lunch at CBS headquarters in New York. It was their first meeting since the abortive takeover discussions in 1981. It immediately became apparent that CBS would pay a high price for all of Turner's holdings — as much as $500 million or more, three or four times what Wyman could have offered for TBS less than two years earlier. CBS had a lot to gain from the deal. By using CNN's elaborate news-gathering network, it could lower its "average" costs, making it a "low-cost" news operation compared with ABC's and NBC's. It would also give CBS a dominant role in cable television. According to Turner's figures, more than 60 percent of the American cable-viewing audience was tuning in to WTBS, CNN, or

CNN Headline News. TBS could also turn a profit quickly by reducing some of its overhead, notably by using CBS salespeople to sell time on Turner's channels. In short, CBS and TBS would be a perfect fit.

The only real drawback was Ted Turner himself, who came along with the deal. As in 1981, Turner wouldn't sell his shares in TBS for cash. He wanted CBS stock and, since his own shares in the company could be worth over half a billion dollars, a payment in stock would turn him into CBS's single largest shareholder, the owner of up to 30 percent of the company's shares. CBS founder William Paley owned or controlled less than 10 percent of CBS stock, so Turner would almost certainly have become the network's new chairman. That position, in turn, would make him the most powerful man at the top of the most powerful TV network in America.

When it became clear that Turner wouldn't change his mind, Wyman again broke off the talks. Turner made similar overtures to ABC president Frank Pierce, and at other times to executives representing NBC, Time Inc., Gannett, and Metromedia. With all of them, Turner demanded stock in return for a TBS merger. He was in the TV business to stay, and he had every intention of staying on as a major force, whether the networks helped him or not.

Although TBS lost money for all of 1982, it eked out a small profit in the last two quarters of the year despite continued, though smaller, losses at CNN. Revenues were growing at a rapid 50 percent annual clip, and even as Turner was sitting down with Wyman, TBS was racking up its third consecutive quarterly profit in more than five years. His SuperStation was growing by leaps and bounds, reaching into more than 25 million homes — over a third of all U.S. dwellings, and CNN was in nearly 20 million. Although ad revenues were not surging ahead as fast as subscribers, Turner knew that the situation could be remedied. He bought back the advertising sales rights on CNN from Warner Communications.

In May Ted Turner gave up his quest for a major network. For the foreseeable future, he announced, Turner Broadcasting would remain an independent company. Turner was also convinced that he would win his court battle with ABC and Westinghouse, based on a wealth of incriminating documents turned over by SNC to the court. Still, the legal battle was draining $100,000 a month from CNN's earnings.

If CNN was to prosper, Turner knew, he needed to extract himself from the costly battle with SNC. In June, by chance, he saw a way out after Bob Wussler ran across ABC Video president Herb Granath at a convention in Las Vegas. Granath bemoaned the legal and competitive tangle that was hurting CNN, SNC, and their respective parents. Wussler

> *There has never been a protracted war from which a country has benefited.... What is essential in war is victory, not prolonged operations.*
>
> —Sun Tzu

agreed. Wouldn't it be nice, he continued, if we could find a way out of this? Granath said it would, and there the conversation ended. Immediately, Wussler tracked down Turner and told him what Granath had said. ABC had softened its position, Wussler believed, and might be willing to negotiate a truce with Turner. "I think that if we came up with a fair proposal," Wussler suggested, "ABC might be willing to cash in its chips on SNC." Turner agreed, deciding to seize the opportunity to end the protracted battle. Within days Wussler heard from Granath, but it was bad news. Group W boss Dan Ritchie didn't want to negotiate, but the matter still had to go to the Westinghouse board of directors, which was uneasy at the prospect of further losses at SNC. The cable channel was supposed to pull in at least $15 million in advertising revenues in its first year of operation, but nine months into service, SNC had less than one million dollars' worth of ad contracts on its books. Turner, meanwhile, was attempting to bleed his rival even further, offering to pay cable systems $1.00 per subscriber per year for the next three years if they would carry all three of his cable services. It was a risky, costly gamble, but Turner figured that the irresistible offer would hammer another nail into SNC's coffin. When it met, the Westinghouse board decided to negotiate.

Ritchie refused to sit down personally with Turner. When

the talks got under way in Atlanta, former Carter administration attorney general Griffin Bell represented SNC and Turner's emissary was his long-time attorney and TBS board member Tench Coxe. A month later the two sides agreed to a mediator who would have a solid working knowledge of the cable industry. Technically, Bill Daniels would be working for SNC, but Turner implicitly trusted the cable consultant and venture capitalist who, in the early days of CNN, had been willing to put up his own money and clout to help get Turner's news channel off the ground. Turner knew Daniels would do his best to devise an agreement that was fair to both sides.

In the end the deal was clean-cut and final. ABC and Westinghouse were seeking to get out with as little financial loss as possible. As Turner had suspected, they had been concerned all along that their shareholders wouldn't stand for the protracted losses that an operation like CNN was continuing to pile up. So on October 12, Turner Broadcasting announced that it was buying out SNC. That evening TBS put $25 million of borrowed money into an escrow account. The next morning ABC and Westinghouse each withdrew $12.5 million from escrow. They also signed a pledge to stay out of the cable news business for three years, and existing SNC subscribers would be offered either or both of CNN's services. Two weeks later Satellite News Channel stopped broadcasting after just seventeen months and six days of continuous operation.

Ted Turner had won! The victory over ABC and Westinghouse had not come cheaply, but CNN was now the only cable news game in town. During the next couple of months NBC would join the ranks of other networks in closing down its overnight news show after having failed to beat back CNN's assault on the late-night audience. And one or more of Turner's three channels was now available in almost every home with cable. For the first time in five years, Turner Broadcasting made a profit in 1983.

Uncharacteristically, Ted Turner wasn't around to bask in the media's congratulatory blitz when the SNC buyout was announced. The undisputed king of cable was hunting in Winnipeg. Soon he would be hunting even bigger game. The merger negotiations with CBS had foundered, but not Turner's ambition to control and dominate America's number one network.

In January 1985 Turner approached CBS for the third time. Chairman Tom Wyman took the call, briefly listening to Turner's suggestion that the two companies revive discussions on a possible "business combination" of CBS and TBS. The phone conversation was brief. Wyman said that CBS was simply not interested as long as Turner wanted a say in running the network.

War is an act of violence intended to compel our opponent to fulfill our will.

—Karl von Clausewitz

The snub didn't deter Turner. He asked Bill Bevins to explore other options open to TBS, including a possible reverse bid, with TBS acquiring CBS rather than the other way around. Since CBS was much bigger, a Turner bid would probably have little chance of succeeding in ordinary times. But for CBS, these were no ordinary times. The company was considered to be "in play" on Wall Street because of Jesse Helms. In December the North Carolina senator had publicly urged conservatives to buy stock in CBS. Helms's objective was to end what he called the "liberal bias" of the media in general, and of CBS News in particular. Helms followers subsequently set up an ad hoc committee called Fairness in Media (FIM), pledging to mount a proxy campaign at the 1985 annual meeting of CBS shareholders to unseat the network's senior management.

Turner was reluctant to join forces with the archconservative Helms and FIM, but he wasn't above using his fellow Southerner's rabble-rousing attacks on CBS to his own ends. At the same time, Turner asked Bevins to run the numbers on another broadcast target, ABC. It was smaller than CBS, and unlike RCA's NBC subsidiary, it was independent. But almost as soon as Turner showed an interest, the network was taken off the market. In March 1985 ABC agreed to sell out to Capital Cities Communications in a friendly merger. And since Cap Cities was willing to pay top dollar, a competing bid by cash-poor Turner was out of the question.

The ABC acquisition galvanized Turner into action. With one network changing hands, it was clear that federal regulators were unlikely to put any obstacles in the way of a CBS takeover, long considered the principal deterrent to hostile suitors. Now was the time to strike.

Ted Turner faced reporters and television cameras on April 18, with Bob Wussler standing in the back of the crowded New York conference room. Wussler smiled quietly as his boss announced to the world that Turner Broadcasting was going after CBS, the company that had ousted Wussler five years earlier — after his twenty-one years of service. Getting to the details, Turner announced that his company was bidding what would amount to $5.4 billion for all the CBS stock, worth an estimated $175 a share. At the time CBS was trading on Wall Street for less than $100 a share. But again there was a catch: not only did Turner come with the package, but TBS was offering no cash at all as part of the transaction. Turner's offer would pay shareholders in bonds, which, according to Turner, would earn their holders substantially more over the next decade than they could hope to earn in dividends and stock appreciation under existing CBS management. In his S-1 registration statement filed with the Securities and Exchange Commission, Turner called the bonds high-risk, high-yield securities. CBS and most of Wall Street called them by their common nickname, junk bonds.

The subsequent offer that went out to twenty-four thousand CBS shareholders promised a drastic overhaul of CBS. To repay some of the debts incurred in the buyout, Turner said he would sell most of the company's non-broadcast properties, such as its publishing, toy, and record ventures, as well as many of its radio stations around the country and a Philadelphia TV station.

In response, CBS did its best to put Turner and his offer in a bad light. In a 128-page brief filed with the FCC, the network claimed that TBS's takeover plan would push CBS into financial ruin. At the core of CBS's allegation was a projection by TBS that it could run CBS profitably, pay off the debts, and still be in the black to the tune of more than $1 billion in 1989. In its filing, CBS claimed that the Turner estimates were inflated and that the debt incurred in the takeover would result in just under a $100 million loss in 1989. CBS also quoted the correspondent it had spurned years earlier, Daniel Schorr. CNN's former senior correspondent charged that Turner was no longer willing to live up to his commitment that Schorr would have complete freedom to report what he wanted. CNN, in response, claimed that the real reason for the rift was Schorr's unhappiness at losing a prime-time call-in show that had been a showcase for his talents but a bomb in the ratings. Schorr replied with an article for the *Los Angeles Times* that was critical of Turner's style and especially of his willingness to encourage companies "to sponsor features associated with their products." It was a common practice in cable TV, but one which Schorr deplored — to CBS's delight, in print.

In its brief, CBS blasted Turner, with Wyman charging openly that Turner was morally unfit to run the network. "In light of a number of pejorative statements by Mr. Turner about various minority, religious, and ethnic groups," Wyman claimed, "we believe that TBS's acquisition of CBS would undermine the CBS network's present broad acceptance by the American public." To back up those remarks, CBS encouraged minority and labor organizations to file briefs with the FCC opposing the takeover. However, the National Black Media Coalition filed a pro-Turner statement. "We agree that Mr. Turner has done a reasonably good job at times of making a public ass of himself when it comes to racial matters," the coalition told the FCC. "[But] one's deeds, rather than one's words, count more in evaluating the prospective operation of a TV network," and the black group went on to call Turner's deeds "exemplary" and CBS's "better-than-average." "[We] know Ted Turner fairly well," the statement concluded, "and we do not, to this day, know whether he is a liberal or a conservative. Nor do we care."

CBS swallowed hard. Faced with the prospect that Wall Street could conceivably swing in Turner's favor, especially if he sweetened his offer with cash, CBS offered to buy back 21 percent of its own stock in cash and bonds worth just under $1 billion. The total value for shareholders came to $150, $40 of it in cash. But several legal provisions not included in the first press release announcing the buyback offer would, in future, prevent any other company from buying CBS if it resulted in creating a debt-to-equity ratio of more than 3 to 4. By any reckoning the TBS offer would have geared up CBS debts to well above that level.

Turner immediately lashed out at the "poison pill" defense by CBS, warning that it would "take away the shareholders' control" over future CBS decisions. Turner also charged that the terms of the buyback would put less in the pockets of shareholders than his bid, even though cash was involved. Turner also tried to get the FCC to block the CBS offer on the ground that it constituted transfer of control of CBS's five owned TV stations, thus requiring FCC approval. But the FCC disagreed, and it quickly became clear that most CBS shareholders preferred some cash up front to Turner's no-cash offer.

Turner knew the network was out of his grasp less than a week after CBS's retaliatory bid. "For all practical purposes," he told the National Press Club in Washington, "if the CBS offer is successful, it would make it extremely difficult, if not impossible, for our offer to have any chance whatsoever." But he refused to admit defeat, threatening to mount a new bid at some future date. The expression "if we fail," he declared, raising both arms and flexing his muscles in a physical display of strength, "is not in my vocabulary." He also used the opportunity to lambaste CBS's tactics, and he especially took aim at CBS Broadcast president Gene Jankowski for openly worrying that ABC's ratings slide might force all the networks to charge less for commercial time, a signal to Turner that the networks were engaging in illegal monopoly practices in pricing their air time for advertisers. "Can you believe that?" Turner asked reporters. "They ought to show that to the Justice Department. I mean, they ought to lock them all up. It's what I've been saying for years."

CBS quickly amassed the 25 million shares it wanted to buy back from shareholders, among them one quarter of the 128,250 shares acquired by Turner Broadcasting in advance of Turner's failed bid for the network. The sale helped defray only a part of the $15 million Turner spent in pursuit of CBS, but the real return on Turner's investment came in the form of what Wall Street liked to call good will. In making the rounds of investment groups, Turner and Bill Bevins found several major institutions unwilling to finance his CBS bid but eager to bankroll future ventures. The good will would come in handy sooner than anyone on Wall Street expected. Ted Turner had lost a round at the hands of the much richer CBS, but he wasn't going to let his failed bid sidetrack plans for expanding the Turner empire.

Even before the CBS buyback was complete, the chairman of TBS made a little publicized visit to MGM's forty-four-acre studio lot in Culver City at the invitation of Las Vegas tycoon Kirk Kerkorian. It was an open secret in Hollywood that Kerkorian was looking to sell MGM if the right bid came along. He had acquired the studio in the seventies, then purchased United Artists in 1981 after the failure of *Heaven's Gate* pushed UA to the brink of bankruptcy. Kerkorian wanted to stay in the movie business, refusing to write off UA completely, but he didn't need to hold on to MGM as well.

Two weeks after the studio tour, a deal was struck. Ted Turner would pay $1.5 billion for all of MGM/UA. He would then automatically turn around and sell UA, its film library, and a half interest in the two firms' distribution company back to Kerkorian for $480 million. Scarred once by Wall Street's reception for his no-cash offer, Turner and Bevins switched tactics to finance the MGM bid, at least partially. This time he would pay in hard cash. He asked one of the most innovative brokerage firms and the prime mover of junk bonds on Wall Street, Drexel Burnham Lambert, to arrange the sale of TBS securities. The proceeds would be used to pay MGM/UA shareholders, principally Kerkorian, in cash.

The MGM deal surprised even Turner's bitterest critics at the networks, most of whom were crowing about the entrepreneur's failure to pull off the CBS deal. Yet on the day Turner quietly withdrew his offer for CBS, the MGM acquisition was announced. Turner was unavailable for comment: he was off fishing in

> *The guerrilla invents his own tactics for each moment of the battle and constantly surprises his enemy.*
>
> —Che Guevara

Alaska. But the subsequent headlines, all of them about the MGM deal, underscored Turner's ability to snatch victory from the jaws of defeat. It did not give the cable king what he most wanted, a full-fledged broadcasting network of his own. But it gave Turner something that the over-the-air networks were legally prohibited from acquiring, a movie studio or programming syndicator. It would also substantially bolster TBS's programming clout, adding twenty-two hundred MGM movies to the film library of the SuperStation that was now reaching into more than 35 million homes.

The acquisition did not go smoothly. Technically Turner committed himself to buying the studio in early August, although it would probably take months to work out details for the financing. Meantime, movie after movie flopped at the box office — *Marie, Code Name Emerald, Fever Pitch, Dream Lover*. Each failure reduced the net value of the studio, which Turner had agreed to buy at a set price. The box-office bombs also made it harder for Drexel Burnham to find takers for Turner's bonds. Although Turner was willing to pay as much as three points above the prime rate that blue-chip corporations paid to borrow, there were increasing worries that Turner wouldn't be able to pay off the debt.

Under pressure from Drexel Burnham, Turner got Kerkorian to accept less cash in the deal, with the difference made up in TBS preferred stock. He also went looking for a buyer of the MGM production studio. In late 1975 a major TV producer, Viacom International, agreed to pay $175 million for a 50 percent stake in the studio. Turner distrusted joint ventures but knew that Viacom had the know-how to run the production operation, and besides, he needed the money. But almost as quickly as the Viacom deal happened, Turner pulled out, claiming that Viacom was trying to welch on its agreement by paying less. Rather than concede, Turner said no. There was a risk of blitzing Drexel Burnham's attempt to raise money for the MGM acquisition, but it was a risk Turner had to take. If he could just hold on, the MGM studio operations would be worth a lot more than the fire-sale price Viacom was offering.

Turner got the financing he needed. When more than six hundred pages of documents were finally signed and sealed in late March, the borrowings arranged by Drexel Burnham carried higher than normal interest rates. But it was the price Turner knew he would have to pay, even if it eventually forced him to sell off parts of MGM to retire some of the burgeoning debts he had taken on to acquire the studio. By not agreeing to a sale in advance, he would at least be able to negotiate on his own terms.

The one asset Turner wouldn't be selling was MGM's film library. At whatever price, he had secured one of the most extensive collections of Hollywood movies, locking in years of future programming for his cable SuperStation. The MGM library, ironically, included the classic riches-to-rags-to-riches tale of an earlier Georgia empire, *Gone With the Wind*. Turner had drawn the names of two of his five children, sons Beauregard and Rhett, from the 1936 movie. And he saw some of himself in the Clark Gable figure. The square jaw and trim mustache. The rugged individualist. The fighter against all odds. Turner had failed to take over any of the networks, so he was not part of the establishment. But CNN assured him a new respectability in the news business, and Turner was taking away hundreds of millions in advertising dollars from the networks. The cable guerrilla was inflicting heavy casualties on the TV giants that had once dismissed him altogether, and the battle was far from over.

CHAPTER 2

Clash of the Colas

COKE VS. PEPSI

THE June 12, 1978, copy of *Business Week* landed on the cluttered desk of the new president of Coca-Cola USA. Brian Dyson had moved into the office atop Coca-Cola's ten-story office building in Atlanta just four weeks earlier. The words on the magazine cover banner irritated him: "Pepsi Takes On the Champ." Dyson knew what was inside. Coke's public relations department had gotten wind of the story the previous week. The premise: Pepsi-Cola was fast closing the gap in sales between its line of cola drinks and Coke's. In A. C. Nielsen's monthly surveys of soft drink purchases at grocery stores, in fact, Pepsi had just taken the lead from Coke for the first time ever. "We're number one!" Pepsi's president boasted in the article. No way, Dyson thought to himself. But what has Don got me into?

Don was Donald Keough, Dyson's boss. An engaging Iowan in his fifties, Keough was president of Coca-Cola's Americas Group, overseeing all soft drink sales in the Western Hemisphere from Coke's red brick headquarters down the block from Coca-Cola USA. Ever since landing the job in 1977, he'd badgered Dyson to take on Pepsi's "Challenge," the marketing campaign that Pepsi had launched one year earlier, using TV commercials to compare Pepsi and Coke in blind taste tests. This challenge was helping Pepsi overtake Coke in domestic U.S. sales. Coca-Cola needed to fight back or risk losing its century-long lead in the soft drink market.

Dyson wasn't easy to convince. Born and raised in Argentina to expatriate British parents, he had lived virtually all his life in Latin America. He was in charge of Coca-Cola's Brazilian operations when Keough took over the Americas Group the year after the Pepsi Challenge began. Dyson wanted to stay put in Rio de Janeiro. His aggressive management style and marketing savvy had helped Coke hold on to a virtual monopoly in the Brazilian market, despite repeated attempts by Pepsi to gain a stronger foothold. It was that success which caught Keough's eye. Executives in Atlanta, he felt, had become complacent despite clear evidence that Pepsi was coming on strong. The domestic operation needed someone with no ties to the past, someone who could re-invent a strong marketing appeal for Coke and simultaneously take some shots at Pepsi. Dyson had done just that in Brazil, and Keough felt he might be able to repeat it in the United States.

For months Keough tried to persuade Dyson to take the job as president of Coca-Cola USA, and for months Dyson kept saying no. Finally, Keough prevailed. Invoking Dyson's loyalty to the firm, he *ordered* the Argentinian to Atlanta. Keough was taking a big chance on Dyson. Tall and thin, with a ruddy complexion and an angular face, Dyson was an animated man who peppered his speech with frequent profanities. He was viewed as brash in a corporate hierarchy that had become sedate, even staid. When he arrived in Atlanta in May 1978, some of the younger executives, and certainly Don Keough, knew Coke was in trouble. A month later, after the *Business Week* cover story, almost every businessman in America knew it too.

Dyson prided himself on being something of a strategic thinker, keeping a copy of Clausewitz within ready reach on his office bookshelf. And he knew it wasn't good enough to lay down a purely defensive strategy. Coke still held the high ground, outselling Pepsi despite losing what had once been a virtual monopoly in the soft drink market. First Coca-Cola

---

The defensive is a relative state, and consequently impregnated more or less with offensive principles.

— Karl von Clausewitz

---

would keep Pepsi at bay, then the soda giant would have to counterattack, taking back some of the market its rival had grabbed already. Dyson and Keough agreed on the need for a carefully designed but aggressive defense.

At first, however, they were alone. Keough's superiors, especially Chairman Paul Austin, were skeptical of any attempt to trade overt punches with Pepsi. Caution was the watchword at Coca-Cola headquarters, a posture that the new head of Coca-Cola USA quickly learned would be almost as hard to surmount as the Pepsi Challenge itself.

History and tradition dominated Coke's corporate culture. There was no premium placed on doing things differently in a company that, in 1978, was still making the same cola with the same secret formula — known as Merchandise 7X — first developed in 1886 by an Atlanta pharmacist, John Styth Pemberton. His bookkeeper, Frank Robinson, devised the name after two key ingredients, the South American coca leaf and the African kola nut. He also designed the distinctive Spencerian script that remains the company's official trademark a century later. Coca-Cola wasn't the first soft drink; Hires root beer was first served ten years earlier, and Dr. Pepper a few months before Pemberton happened on his concoction.

By 1893, when the U.S. Patent Office awarded it a registered trademark, Coca-Cola was the leading soft drink sold at soda fountains. The same year Caleb B. Brabham changed the name of *his* drink — a kola-flavored tonic he was selling at his drugstore soda fountain in New Bern, North Carolina, with the name Brad's Drink — to Pepsi-Cola. Meanwhile, Pemberton had sold all his shares in Coca-Cola to an Atlanta businessman, Asa Candler, for $2300. By 1919, when Candler's heirs sold out to a consortium led by the Trust Company of Georgia, Coca-Cola was worth $25 million. The new owners, led by Trust Company president Ernest Woodruff, listed Coca-Cola on the stock exchange, and in 1923 Woodruff's son Robert was elected president, beginning an era of personal domination of an American corporation that would continue for more than sixty years. When Robert Woodruff officially stepped down as chairman of the board in 1955, Coca-Cola was still selling exactly the same concoction in exactly the same six-and-a-half-ounce bottle it had used at the turn of the century.

Pepsi had been offering several bottle sizes for years, one factor behind the Purchase, New York, company's inroads into Coke's traditional markets. Between 1950 and 1958, Pepsi-Cola tripled its sales; where Coke used to outsell Pepsi by five to one, Pepsi was then selling two bottles for every five sold by Coke. Then, in 1960, Pepsi put its advertising in the hands of Batten, Barton, Durstine and Osborn (BBD&O). Zeroing in on Coke's "traditional" image, BBD&O did everything to paint Pepsi as the soft drink for the young and, as its first slogan screamed from billboards across the country, "For those who think young." When the official "Pepsi Generation" slogan surfaced in 1964, a slogan that recurred regularly in Pepsi advertising over the next two decades, Pepsi had the self-proclaimed taste of the "new" generation — the baby boomers just growing up, with their thirst for soft drinks growing too.

It wasn't until 1960 that Coca-Cola introduced its first non-cola drinks, under the Fanta brand, followed by Sprite. That same year it diversified into orange juice, acquiring Minute Maid. In 1963 Coke responded to market newcomer Diet Rite with its own sugarless cola, Tab. The following year it bought a large coffee producer, Duncan Foods. The moves were part of an overall diversification strategy dictated by a huge increase in earnings, especially from Coke's overseas operations. The Atlanta company was awash in cash and felt compelled to follow much of corporate America down the road of diversification — cautiously. The acquisitions and new divisions were all structured to mix well with Coca-Cola's basic mission: to sell soft drinks and, specifically, Coke.

Even as Coca-Cola diversified, its share of the cola market continued to decline. While looking for a response to Pepsi's generational advertising, Coke saw its sales lead dwindle to two to one over Pepsi. Then came the Pepsi Challenge, with its test debut in Dallas in 1975 and a national advertising campaign in 1976. Pepsi's research had shown that, in blind taste tests, more people preferred Pepsi than Coke, and BBD&O came up with a commercial showing loyal Coke drinkers choosing Pepsi, labeled *M*, over Coke, identified as *Q*. Executives at Coca-Cola impugned the ethics of the challenge and tried to discredit Pepsi's test by arguing that people have a natural bias for the letter *M* over the letter *Q*. It was nit-picking, because the ad campaign had already achieved what Pepsi and BBD&O set out to achieve: to make consumers reconsider their allegiance to the "old" cola and compare it with the "young" one. Pepsi sales jumped: for every two bottles of Pepsi, Coke was now selling only three. And less than three years after the Pepsi Challenge was launched, *Business Week* was wondering in print whether Coca-Cola had the defensive skills and marketing wherewithal to fend off Pepsi's onslaught.

The Young Turks inside Coca-Cola blamed many of the company's problems on an unwillingness by patriarch Robert Woodruff and chairman Paul Austin to keep step with the times. At eighty-nine, in mid 1978, Woodruff remained chairman of Coke's finance committee, but he was nearly deaf and blind and spent only two weeks a year in Atlanta, calling shots the rest of the time from his country estate hundreds of miles away. The day-to-day running of Coca-Cola worldwide fell to Austin, a native Georgian educated at Harvard College and Harvard Law School. He became an assistant to the president of Coca-Cola's export division, later heading up the company's African subsidiary before returning to a series of senior staff assignments in Atlanta. Reserved and patrician, Austin was considered an aloof manager by even his closest lieutenants. He was more at home talking with lawyers than marketers, doing battle with regulatory agencies in Washington than with Pepsi in the marketplace.

Even at fifty-one, Don Keough was considered one of the Young Turks. With Coke for twenty-eight years, he had been in Atlanta for only the last five after transferring from the company's food division in Houston. He, too, blamed many of Coke's problems on Austin. Specifically, he was concerned that a lot of the company's marketing energies were being sapped by internecine fights with Coke's own bottlers and the U.S. government.

In Washington, Coca-Cola was lobbying against a ban on saccharin, an artificial sweetener used in diet soft drinks, including Coca-Cola's Tab brand. The Food and Drug Administration (FDA) was considering the ban after finding saccharin a possible carcinogen. Again, Coke executives did the work. And more and more senior officers found themselves commuting to Washington for hearings, thus taking their attention away from the marketing challenge posed by Pepsi-Cola.

In 1978 Coke was also in its seventh year of fighting a Federal Trade Commission (FTC) challenge to the soft drink industry's franchise bottler system. Austin insisted that Coke executives mastermind the legal fight themselves instead of delegating that authority to outside counsel. Yet the outcome of the fight could drastically change the way Coca-Cola operated. At stake was the practice of allowing bottlers — some of them partly owned by Coca-Cola itself — to maintain a monopoly in Coke products throughout a designated retail area. Whereas most of Pepsi-Cola's bottlers were owned by the company, Coca-Cola was built on synergistic but distinct roles for Atlanta and the various regional bottlers, who also acted as distributors of all Coke soft drinks. The FTC was investigating the decades-old system for possible abuses of the monopoly position bottlers enjoyed in their franchise areas, making it difficult for rival bottlers to enter the market. Under the system, the bottlers had a clout that even Coca-Cola didn't enjoy: "no-cut" contracts. In a 1921 agreement, Coca-Cola's franchise contract gave independent bottlers exclusive rights to bottle Coke in their territories. It also guaranteed a fixed price for the syrup they bought from Coke. The only flexibility in the pricing involved the cost of sugar: syrup prices could rise only as much as the cost of sugar rose. In the inflationary seventies, though, Coca-Cola felt that it had to change the contract or face continually declining profit margins. To do so, it would have to convince more than half its five hundred or so U.S. bottlers to go along with a new contract. Both Woodruff and Austin expected little trouble, since it would be the first major revision in the contract in more than fifty years. But when Keough and other Coke executives first approached the bottlers in late 1977 with a plan to amend the contract, they were told, in no uncertain terms, to get lost.

By the time Brian Dyson took over as president of Coca-Cola USA, only sixteen bottlers — none of them major ones — had agreed to the amendment. To pass, the amendment had to win the support of at least half the bottlers both in numerical terms and in the amount of Coke bottled. Coca-Cola began revising its position, and in August Keough and Dyson scheduled two weeks of meetings with bottlers to push a revised amendment. Over the next several weeks many of the smaller bottlers agreed to the new terms, but Coke was still short of the 50 percent needed.

In December rumors reached Atlanta that its sixth-largest bottler, Crass Bottling, covering Washington, D.C., and parts of Virginia and Pennsylvania, was for sale. That same month Keough received a call from Bud Crass, chairman of the bottling company, who denied the rumor. The following weekend, Keough was having a sandwich at an Atlanta delicatessen when he got another call. This one was from the head of a company he'd never heard of, Simplicity Patterns. Simplicity, he was told, had just signed a letter of intent to buy Crass Bottling. Simplicity had the cash to buy Crass, but Keough was worried that it had no experience as a bottler. What would prevent Simplicity from screwing up? If it did, Coke risked losing its edge in the Washington area over Pepsi, making it that much harder to regain ground it had already lost to what was unaffectionately known as Brand X at Coke headquarters.

The question was never answered. Within two weeks the deal fell through when attorneys for the two companies couldn't agree on the details. But the Crass episode did bring home to Coke executives that the company's relationship with its bottlers had become both precarious and outdated. Unlike Pepsi, Coke had almost no say in how its bottlers ran their businesses.

Brian Dyson made the bottlers his top priority when he assumed the top job at Coca-Cola USA, and he believed that the company's hitherto kid-gloves handling of the relationship was misguided. As long as Coke appeared willing to acquiesce without demanding more of the bottlers, there was little incentive for them to become more aggressive in marketing Coke — and presenting a united front. The company usually held a bottlers' convention every two or three years, but under Austin's management Coca-Cola had gone without such a meeting since 1969. Now Dyson decided it was time to bring Coke's bottlers together again for a pep talk, and he scheduled the convention for June, just seven

He whose ranks are united in purpose will be victorious.

— Sun Tzu

months away, in San Francisco. "The Great Get-together," Dyson figured, would have to be a watershed for Coke and its relations with bottlers, solidifying Coca-Cola's ranks in advance of any counterattack against Pepsi.

At the same time, Dyson knew that Coke couldn't afford any open rebellion in San Francisco. Coca-Cola had to get bottlers to amend the 1921 contract, and the issue had to be settled before the convention. Dyson and Keough stepped up their efforts to get a new agreement with Coke's two biggest bottlers, who between them controlled nearly one quarter of the U.S. market. The Coca-Cola Bottling Company of New York was determined to pay as little for syrup and concentrate from Coke as it could in return for agreeing to more flexibility on future changes in prices. In April Coke made a tactical concession, agreeing to New York's demands. The following month the Associated Coca-Cola Bottling Company, which distributes Coke in much of Florida, upstate New York, Philadelphia, and southern New Jersey, also agreed to sign the '78 Amendments. With that, more than 50 percent of Coke's bottlers were signed, sealed, and delivered. The stage was set for San Francisco.

Some three thousand Coca-Cola and bottling company executives met for Coke's Great Get-together the second week in June. Dyson promised stepped-up marketing assistance for all the "amended" bottlers — those who had already signed the '78 Amendments. At the same time, he and other Coke executives urged bottlers to reassess their own marketing strategies in an effort to increase their market shares in the face of stiff competition from Pepsi-Cola and, increasingly, from 7-Up. The Philip Morris Company had bought 7-Up in the summer of 1978 and was quickly gearing up to pour its enormous marketing resources into the "UnCola." Coke, in response, wanted the bottlers to spend more money on marketing, providing shelf displays for grocery stores, making more frequent deliveries, and the like. To assist, Coke announced creation of the Coca-Cola Finance Company, making $100 million available on easy terms, much of the cash earmarked to help bottlers buy vending machines and thereby boost their number of sales outlets.

Almost as important, Dyson knew, was Coca-Cola's offer to give bottlers something they'd been demanding for months: a new advertising campaign. The lackluster "Coke Adds Life" had been the company's standard for the previous three years, and bottlers considered the campaign so "tired" that there was even talk that Coke's long-time ad agency, McCann-Erickson, was in danger of losing the account.

On Friday June 15, 1979, at San Francisco's Civic Auditorium, however, McCann delivered a new message, "Have a Coke and a smile." The slogan was everywhere: emblazoned on a helium balloon tethered to the top of the Hyatt Hotel in Union Square; on banners around town; even in window displays at some retail stores featuring Coke memorabilia. But the star was one TV commercial in particular. In it, Pittsburgh Steeler defensive lineman "Mean" Joe Greene, limping to the locker room after a bad day on the field, passes a young boy who offers him a Coke. Reluctantly, Mean Joe takes the drink and quaffs it down in one swig. Refreshed, he calls after the boy, who is already leaving the tunnel, "Hey kid, catch!" He tosses the boy his soiled jersey and cracks a wide smile. The commercial became a classic, and it delivered strongly on Coke's new "smile" slogan.

The bottlers were ecstatic. The new ad campaign was clearly a winner, and a pep talk by the new president of Coca-Cola USA signaled a significant shift in strategy for the company. Atlanta was becoming more aggressive itself, readier to take on Pepsi face to face, and the $100 million made available in low-interest loans was proof that Coca-Cola was willing to put its money on the line even as it demanded more from the bottlers. Even those executives who had not signed the '78 Amendments left San Francisco convinced that Coca-Cola was on a roll.

A month later Crass Bottling was again looking to sell out. This time, though, the prospective buyer was Northwest Industries, a bottling company that was interested in adding Crass to its stable of Coca-Cola markets, which included Los Angeles, Kansas City, and Madison, Wisconsin. The possible acquisition scared Dyson for two reasons. First, Northwest was one of the holdouts among bottlers refusing to sign the '78 Amendments, so by expanding its territory, Northwest would have an even stronger adversarial position vis-à-vis Coke headquarters. Second, Coca-Cola remained worried that the FTC might torpedo the exclusive territorial bottling system, and if it did, the much larger Northwest would be well equipped to expand into other markets as well, trampling over smaller bottlers who may already have signed the amendments. If so, Coke would face the possibility of a permanent foe among the ranks of its bottlers, one with the clout to undermine Atlanta's attempts to get a better deal from its bottlers *and* push them into stepped-up marketing efforts.

Don Keough and Brian Dyson agreed that Coke either had to buy Crass itself, or at least arrange that it fall into the proper hands. With the help of Citicorp, they put together a consortium that included Coca-Cola, the Prudential Insurance Company, and Citicorp's venture-capital unit. Chairman Paul Austin was at first opposed to the buyout because it was mostly based on borrowed capital and interest rates were rising rapidly. But Keough and Dyson argued that Coca-Cola had to look beyond the cost of this one transaction to an overall strategy that was essential to repositioning Coke in the U.S. market. Finally, with Austin's blessing, Coca-Cola's board of directors approved the buyout in December 1979. Coca-Cola would now run Crass Bottling, most of the bottlers had accepted the '78 Amendments, and Atlanta had made clear to other bottlers that it would brook no major dissension in the ranks. Barely days after the board approved the buyout, Coke executives would see in a new year as well as a new decade. At last, Keough and Dyson figured, they could turn all their attention to the real problem at hand, Pepsi.

The authors of the Pepsi Challenge were watching Coke, too. Slowly but surely, the sales figures for Pepsi showed gains both in supermarket sales and at soda fountains. And the head of Pepsi-Cola USA, John Sculley, still in his thirties, was convinced that Pepsi could ultimately overtake Coke for two fundamental reasons, taste and marketing. Test after test showed that consumers, especially younger ones, preferred the sweeter, smoother taste of Pepsi. And as the Pepsi Generation grew up, Coke's long-time stranglehold on the market would dissipate. As the industry's number two, Sculley knew from his graduate marketing courses at the Wharton School in Philadelphia, Pepsi-Cola could afford the luxury of comparative advertising, and the resulting Pepsi Challenge went even further than comparative: it was downright combative! Sculley also had the luxury of taking on a slumbering giant, one that was visibly set in its ways and unlikely to fight Pepsi's fire with fire of its own. Unlike Coke, which had steadfastly refused to put the Coca-Cola name on any of its other soft drinks, Pepsi had no compunction about putting its brand name on Diet Pepsi. And unlike Coca-Cola, Pepsi didn't have large, independent bottlers to contend with, making it easier to execute tough marketing tactics from its headquarters.

Brian Dyson was not above taking a page out of Sculley's marketing notebook. The buyout of Crass Bottling and the '78 Amendments represented the best deal Atlanta could get from its bottlers, given the system's history. In November 1978 Dyson began to write a strategic plan for Coke's U.S. operations. Until then, any plan had been eschewed by such corporate higher-ups as Austin. Working with Bryan Hiller, head of the headquarters planning staff, Dyson hired the Arthur D. Little consulting firm to help with the study that surfaced six months later. Boiled down to basics, the strategy called for a strengthening in Coke's overall line of soft drinks. Only Sprite, Tab, and Coke were flourishing. The Fanta line of sodas wasn't doing well, nor was Mr. PiBB, Coke's answer to Dr Pepper (the period in Dr. had been dropped in the 1950s). The company also needed a reformulated and repackaged Fresca, and it decided to halt the introduction of its Mello Yello brand, keeping it east of the Mississippi.

In early 1979 Brian Dyson began seriously assessing the impact Diet Pepsi was having on overall Pepsi sales. Low-calorie sodas represented a market that promised the greatest growth in sales and profits in the 1980s. Tab was still the best-selling diet drink, but Diet Pepsi was closing the gap, largely on the strength of what consumer tests showed was a milder, less "diet" taste. With the market expanding exponentially, Dyson was worried that Tab might continue to sell well but would soon be displaced by a Diet Pepsi that appealed to younger drinkers as they gradually switched from sugared colas to diet versions.

If Tab wasn't the right product to stay ahead of the growing pack of diet colas, the formula wasn't the only problem. Dyson was convinced that much of Diet Pepsi's strength came from the Pepsi name, at a time when Coca-Cola wasn't even using the Coke name in the fastest-growing segment of the market. Dyson felt, in early 1980, that it was time to take the plunge with a new diet soft drink called Diet Coke.

No issue could have touched off more heated debate at headquarters in Atlanta. The opposition to extending the Coke name was almost institutional. Nearly two decades earlier, a few executives had suggested calling the company's new low-calorie drink Diet Coca-Cola. That suggestion was ignored by Coke's top brass, on the ground that it would devalue the Coke name, the company's premier asset. Instead, the company called its new soda Tab, one of thousands of prospective brand names generated by an IBM computer. Several times in the intervening years there had been talk of changing the Tab name or introducing a new diet drink with the Coke name, but it turned out to be idle talk. Now the reception to Dyson's plan was equally chilly. Paul Austin himself was critical, but he authorized an experimental project to see whether Keough, Dyson, and Coke's scientists could come up with a product that might be worthy of the Coke name. With that, Dyson began doing market research, and Coke's chemists started experimenting.

As the Diet Coke project got under way, Dyson had no illusions about how much support he could expect from the Old Guard. Austin, after all, really didn't want to give a go-ahead on the project. The chairman wasn't sure it was the right direction for Coke to go in. And he himself wouldn't be able to see it through. Already past the mandatory retirement age of sixty-five, Austin had been granted a one-year extension by the board of directors in the absence of any clear successor as chief executive. He was also becoming increasingly alienated from Coke's senior staff. Although few people knew it at the time, Austin was suffering from the early onset of Alzheimer's disease, an explanation for his fits of memory loss and unexpected flip-flops in decisions from one day to the next. In August 1979 his second in command, J. Lucian Smith, had resigned as president. In his place, Austin created an "Office of the Chairman" and promoted six top corporate officers to the post of vice chairman. The Vice Squad, as they came to be known inside the company, would slug it out to determine the winner.

Ian Wilson, the South African–born head of Coke's Pacific operations, was Austin's pick. Along with another new vice chairman, Albert Killeen, boss of Coke's new wine group, Austin and Wilson were known inside the company as the South African Mafia, Killeen because he, too, was South African and Austin because his only overseas assignment had been as the head of Coke's African operations, based in Johannesburg. Rounding out the race for the chairman's job were Don Keough; Claus Halle, a German who was then head of Coke's European and African operations; Ira Herbert, president of the foods division; and Roberto Goizueta, the Cuban-born boss of Coke's administrative and technical staffs.

In May 1980 Coke's board of directors held a special meeting in Atlanta to end some of the internal feuding that was clearly affecting the senior management team. Killeen, an ardent opponent of the still-secret Diet Coke project, had gotten Austin to kill the project in March. Keough heard of the decision in a telegram delivered to his Buenos Aires hotel room one morning during a swing through some of Coke's South American operations. The telegram was short, to the point, and gave no explanation for the order to "stop all work ... immediately." The telegram was signed by Paul Austin himself.

At the board meeting on May 30, 1980, the South African Mafia was by-passed, and the board's pick was, by many accounts, the least likely choice among the Vice Squad contenders. Roberto Goizueta, then forty-nine, was appointed president and chief operating officer. Although it wasn't made public at the time, Coke's directors, at the order of Robert Woodruff, also decided that Goizueta would take over as chairman and chief executive officer when Austin's term was up in March 1981. At the same time the board promoted Don Keough, elevating him over the other five vice chairmen in the old management structure. The Office of the Chairman was disbanded. In its place, Keough became Coke's senior executive vice president. Wilson, Halle, Herbert, and Killeen became executive vice presidents, along with John Collings, the company's chief financial officer.

At first Goizueta seemed an unlikely choice to lead an All-American company called Coca-Cola. He had never had direct charge of any of the company's products. In a company that depended heavily on marketing, Goizueta had been in charge of Coke's administrative, legal, technical, and public relations departments. He was also an unassuming man who, despite twenty years in the States, still spoke with a trace of a Spanish accent. In fact, Goizueta first came to the United States in 1949 at the age of eighteen to attend a prep school in Connecticut. In 1954 he graduated from Yale with a degree in chemistry and went home to Havana. An only son, he went to work for the family sugar business. A year later, eager to be on his own, he answered a blind ad in a local newspaper for a chemist position with a large multinational firm, which was Coca-Cola. When Fidel Castro nationalized Coke's operations in 1961, Goizueta moved first to Miami, where he had sent his family at the time of the revolution, then to Nassau, to work in Coke's Caribbean office for three years before being transferred to Atlanta. Two years later, at the age of thirty-five, he became Coca-Cola's youngest vice president, and, from his position in charge of Coke's technical operations, began climbing the corporate ladder.

"Partner." Coca-Cola's chairman emeritus Robert Woodruff used the word sparingly, but from early on it became Woodruff's nickname for Goizueta. Insiders saw no great ambition in

Goizueta, but Woodruff took to him like a father to a son. Like Woodruff, Goizueta appeared to have no enemies. It was Woodruff, not Austin, who placed the call to Goizueta's office to inform his favorite that he was now president.

Although Goizueta had a reputation for striking compromises, he was also quick to resolve disputes, and unyielding in having senior management toe the line once a course of action was decided. From the first discussions prompted by Dyson's proposal, Goizueta favored the Diet Coke project, and as soon as he was named president, he put the project back on the front burner. He urged Keough and Dyson to work quickly but quietly on the project; if word leaked too early, Coke's rivals might make some sort of strike. There was still considerable opposition from within the company, opposition that Goizueta couldn't afford to let out in the open until Austin had retired and he, Goizueta, was sitting in the chairman's office.

With Goizueta egging them on, Keough and Dyson needed a strong point man to organize the Diet Coke project, which had quickly become the centerpiece of their strategy vis-à-vis Pepsi. With Pepsi only gradually eating into the market for regular Coke, the real spoils of the cola wars belonged to whichever company could capitalize on the growing demand for diet soft drinks. And for that, Coca-Cola needed a more powerful offering than Tab.

> *It is essential to understand the flow of the opponent's personality, to find out his strengths and weaknesses.*
>
> — Miyamoto Musashi

It became clear that the point man for Diet Coke would be best served if he was familiar with Pepsi's strategy in the market, and they didn't have to look very far for the right person, one with whom both Goizueta and Dyson felt comfortable. After all, he was a Latin. He also represented the new blood Goizueta was eager to promote into more senior jobs as he himself made the transition from the presidency to the chairmanship he would inherit in only a few months.

When Sergio Zyman, a Mexican Jew, was plucked by Roberto Goizueta and Brian Dyson to mastermind the Diet Coke project, he was Don Keough's main assistant. He got his first experience with Coca-Cola working on the company's advertising account at McCann-Erickson's office in Mexico City. Later he joined Pepsi-Cola in South America, and when he was recruited by Keough in 1978, he had been in charge of marketing at Pepsi. If anyone knew how to respond to Pepsi's challenge, it was Zyman.

When he was first offered the plum Diet Coke project, he turned it down because he had been planning to spend the summer at Harvard's Advanced Management Program, but Keough and Dyson prevailed. For his pains, Zyman got to label the top-secret undertaking with his code name, Project Harvard. And top secret the project was. Over the next forty-eight months no files were kept, no letters written, no photocopies made. Most of the key meetings took place in Atlanta hotel rooms, *not* at Coke's plush new Corporate Tower.

In August 1980, the same month that Coca-Cola announced that its president would take over as chairman the following March, Roberto Goizueta escalated his raid on the ranks of Pepsi alumni. He announced that John Bergin would assume control of the company's account at McCann-Erickson in New York. Bergin hadn't been involved in soft drinks for over six years, but he was a legend in the industry, having created the memorable Pepsi Generation campaign at BBD&O. When he moved into the Coke account, he was vice chairman of SSC&B, McCann's sister agency in the Interpublic Group, the largest holding company on Madison Avenue. He was handed the job only after Coke, and specifically Keough, threatened to pull the account from McCann, not necessarily because McCann's ads weren't doing the job, but because of the agency's complicity in Austin's earlier decision to kill the Diet Coke project. When Bergin took the job, he was unaware of the feud over Diet Coke and McCann's role in it; McCann had assured him that relations with Coca-Cola had never been better. Either way, it was clear that unless Bergin came up with a winner, McCann-Erickson, which had booked Coca-Cola's advertising since 1955, risked losing the account.

As Bergin set to work on a new ad campaign for Coke, Project

Harvard was progressing under full steam, the veil of secrecy lifted only for a select few senior managers responsible for directing and digesting the research. The company's marketing staff had been regularly surveying the soft drink market since 1953, conducting annual consumer surveys to measure purchasing habits, advertising awareness, and brand loyalty. Zyman and the research department devised three key tests to measure the viability of Diet Coke. First, they needed to find out whether the Coke name would make a big difference.

To do so, some four hundred diet soft drink consumers were put through a series of taste tests in shopping malls in San Diego, Rochester, Philadelphia, and Denver. The first test was a blind one between two diet drinks, say, Diet Pepsi and Tab. Then the test was repeated with clearly labeled cans. There was one hitch: Coke's chemists still hadn't come up with a recipe for Diet Coke. Instead, the researchers substituted either Tab or Diet Pepsi. Asked to compare Diet Pepsi and Diet Coke, for instance, consumers were actually comparing Diet Pepsi and Tab. Similarly, in the Tab versus Diet Coke test, the Diet Coke can actually contained Diet Pepsi. The results showed the value of the Coke name. Consumers were roughly split in their preference between Diet Pepsi and Tab, but overwhelmingly chose Diet Coke (actually Tab) over Diet Pepsi in tests where the brands were identified. Likewise, Diet Pepsi in a Diet Coke can fared better against Tab. Clearly, the Coke name carried clout, seeming to matter even more than the taste of the drink itself. Subsequent tests reached the same conclusion: consumers generally picked cans labeled Diet Coke — no matter what they contained — over Pepsi's offering.

At the same time, Coke executives were surprised and delighted at the relatively low rate of "cannibalization" of Tab. They feared that Diet Coke might simply pull customers away from Tab, hurting Coke instead of Pepsi. Yet all the tests showed Diet Coke pulling a majority of buyers away from Diet Pepsi and other diet soft drinks, and amazingly few from Tab. Dyson and Zyman figured that if Diet Coke siphoned off two thirds of Tab's sales, the new introduction wouldn't be worth the effort. The tests seemed to show, on the contrary, that Tab's loyal base of figure-conscious women — accounting for 70 percent of Tab sales — might prove to be more loyal than consumers of Diet Pepsi. Indeed, Tab had fewer consumers than Diet Pepsi, but those who did buy Tab bought a lot more of it, making it the best-selling diet soft drink in the world.

To keep Diet Coke distinct, the company's chemists worked on a concoction that would have broader appeal than Tab. Consumers identified Diet Pepsi with a clear, mild, smooth taste. Tab was a dieter's drink, with no calories and no sugar. The concept that Zyman and Dyson took to their chemists was simple: "Diet Coke. A clear, smooth, light, real cola taste."

On March 1, 1981, Coca-Cola announced disappointing earnings for 1980. Profits were flat despite higher sales. The same day, promising to restore the profit ethic that had once made Coke a darling on Wall Street, Roberto Goizueta, just short of his fiftieth birthday, took over from Austin as chairman and chief executive officer.

From his plush, modern, twenty-fifth floor office atop the Coca-Cola tower, Goizueta moved quickly to end the division between the Old Guard and Young Turks within the company. Unlike the matador cast in bronze, part of a statue that adorned a fake Chippendale in one corner of the office, Goizueta knew he couldn't take the bull by the horns on his own. He was committed to uniting his management team behind one purpose: to counter Pepsi's challenge. He named Don Keough, fifty-four, president. Dyson and Zyman kept their jobs, now enhanced by direct access to the chairman's office.

The team was in place to guide Coke through the rest of the decade. Three days after taking over, Goizueta personally put the finishing touches to a nine-hundred-page position paper he had been drafting for more than six months. He asked, and got, the board of directors to endorse his "Strategy for the 1980s." The position paper put a premium on reassessing even the most ingrained corporate traditions. "Intelligent, individual risk-taking," Goizueta wrote, was to be encouraged. The new chairman, in short, was ready and willing to rewrite the rule book at Coca-Cola.

Goizueta knew that nothing less was needed to revive Coke's profits. And the Diet Coke project was a key component in the new strategy. Goizueta also felt that the company should get out of unrelated businesses, notably Aqua-Chem, which manufactured water-purification systems. Finally, Goizueta believed that Coca-Cola should diversify its holdings through a strategic acquisition in a related industry, probably entertainment.

The new chairman invited Coca-Cola's top fifty executives to a meeting in Palm Springs to iron out details of the new plan. "Tell me what we're doing wrong," Goizueta asked his team. "I want to know it all, and once it's settled, I want 100-percent loyalty. If anyone is not happy, we will make you a good settlement and say good-bye." By the time the meeting broke up, Aqua-Chem was on the block, the planning staff was charged with finding an acquisition in the entertainment business, and Project Harvard acquired a new urgency — and backing — in Atlanta.

That spring of 1981, Coke chemists devised five different formulas for Diet Coke and tested them against Tab and Diet Pepsi. None seemed to fit the smooth, light formula Zyman considered essential to positioning the new diet drink alongside Coca-Cola's other offerings. The one time a formula beat Diet Pepsi handily, it turned out that Coke's concoction had been tested against a bad batch of syrup. The mistake caused a two-month delay for new testing. This time, however, the Diet Coke formula beat a *good* sample of Diet Pepsi, by a respectable seven or eight percentage points. The taste was close enough to Diet Pepsi not to threaten Tab.

Less than five months after Project Harvard began, Dyson and Zyman had a product to sell. The next move was to create the packaging. In May Zyman asked industrial designer Alvin Schechter to work on a Diet Coke "look," requiring as part of the commission that the designer pledge total secrecy. Zyman remained worried about the impact on sales of Tab — and a possible surprise attack by Pepsi — if word of Diet Coke leaked out.

Schechter was best known for his work on Budweiser beer and Camel cigarette packaging, as well as Coke's own Wine Spectrum products. Handed the Diet Coke assignment, Schechter was asked to preserve the Coca-Cola logo in Spencerian script, as well as the "dynamic curve" that runs from top to bottom on all Coke cans and bottles. In short, he was being asked to blend innovation and tradition, giving Diet Coke a fresh look while capitalizing on the most widely recognized brand name in the world. Over the next two months Schechter showed Zyman nearly 150 different versions. Zyman rejected all of them: red backgrounds were too close to mainstream Coke cans; blue was too closely identified with Pepsi, silver with Diet Rite. The name was tried horizontally, vertically, diagonally. There were thin-, medium-, and fat-letter versions, as well as a variety of type faces and sizes. In the end, Schechter and Zyman agreed on a style that neither of them had originally thought would work: red printing on a white background, essentially a reversal of Coke's original colors. To enliven the white background and keep the package from appearing generic, Schechter added diagonal silver pinstripes to the design. Combined with a larger type face than the one used on Coke cans, the "diet Coke" — with a small *d* — design was fresh and bold.

All this time, the Rabbi of Diet Coke, as Sergio Zyman was dubbed in Atlanta, kept his project a secret, even inside Coca-Cola, from all but those most directly involved. Project Harvard gave way to a succession of code names designed to throw off nosy Coke employees. Zyman's top assistant filled his office with orange juice cartons and jars, and Zyman occasionally referred to the project as Tampa, to promote rumors that the project was connected with the company's Minute Maid subsidiary. Subsequently, the code names varied: Lucy, Shrimp, and BPS, the last three meaningless letters that some Coke executives later speculated stood for "Beat Pepsi Soundly," "Bottler Productivity Study," or "Best Product under the Sun."

Partly because of McCann-Erickson's earlier doubts about Diet Coke, Zyman hired SSC&B to work on the Diet Coke account. On July 31, 1981, he met with Dyson in New York and boldly suggested that all systems were in place to begin marketing the new drink as early as the autumn. Dyson was surprised: he had been periodically apprised of the project's progress, but had not expected Zyman to bring everything together so quickly. The bottlers, he knew, would be reluctant to gear up for a major new product introduction during the fourth quarter. Millions of dollars would have to be spent to retool bottling plants and advertise the new entry, without any hope of making it all back before the end of the year, depressing earnings for the second year in a row. Bottlers wanted to report higher profits for 1981, and Goizueta, in his first year as chairman, was eager to comply.

Caution was essential. Pepsi was unlikely to be working on a new entry in the diet market, since its name was already on the second biggest seller. So there was no immediate threat from the enemy camp, and rather than risk any faux pas in rolling out Diet Coke, Dyson decided to postpone its debut until the spring. The delay would also give Zyman more time to work on a long-term marketing campaign for the diet soda.

The more slowly military action proceeds ... mistakes can be more easily repaired.
— Karl von Clausewitz

Zyman was disappointed, but not for long. He was splitting his time between "BPS" and a major overhaul of Coke's mainstream advertising. John Bergin had amassed hundreds of suggested slogans and phrases and commissioned several music houses in New York to write songs for the nineteen slogans he liked best. Zyman pored over the results and settled with Bergin on five trial campaigns for intensive testing. "Coke makes it better" was the most conventional; the others were "You've got a Coke comin' to ya," "Just like you, Coke comes through," "Going all out. Going with Coke," and, finally, "Coke is it!"

The song "Coke Is It!" was originally written by McCann copywriter Ken Schulman for Coke's Canadian subsidiary, with a refrain that went, "The biggest taste in Canada." Bergin changed the refrain to "The biggest taste you've ever found" and set the slogan to snappy, fast-paced music. What emerged was a fight song, lively and aggressive, precisely the positive statement Bergin knew Coke, with Pepsi snapping at its heels, was trying to make. Zyman went for it immediately, but told Bergin to put together the other trial campaigns as well, using existing footage to create sample TV commercials. "Coke is it!" predictably came out on top in several test surveys.

Armed with the survey results, Zyman and Bergin took the whole set of commercials to Ira Herbert, Coke's head of marketing, and Roberto Goizueta. "You're bringing us four straw men and a campaign," Herbert told Bergin after seeing the five campaigns. Goizueta was even more impressed. The usually soft-spoken Cuban was excited. Turning up the volume on the cassette player, he pounded his fist to the emphasized one-two-three beat, occasionally punctuating the music with his own, "Coke-is-it!"

"Hit it hard," Goizueta advised Bergin. "The phrase really has to stand out." The words and the music achieved just what Coca-Cola's chairman was looking for to characterize his company's aggressive new posture, a counterpoint to the ballads that had dominated Coke's advertising for twenty years. "Did you notice that 'Coke is it' is eight letters long?" Goizueta asked Bergin later. "I guess so," the ad man replied, not quite knowing what Coke's boss was driving at until Goizueta said "So is 'I love you.'"

On February 4, 1981, more than twenty-five hundred Coke executives and bottlers crowded into Atlanta's Civic Auditorium — and loved what they saw. The hall was dark except for a magenta beam of light pointed at a huge screen in front. Dramatically, the Atlanta Symphony rose from the orchestra pit, striking up Coca-Cola's new anthem. Goizueta, Dyson, and Zyman all provided pep talks, but it was the commercials that did the talking. One after another they appeared on the screen, shot from Round Rock, Texas, to Portland, Oregon, and Brooklyn, New York. An exhausted softball team stopping by Joe's Place for an after-game refresher: "Coke is it!" A farmer coming in from the fields to a surprise birthday party: "The biggest taste you've ever found!" A group of young off-Broadway performers launching into an impromptu song during a rehearsal break. "The one that never lets you down!" A teary-eyed boy getting back on the bus for home after a day's trip to a working farm: "Coke is it!" Everyone everywhere in the six spots was drinking a Coke. The bottlers loved it. The next day Coke repeated the show for its own employees. That evening Coke's new campaign debuted at 9:15 on all three networks, a technique called roadblocking. Virtually every television viewer in America saw the commercials. Coke was positioned with the public, Goizueta told himself that evening; now would begin the task of translating the awareness into regaining some of the market that Pepsi had captured in the 1970s.

Even before the commercials appeared, Coke's board of directors had met and approved Roberto Goizueta's ambitious takeover of a Hollywood studio, Columbia Pictures Industries. The acquisition was the follow-up to the decision to branch out into a related industry that could add some pizzazz to Coca-Cola's earnings. For months Goizueta had been scouring Hollywood for the right buy. Columbia was on the block, and its chairman, Herbert Allen, was only too happy to unload the studio in the wake of the David Begelman scandal. Following revelations that the head of Columbia's movie operations had forged checks to cover personal debts, several management shakeups had sapped morale and drastically cut back the pace of film production. Ultimately, Allen, more a Wall Street investor than a movie mogul, wanted to get out. When the Coca-Cola board approved the $750 million purchase in January 1982, accounts in the business press questioned the wisdom of Coke's getting into a highly volatile and apparently tainted business about which it knew nothing. What the press didn't question was Goizueta's willingness to take risks and tamper with Coke's stodgy image. In a matter of weeks, it became clear how Coke could afford the gamble.

The Diet Coke project, meanwhile, had derailed — almost literally, albeit temporarily. Aiming for a March launch, Sergio Zyman and Brian Dyson had been asked to engineer one final test of the product. In late January a truck left Atlanta for Birmingham in the middle of a massive snowstorm. On board was a top-secret cargo of Diet Coke cans and bottles. The truck went off Interstate 20 into a ditch and its precious cargo froze. When news of the accident reached Atlanta, Zyman tried to get Goizueta to allow the launch without the final taste test. Goizueta refused, ordering a delay in the introduction until the summer. He told Zyman and Dyson to repeat the test. Coke could afford the delay; it was certainly better than risking a mistake. Unhappy with the further delay, Zyman took leave of the Diet Coke project in February, eager to spend a few months at the Harvard management program he'd skipped two years earlier. This time Dyson didn't object. Coke's liaison with the bottlers, Marvin Griffin, had warned him that the rollout would go a lot smoother *without* Zyman. Griffin, who didn't like the brash Mexican, believed that Zyman would rub the bottlers the wrong way. Dyson was reluctant to see the Rabbi go, but he also knew there was some truth to Griffin's objections. Rather than over-rule Griffin, he okayed Zyman's sabbatical.

Fortunately, Zyman's work on the Diet Coke project was finished anyway. The product, its packaging, an advertising campaign, and reams of research data were all there. The commercials he developed with SSC&B were in line with the broad-based appeal Goizueta, Keough, and Dyson intended for the drink. While Tab and Diet Pepsi targeted a largely female audience with diet-conscious commercials, Diet Coke's slogan was for everyone: "Introducing Diet Coke. Just for the taste of it." Zyman was pushing the taste element, and the commercials depicted more than the token number of men usually seen in low-calorie soft drink commercials. At the same time, Coke was working on a new campaign for Tab that would focus more than ever before on female dieters.

On July 8, 1982, at a press conference in New York, Brian Dyson announced that Diet Coke would be on supermarket shelves in the Big Apple in August. There would be no test marketing for the new cola, Dyson told reporters. The company would pull out all the stops for a nationwide rollout of the diet drink strictly on the basis of advance taste tests and consumer surveys, a procedure that was virtually unheard of in the soft drink business, where companies typically marketed a new product in small markets, then larger regions, before making it available nationally. The press got Dyson's drift: Coca-Cola was convinced that Diet Coke would be a hit. Dyson also made it clear that his company was looking at new ways to leverage the most widely recognized consumer name in the world. "The introduction of this product means that the Coca-Cola Company is looking at its equities in a totally different light," Dyson said, elliptically referring to the Coke name. "We are turning this company from a warehouse of equity into a factory of equity. Our trademark is our most precious resource. It is the very fiber of this company, and we intend to make use of it from now on."

The decision to launch Diet Coke in the New York market was unconventional, given the tradition of starting in smaller markets where any hitches or marketing gaffes would attract less attention. But having decided not to go the traditional route of region by region marketing, Coke executives were seeking to attract the greatest attention. And the chairman of Coke's New York bottler, Charles Millard, was willing to go all out for the new rollout. He rented Radio City Music Hall for what was billed on the marquee that evening as "The World Première of Diet Coke." Inside, some four thousand employees of Coke and the Coca-Cola Bottling Co. of New York saw one of the most extravagant kick-offs ever, complete with high-kicking Rockettes and a sixty-second TV commercial featuring Joe Namath, Judd Hirsch, and Phil Esposito, all drinking Diet Coke on the streets of New York.

Dyson agreed to pick up part of the tab for the New York "opening." In return, Millard let Coke videotape the extravaganza for an "event" TV commercial that SSC&B wanted to put together for the national introduction of Diet Coke. There were no stars on hand at Radio City, but the video crew put the hoopla on tape, with the Rockettes dancing and kicking their way around a fourteen-foot-tall can of Diet Coke. Then SSC&B rented the Shrine Auditorium in Los Angeles for a day and filled the theater with hundreds of extras and a dozen or so recognizable stars, seated and filmed as though they were actually in Radio City Music Hall watching the Rockettes — and drinking Diet Coke right there in the audience. By the time the sixty-second commercial was shot and edited, it set Coke back a lot more than the $500,000 originally budgeted — five times as much, to be precise, making it the most expensive commercial ever made to that date.

The rollout of Diet Coke went like clockwork. By the end of September, it was available to 15 percent of all Americans; by the end of 1982, 30 percent; and by the following spring, the fig-

ure was up to 90 percent. It marked another superlative for
Coca-Cola: the fastest national rollout in soft drink history. Diet
Coke was well on its way toward passing both Diet Pepsi and
Tab, with sales in most markets running at double the level
Coke had projected. The new product's rate of cannibalization
of other Coke products was far less than the 35 percent Coke executives expected would come at Tab's expense, plus 12 percent
from Coca-Cola itself. In other words, nearly half of Diet Coke's
sales might have come out of the company's own revenues. The
actual rate was far lower. Only 24 percent was coming from
erstwhile Tab drinkers. And all told, only 34 percent of Diet
Coke's sales could be traced to switchovers from Tab, Coca-
Cola, and Sprite combined. Tab drinkers were proving even
more loyal than Coke had hoped. Although it was clear that Diet
Coke was expanding the marketplace, the real cannibalization
was hurting Pepsi's sales more than Coke's.

But less than twenty-four hours before Dyson unveiled Diet
Coke, Coca-Cola was being put on the defensive. Pepsi-Cola
president John Sculley called a press conference, also in New
York, to unveil a new drink of his own, a caffeine-free cola called
Pepsi Free. When Brian Dyson met many of the same reporters
the next day, the questions were disparaging, even acerbic. Why
bring out a new diet cola at all? Wouldn't it cannibalize the
market that was already dominated by Tab? Did Coca-Cola, the
reporters seemed to be asking, really have its act together?

In fact, Sculley's announcement came as no surprise to Coke,
although Dyson thought that the timing of the announcement
had been a calculated attempt by Pepsi to undermine the Diet
Coke release. As early as 1980, research had shown that there
was a definite market for a cola without the caffeine that had
originally been added to colas in the nineteenth century to enhance the taste.

Coke's own economists estimated that caffeine-free soft drinks
could eventually account for 15 percent of the market. The real
question for Coke wasn't *whether* to enter the market, but
how — and when. A full year earlier, Royal Crown had broken
new ground in the industry with RC-100, the first cola free of

caffeine. From then on, both Coke and Pepsi had put their researchers to work tracking how consumers felt about the new
variation. At the same time, Philip Morris's 7-Up subsidiary
started an all-out campaign to enhance its reputation as an alternative to the colas. "No caffeine," proclaimed the new slogan.
"Never had it, never will." Even as Coca-Cola was preparing to
introduce Diet Coke in the spring of 1981, its chemists were
working on caffeine-free formulas for Tab and Diet Coke as well
as Coca-Cola itself. Without the caffeine, Coke had a somewhat
bitter taste and required more sugar to resemble the flavor of
regular Coke. The adjustments in the formulas for the company's diet colas had been easier to make. When it became clear
that Coke could produce caffeine-free colas that maintained the
taste of "the real thing," Goizueta and his lieutenants faced a
tough decision.

There were three principal alternative marketing strategies
available to Coca-Cola in its response to Pepsi Free. First of all,
it could produce an entirely new brand of cola sans caffeine like
RC-100. Or it could convert
one of its existing brands, the
obvious candidate being Tab.
It was already an established
brand among health-conscious

*True concentration is the prod-
uct of calculated dispersion.*
— B. H. Liddell Hart

consumers, and the transition to a diet, caffeine-free offering
would not be difficult to accomplish. In Atlanta, Sergio Zyman,
back from his sabbatical at Harvard, seriously considered the
option, not least because it would further differentiate Tab from
Diet Coca-Cola. The other alternative was to respond with caffeine-free versions of all its cola drinks: Coca-Cola, Diet Coke,
and Tab.

It was Dyson who vetoed turning Tab into the company's
only caffeine-free offering. He worried that such a move would
be tantamount to gambling Tab's hard-earned, billion-dollar
market on an untested cola that could turn out to be just a fad.
Dyson also nixed a new brand of cola: he felt that Coca-Cola
couldn't afford to spend the millions necessary to establish a
completely new brand, especially at a time when it was making a
big push for Diet Coke. So "line extension" was the answer, he

decided, as long as it could be done without jeopardizing the appeal of the existing brands. By spreading the risk and offering caffeine-free versions of all three main brands, Coke was creating a more effective concentration of its marketing resources against Pepsi, with its Pepsi Free and a diet version.

Rather than respond immediately to the Pepsi Free announcement, however, Dyson waited. Coke could probably have put its decaffeinated colas on grocery shelves as quickly as Pepsi could, but Dyson was in no rush. He didn't want to dilute the marketing effort that was just getting under way for Diet Coke, a product that was almost certain to become a bigger seller in the market than any of the caffeine-free versions. The delay would also give Coke a chance to see how Pepsi Free, in both forms, fared in the marketplace.

By November the answer was clear. Pepsi Free had already overtaken RC-100 in the non-caffeine cola market. With the Diet Coke marketing proceeding smoothly, Dyson took his proposal for three caffeine-free offerings — Coke, Tab, and Diet Coke — to Goizueta and Keough. By January, when the decision was made, it was a foregone conclusion, because there were already signs that Pepsi Free was eating into Coke's line. Meetings with bottlers on the new products began in February. On the heels of the big Diet Coke introduction, three new Coca-Cola drinks would be a shock to the system. For the past twenty years, the company had distributed two colas, Coke and Tab. In less than a year, it was introducing four more. Some bottlers and retailers balked. The bottlers worried about the logistics as well as the need for three caffeine-free brands, while some retailers refused to give more shelf space to Coke products. To help, Coke decided to give away the first delivery to some retailers. For some stores, it meant as much as $400 in free merchandise — and a lot of good will — which guaranteed the shelf space Coke was after. To help the bottlers, Coke executives revamped its entire line of TV commercials, shortening its regular thirty-second spots for Coke, Tab, and Diet Coke and filling the extra ten seconds with a "tag" pitching the caffeine-free versions. The gimmick underscored that the caffeine-free colas were essentially variations of the main brands, not separate brands. They also downplayed the caffeine issue, focusing on caffeine-free colas as a choice rather than a necessity.

By May Diet Coke was available throughout most of the country and Dyson felt it was time to begin marketing the company's caffeine-free drinks. At a press conference in New York, he told reporters that caffeine-free colas would represent more than 15 percent of the soft drink market by the end of 1984, and he predicted that Coca-Cola's offerings would capture at least half those sales. It was an ambitious boast, given Pepsi Free's ten-month lead, but given the speed with which Diet Coke was clearly catching on with consumers, it was a boast that Coca-Cola seemed capable of fulfilling.

A month later Coca-Cola suffered a very public, if not particularly major, setback. It involved Brand Coke (industry jargon for the original soda), not its diet or caffeine-free derivatives. Ever since winning a franchise in 1979 to supply Diet Pepsi as the "official" diet drink at Burger King's restaurants nationwide, Pepsi-Cola had been lobbying to displace Coke completely as the fast-food chain's beverage supplier. Unhappy with what it viewed as preferential treatment Coke was giving to McDonald's, Burger King finally made the switch, handing Pepsi a contract to provide its thirty-two hundred restaurants nationwide with eight million gallons of Pepsi syrup a year. The deal was worth $30 million in annual revenues to Pepsi, and the publicity generated by Burger King's "defection" from Coca-Cola may have been worth even more than that to the Pepsi camp.

The setback was embarrassing for Coca-Cola, but it wasn't cataclysmic. The company still owned the rights to supply ninety-five of the top one hundred "fountain" accounts in the country — mainly fast-food and other restaurant chains, the largest of them being Burger King's archrival, McDonald's. The loss of the Burger King account forced Coke to reassess its fountain operations, paying more attention to its clients despite the fact that such accounts represented a declining share of its market.

Goizueta recognized that the real growth would come from Diet Coke and new extensions of the Coke line. The company couldn't afford to overlook either, and after letting Pepsi take the lead in caffeine-free colas, Goizueta was convinced that from now on, Coke had to be the innovator, the aggressor. Since taking over, Goizueta had contented himself with a series of moves to contain Coca-Cola's declining market share, and it was time to go on the offensive.

Goizueta fired the opening salvo almost exactly one year after Dyson announced Diet Coke. The U.S. Food and Drug Administration announced in July 1983 that it had approved the use of aspartame — the artificial sweetener developed by G. D. Searle & Company under the brand name NutraSweet — in soft drinks. First discovered in 1965, it had been held up in FDA testing for years. For months before the FDA's announcement, however, Coke and Searle had been in negotiations on a worldwide pact to sweeten Diet Coke, and eventually Tab, with NutraSweet. At $90 a pound, NutraSweet cost about twenty times as much as saccharin, so Coke was reluctant to convert 100 percent from saccharin. For its part, Searle objected to any mixture that wouldn't do away with the bitter aftertaste of saccharin. On August 2, 1983, Searle and Coke jointly announced a compromise: NutraSweet would account for about half the sweetener in Diet Coke. And, when Searle could produce enough NutraSweet — thereby reducing the cost per pound — Coca-Cola said, it would begin putting the artificial sweetener in Tab as well. Eventually the cost of aspartame would come down and Coke would switch to 100 percent NutraSweet for sweetening its diet drinks.

> *Invincibility lies in the defense, the possibility of victory in the attack.*
>
> — Sun Tzu

Coke's pre-emptive strike was successful. It took Pepsi-Cola two more months to hammer out a deal with Searle, partly because Coke was immediately taking most of the available output for use in soft drinks. As a result, Diet Coke with NutraSweet had a two-month lead over Diet Pepsi in most markets, just enough time to woo even loyal Diet Pepsi fans to sample the new concoction from Coca-Cola.

Nineteen eighty-three was a banner year for Coca-Cola. Once viewed as a sluggish corporate giant, it was now winning raves on Wall Street. Relations with bottlers were better than ever. The Columbia Pictures acquisition was paying off handsomely, thanks to a steady stream of box-office bonanzas such as *Tootsie* and *Gandhi*. In September Roberto Goizueta had engineered the sale of the company's only remaining money loser, its wine group, which Coke sold to Joseph E. Seagram & Sons for a hefty $200 million. The same year, Diet Coke became the third best-selling soft drink in the country, overtaking both 7-Up and Dr Pepper, and Tab held its own as the number three diet drink after Diet Coke and Diet Pepsi. Overall, Coke's soft drink sales were growing at a 7 percent annual clip compared to half that rate for the industry as a whole. And in a company that hadn't won plaudits for its marketing savvy in nearly twenty years, *Ad-Week* magazine named Roberto Goizueta its Marketer of the Year, and *Fortune* magazine called Coca-Cola the second most admired corporation in the United States, second only to IBM.

Roberto Goizueta was unwilling to rest on those laurels. Nor was the aggressive team that was running Coca-Cola. The company still faced one basic problem: the continuing erosion of Brand Coke's share of the soft drink market. Consumer and scientific research on the Diet Coke project had confirmed what Pepsi had been claiming all along: that younger Americans tended to prefer the sweeter, with nearly ten calories more per can, but smoother taste of Pepsi. The findings flew in the face of brisk sales of all diet colas, and from the very start, even Goizueta was biased against toying with the secret formula for Brand Coke. But when Diet Coke researchers happened on a non-diet formula that appeared to have all the makings of a cola that could beat Pepsi hands down in taste tests, Goizueta saw at least the possibility of killing off the seven-year-old Pepsi Challenge and its incessant taste tests once and for all. The new formula also held out the prospect of building Coca-Cola's constituency among the Pepsi Generation.

Brian Dyson and Sergio Zyman began secretly testing the sugared cola formula based on the taste built into Diet Coke. In the laboratory, the formula appeared to be an important advance over Merchandise 7X, the secret recipe for Coca-Cola that had been locked in a Trust Company of Georgia vault for nearly a century. Its smoother taste would go down easier, convincing Zyman that it might induce drinkers to quaff more of the beverage at a sitting, and sell more Coke in the process. It was also sweeter, with ten more calories per twelve-ounce serving, giving it a taste closer to Pepsi-Cola's even sweeter formula. In short, the new formula had the makings of a strong new entry in the cola wars, one that Coke could use effectively to combat Pepsi's taste claims in blind tests.

At first, neither Zyman nor Dyson saw the new formula as a replacement for the original Coke formula. The company was seeking to leverage its name on new soft drink products, including a cherry-flavored formula that would compete more directly with Dr Pepper than Mr. PiBB was doing in selected regional markets. Dyson and Zyman decided that the best way to test the new formula — tentatively dubbed 7X100 in honor of the company's upcoming centennial in 1986 — would be through extensive consumer taste research rather than marketing the new product in local markets. Similar research had proved successful in advance of the nationwide Diet Coke launching, and if researchers got similar results with the new sugared formula, they could expect to do away with the necessity of test marketing that had traditionally marked the rollout of new soft drinks.

Thus began, in mid 1983, eighteen months of taste tests around the country. More than 190,000 consumers were surveyed at a cost to Coke of $4 million — the most expensive research campaign in the company's history. In "blind" tests, the results were overwhelming. Soda drinkers typically preferred the new formula to the old by a margin of at least 20 percent. In the final tests, consumers were told that one was the taste of existing Coke, the other a *new* formula, and the margin was even more convincing. On average, those surveyed picked the new taste by a margin of 61 to 39. By early 1985 the evidence was clear. Coca-Cola had a new formula that could take on the Pepsi Challenge and beat it.

In January, on one of his regular, twice-weekly trips to visit patriarch Robert Woodruff at his plantation in south Georgia, Roberto Goizueta explained the thrust of the research findings. To Goizueta's surprise, Woodruff — at ninety-five in failing health but still mentally alert — wasn't unalterably opposed to a change in the formula. Years earlier, Woodruff had ruled out all research on the product on the ground that the money would be wasted, since Coca-Cola would never change the formula anyway. Now he seemed to accept that change was inevitable. Returning to Atlanta, Goizueta was well aware that the switch in formulas would encounter stiff resistance among traditionalists inside Coke. But with his mentor at least willing to entertain the notion, Goizueta decided that it was time to think the unthinkable: a new formula for Brand Coke.

By January Sergio Zyman was convinced that Coca-Cola couldn't simply introduce a second version of Coke — Coke II or Son of Coke, as one of his colleagues had taken to calling it. There would be confusion, and inevitable comparisons between the two products. In early discussions with several key bottlers, the same worries surfaced: How could Brand Coke remain the standard-bearer if the company was bringing out a new version that, by the company's own admission, tasted better?

Zyman knew that the experience of Diet Coke indicated otherwise. The new diet cola quickly outsold Tab but, true to internal forecasts, Tab had its own bedrock constituency. In 1984 Diet Coke took 5.4 percent of the soft drink market, with Tab holding on to 1.8 percent, a small but still highly profitable segment. Diet Pepsi, by contrast, had a total 3 percent of the market. Nevertheless, Zyman argued against introducing "Coke II" while keeping Brand Coke on the market. The company's original diet drink, Tab, had a brand recognition all its own; Diet Coke would have an appeal all its own, taking drinkers away from all other diet colas, not just Tab. Just as important, Diet Coke was a new offering in a market that was growing exponentially. Sales of sugared colas, on the other hand, were growing at only a modest pace every year, and most of that growth was coming from overseas sales. So the company couldn't count on a Coke II to capture entirely new markets. Two brands would compete directly with each other as much as they would with Pepsi.

Roberto Goizueta faced the single most important decision he expected to make during his entire career at Coca-Cola when he was told that Robert Woodruff had died on March 7, 1985, ten days after entering Emory University Hospital. Almost certainly, he knew, Woodruff wouldn't have welcomed a change in the secret formula for Coke. But Goizueta believed that Woodruff wouldn't have vetoed it either. The man who built Coca-Cola for more than fifty years had approved the introduction of Cherry Coke barely weeks before going into the hospital. After all, The Boss, as Goizueta still called him, considered himself a good salesman; what Coke hoped to do with 7X100 was to take that salesmanship one step further — into Coca-Cola's second century.

Woodruff's death catalyzed Coca-Cola's board of directors. Within days, Goizueta gave Brian Dyson and Sergio Zyman their marching orders to gear up for a national introduction of 7X100 in the spring. By midsummer, the "new" Coke would replace the "old" one nationwide. An international rollout was put on hold until the new formula was firmly established in the U.S. market.

On April 23, at a huge convention hall in midtown Manhattan, Roberto Goizueta and his colleagues from Atlanta dropped their bombshell. Armed with a $70 million advertising budget for the first year, Coca-Cola was putting a new, improved formula into the old Coke can. New Coke, as it quickly came to be called, would replace the old Coke with a smoother, better-tasting cola that was second to none in taste tests. It was, Goizueta told a packed press conference at the New York Coliseum on Columbus Circle, "the surest thing" the company had ever done. The $4 million in market research said it was. Gut instinct at Coke's headquarters in Atlanta said it was. And soon, he promised, New Coke would be available nationwide for consumers to judge for themselves.

At headquarters Pepsi-Cola USA's president, Roger Enrico, was jubilant. Tipped off two days earlier, Enrico ordered his New York sales staff to arrange a free Pepsi giveaway and taste test just outside the Coliseum. Two days later he placed full-page advertisements in newspapers around the country to claim victory. "Coca-Cola is withdrawing their product from the marketplace, and is reformulating brand Coke to be 'more like Pepsi,' " the ads boasted. "Maybe they finally realized what most of us have known for years: Pepsi tastes better than Coke. . . . After 87 years of going at it eyeball to eyeball, the other guy just blinked." With that, Enrico declared the following Friday a company holiday. "Victory is sweet," the copy concluded, "and we have earned a celebration. . . . Enjoy!"

Enrico's ebullience was partly cosmetic. Given the results of Coke's marketing research, Pepsi could only assume that its archrival had come up with a formula that would, at the very least, make it difficult to count on taste tests and the Pepsi Challenge as a bulwark of the company's marketing strategy in the future. From the start, therefore, Enrico knew that Pepsi's response would have to be targeted at the reason behind Coca-Cola's move — and its apparent admission of what Pepsi had claimed all along: consumers prefer the taste of Pepsi.

On that Tuesday in April, however, neither Enrico nor Goizueta fully appreciated the extent or nature of public response to the switch. Over the next ten weeks, 150 million Americans tried New Coke, and the company's surveys indicated that 75 percent of them were going to buy it again. But for a vociferous minority, Coca-Cola's decision to discard its ninety-nine-year-old secret formula amounted to betrayal, and their reaction was immediate. Some began hoarding bottles of "old" Coke. In Seattle, a retired hotel owner formed Old Cola Drinkers of America to lobby for the return of 7X.

At first the reaction was anticipated. Goizueta knew there would be a sentimental backlash. But once consumers had a chance to taste the new Coke, he felt, they would go with the change, and Pepsi drinkers, tempted by all the hoopla, would taste the new formula and possibly switch. Blind taste tests, carried out on a weekly basis through the spring, confirmed Goizueta's gut feeling. New Coke beat both old Coke and Pepsi by even wider margins than it had prior to the product's introduction. Four weeks after New Coke's debut, Dyson continued to harp on the company's optimistic expectations and newfound willingness to take risks. "We're not following the lead of others, we're setting the pace," he told bottlers. "We are on the front lines of change."

Two months later, however, it was clear that the controversy wouldn't go away. The furor continued to make headlines and had become a staple of TV coverage. By mid June operators at Coke's headquarters in Atlanta were recording fifteen hundred calls daily, almost all demanding the return of old Coke. Some bottlers reported that their deliverymen were being harassed by retailers and shoppers. In a few markets shipments of New Coke were down 15 percent after the May surge. Supermarket surveys every Thursday showed that the tide had changed: in June, more than half of those responding didn't like New Coke, and the ranks of the disenchanted appeared to be growing daily. At a regional meeting of Coke bottlers in Dallas on June 18, disgruntled bottlers signed a petition asking Atlanta to bring back old Coke. Goizueta got the same advice from a fellow Atlanta businessman, Ted Turner. "You don't cancel a winner," Turner would say later, recounting the meeting with Goizueta, "just because you are bringing out a new product."

On the first Wednesday of July, Roberto Goizueta and Don Keough met with senior executives from Coke's five biggest bottlers. The meeting went badly. If the barrage of bad publicity continued, the bottlers claimed, Coke — by whatever name — risked losing market share overnight to Pepsi, a share that would be that much harder to regain. Goizueta promised to have a decision by the following Monday.

To all intents and purposes, Goizueta had already decided that Coca-Cola would have to change tactics dramatically. Going back to work the following day, he ordered all departments to prepare for the return of old Coke. Even the bottlers agreed that New Coke should remain the standard, given the amount of publicity and consumer awareness generated by the controversy. Old Coke would therefore be aimed at die-hard fans of the original formula, New Coke at younger consumers and Pepsi drinkers. That decision taken, Keough ordered the research department to test several possible names for the old Coke, among them Original Coke, Coke I, Coke 1886, or, simply, Old Coke.

On Monday morning Sergio Zyman argued against Goizueta

> *[The general] able to gain victory by modifying his tactics in accordance with the enemy situation may be said to be divine.*
>
> — Sun Tzu

and Keough's decision. He felt that the company was caving in too quickly. The marketer was still convinced that the furor would subside as quickly as it arose and the red-and-silver "New" banner was removed from Coke cans. But Goizueta and Keough had made up their minds. Dyson agreed, especially after a meeting early Monday morning with bottlers who were urging the company to cut its losses and do it quickly. It was the last straw. Goizueta made the decision official and ordered Zyman to call Alvin Schechter in New York.

Schechter, who had designed the Diet Coke can, was given forty-eight hours to come up with a package design for Coca-Cola Original, one of the names that had tested best among those used in surveys taken over the weekend. Working late into the night, Schechter devised half a dozen styles, all using the same basic red motif that runs through all of Coke's cola offerings. The next morning a colleague flew to Atlanta with the drawings, returning the same afternoon. Coke executives asked for minor changes in one of the drawings, and one big one: instead of Coca-Cola Original, Goizueta wanted to go with the more alliterative Coca-Cola Classic, which had also tested well.

The next day, Schechter shipped the final version to Atlanta: a can wrapped in a distinctive red wrapper, *Coca-Cola* in the company's bold, white, Spencerian script, the word *Classic* in capital letters, also in white, floating just below. With no time to devise a sophisticated advertising campaign to accompany the stunning reversal in Coke's plans, Zyman asked McCann-Erickson to send a TV crew to Atlanta and booked a local studio to tape an announcement by Keough. With the New Coke and dummy Coca-Cola Classic cans on a desk, Keough sitting behind it, the thirty-second spot began with Coca-Cola's president thanking "the millions" of consumers who had made New Coke a success. He also apologized to "the millions" who preferred the taste of old Coke. Then he announced that the old Coke was coming back in a new can labeled Coke Classic. Several takes were required before getting a good version on tape.

Keough returned from the studio to pandemonium at Coke headquarters. Rumors that it was bringing back old Coke were awash on Wall Street, and the company's public relations office was flooded with calls from reporters around the country. Plans were already under way for a press conference in Atlanta the next day, Thursday, but Goizueta and Keough decided to end the confusion before it got out of hand. Late in the afternoon they ordered Zyman to contact the sales departments at all three major broadcasting networks and asked for last-minute time on the evening newscasts. The final thirty-second spot — shot in one continuous take with no editing — was beamed to New York via satellite, with only minutes to spare before the first 6:30 P.M. newscasts.

At Coca-Cola headquarters, the decision to bring back the old formula as Coke Classic radically altered the downbeat mood that had been building. "Thank you for bringing old Coke back," read the letter from a sixty-eight-year-old woman. "The only thing better is sex!" Within days Coca-Cola was flooded with calls, telegrams, even bouquets of flowers. Overhead an airplane trailed a banner that read THANK YOU, ROBERTO!

By Roberto Goizueta's own admission, it would take months to assess whether the decision to market two Coca-Colas was the right one. But he refused to call the original launch of New Coke a mistake. "Consumers were so mad, but they were not reacting against the taste of New Coke," he told a reporter after the Coke Classic announcement. "It was the idea that 'somebody took away my soft drink.' " Don Keough readily admitted that the events of the past three months were not, as some skeptics conjectured, a finely tuned strategy to hype the introduction of New Coke. "Some critics will say Coca-Cola made a marketing mistake; some cynics will say that we planned the whole thing," Keough told reporters the day after his thirty-second spot announcing the change was beamed into millions of American homes. "The truth is, we are not that dumb — and we are not that smart."

In fact, Coca-Cola was that dumb *and* that smart. Goizueta admitted that the company knew all along that it could reintroduce the old formula, without actually expecting to have to do so. But once public sentiment shifted decisively away from New Coke, for whatever reason, Goizueta was quick to change course. Coca-Cola had proved once again and this time successfully that, under its new leadership, it could adapt quickly to the marketplace.

The payoff was almost immediate. Despite three months of bad press, the awareness of Coke's advertising around the country had hit an all-time high. Retailers began stocking their shelves with Coke Classic alongside New Coke. Had the company opted to introduce New Coke the way it had Diet Coke, without scrapping Tab, retailers may have been less willing to carry the new product. In the end, Coca-Cola got the best of both worlds — a product to satisfy Coke's die-hard fans, and a product to meet the Pepsi Challenge. By September Coca-Cola was reporting that sales of its three sugared colas, including Cherry Coke, were running 10 percent higher than Coke sales a year earlier, when Coke was growing by only 3 percent. And an *Advertising Age* survey the same month showed that the company's overall market share was up almost two points; Pepsi's was *down* just under a point.

Roberto Goizueta's problems weren't over though. In some markets, sales of Coke Classic were outgrossing the new version by a wide margin. The company now had to grapple with positioning its three sugared colas in a crowded market. The "megabrand" strategy Goizueta had begun to develop, first with Diet Coke and then with Cherry Coke, became even more crucial. At its bottlers' convention in early September 1985, the company disbanded its "Coke is it" TV campaign under pressure from bottlers who felt the otherwise successful slogan had been tarred in the fiasco that followed the introduction of New Coke. Jokes about changing the anthem to "Coke *Are* It!" were making the rounds at headquarters in Atlanta. In its place, Coca-Cola began a megabrand commercial campaign to plug the entire line of colas. In an ad blitz that delivered on the promise New Coke held early on, Coca-Cola announced that its new cola was beating Pepsi-Cola in taste tests nationwide. "We tried everything — more marketing, more spending," Goizueta told *Business Week*, recalling the original concept behind New Coke. "The only thing we had not tried was claiming product superiority." Now Coca-Cola seemed to be able to make the claim stick, and with Coke Classic also on grocery shelves, the once-sleepy Atlanta company wouldn't lose any partisans in the process.

Diet Coke, meanwhile, was proving a bigger winner than expected. It quickly became the third best-selling soft drink on the market, after Brand Coke and Pepsi. Six months after its reintroduction, Coca-Cola Classic was again the number one soft drink in the country, outselling New Coke by almost three to one. And on its own, Classic was on the verge of overtaking Pepsi as the top seller, a position Pepsi held briefly after the Coca-Cola brand was split in two.

In Purchase, Roger Enrico saw the writing on the wall. Pepsi-Cola couldn't count on its flagship soda to pull consumers away from Classic. If Enrico's company was to overtake Coke, it would have to do it in the overall market. That meant two choices: bring new sodas on the market or acquire existing ones. Enrico had already done the first with Slice, a new line of citrus sodas, which was launched in 1985. Pepsi began pumping more money into the marketing effort at a time when Coca-Cola was still too busy putting out fires to push its rival citrus drinks under the Minute Maid logo.

Then, as 1986 dawned, Enrico went outside the company: Pepsi announced that it was buying 7-Up from Philip Morris. The combination, Pepsi officials boasted, would allow Pepsi to surpass Coke's total market share in a single stroke.

Pepsi's euphoria was short-lived. Roberto Goizueta knew that 7-Up was for sale and suspected that Pepsi was interested. After all, Pepsi had already held secret discussions with the owners of the third largest company in the market, Dallas-based Dr Pepper, but wasn't willing to pay the asking price. Coke itself was looking at Dr Pepper, and Pepsi's announcement galvanized Goizueta into action. The deal took less than a month to negotiate. On February 23, 1986, Coca-Cola announced that it had agreed to pay $470 million for Dr Pepper, pending federal antitrust approval of the deal.

It was a coup de grâce. Henceforth, Pepsi's proposed buyout of 7-Up and Coke's approach to Dr Pepper would be inextricably linked in the minds of antitrust officials. If those authorities proved to be uncomfortable with the deals because they would put 80 percent of the market in Coke and Pepsi's hands, they would have to veto both of them. Which is what they eventually did, in June. Either way, Coca-Cola's premier position was safe. Pepsi's hopes of assuming the top spot were dashed.

As the company's centennial rolled around in May, Roberto Goizueta and his colleagues had every reason to rejoice. Coca-Cola had bounced back from its mistake in introducing New Coke. Shipments of New Coke and Classic together were running substantially higher than those for old Coke before the fiasco began. The Dr Pepper and 7-Up acquisitions were vetoed by federal antitrust officials, effectively thwarting Pepsi-Cola's assault on the top spot.

Even while battling Pepsi-Cola, Goizueta had insisted on diversifying further into the entertainment business. His decision to acquire Columbia Pictures was perceived as canny, especially after the runaway success of *Ghostbusters* at the box office. Coca-Cola bought out Embassy Communications, one of TV's leading production companies, in 1985 and acquired Merv Griffin Productions less than a year later, in the spring of 1986. Wall Street was impressed: the same shares that sold for $29 on the day Goizueta became chairman were selling for more than $100 five years later. And *Business Week,* which had questioned Coca-Cola's ability to defend itself against the Pepsi Challenge in 1978, conceded that Goizueta had turned out to be "a bold agent of change in a once-stodgy corporation," concluding that "the changes Goizueta is making outweigh one spectacular blunder."

If Goizueta had reason to rejoice, he also had the perfect occasion. On May 8, 1986 — as corporate lore had it, exactly one hundred years from the day that John Styth Pemberton mixed the first batch of syrup in his backyard — Coca-Cola celebrated its centennial. Coke pulled out all the stops for the occasion. For four days the company treated Atlanta and its employees to one of the largest corporate spectaculars in history. Some 14,000 staffers flew in from the 155 countries where Coca-Cola does business. Thirty floats with Coke themes and 30 marching bands from around the country snaked through downtown, and the estimated 300,000 people who lined the route were treated to all the free Coke they could drink. To lead off the parade, Atlanta mayor Andrew Young joined Goizueta, backed by a 1000-voice choir and 60-piece orchestra, in a rousing rendition of Coca-Cola's classic anthem, "I'd Like to Buy the World a Coke."

For many, though, the highlight of the festivities took place half a world away, in London. Echoing the latest advertising slogan for New Coke, "Catch the wave," organizers planned to topple some 600,000 dominoes in a single wave that would connect Atlanta, London, Rio de Janeiro, Nairobi, Sydney, and Tokyo. The sites were connected by satellite, and giant video screens were placed around Atlanta's cavernous Omni Center. As wave after wave of dominoes fell flawlessly and the topple in London drew to its finale, a giant Pepsi can came into view. Climbing one last ramp, the dominoes detonated a small explosion, blowing the Pepsi apart. In London Coke employees cheered, but in Atlanta there was silence. Just as the dominoes were climbing that ramp, the satellite transmission went down, and Atlanta never saw the final explosion. Rumors began circulating through the crowd that Pepsi had somehow sabotaged the event. It was a reminder to Coca-Cola employees that the battle with Pepsi wasn't over. But for four days in May, the centennial was also a reminder that the company had fought off its attacker. As it embarked on its second hundred years, Coca-Cola was still number one.

CHAPTER 3

The Pubic Wars

PENTHOUSE VS. PLAYBOY

IT WAS SIMPLE, crude, and deadly: *Playboy*'s hallmark bunny insignia, locked dead center in the cross hairs of a rifle scope. Beneath the bold image, four words neatly summed up the mission. The newspaper advertisement was still roughly sketched, but it got the point across. *Penthouse* — virtually unknown in the United States —was taking aim at *Playboy*'s monopoly among men's magazines. To pull it off, *Penthouse* would have to convince the public and Madison Avenue not only that it could, but that it would, succeed.

Good propaganda, that's what we need, Bill Lyons thought to himself. Make 'em *think* that *Playboy* is vulnerable, and the house that Hugh Hefner built could quickly come tumbling down. Lyons slipped the opaque paper under a sheaf of other drawings. In all his years on Madison Avenue, Lyons had never had an assignment quite like this one. His client wanted to take aim at one of the most successful publishers in America, but he didn't really have the financial resources to get the job done. So what Lyons didn't have in the way of big bucks, he'd make up for in the message: simple, crude, and deadly.

Five-thirty in the afternoon a few weeks earlier, on Thursday, April 10, 1969, Lyons had been looking out his office window at a darkening Manhattan skyline. He reached for his overcoat. Out the door of Nadler & Larimer's offices, he took the elevator down to the lobby of the art deco Fuller Building at Fifty-seventh and Madison and surged into the rush-hour crowd out-side. Whisked along, Lyons took a right on Fifty-sixth Street, then walked briskly half a block east toward Park Avenue. There it was on the right: Le Manoir — discreet, not a usual haunt of his adversaries in the advertising business. After work the French restaurant was usually quiet. It would do just fine for the first meeting, even if it turned out to be the last.

Over the phone he had heard a trace of an English accent, but not quite. It wasn't American, either. She waved from a table along the wall. She was young and sure of herself. But she wasn't what he'd been expecting.

"Kathy Keeton," she said matter-of-factly.

Good for her, he thought. "I'm Bill Lyons. I've been meaning to ask, are you English?"

Laughing, Keeton said, "South African. But that's a long story. A lot of Americans think I'm English."

A lot of Americans probably also think she's older than her twenty-six years, Lyons said to himself. She certainly was strik-ing, with long blond hair. But the features were hard, the accent too guttural.

"Excuse me," Keeton went on. "This is my publisher, Bob Guccione."

If Lyons had been surprised at Keeton, he was flabbergasted at the man who stood up from the table. Lyons had expected an Englishman. He didn't know what type of Englishman, but after all, *Penthouse* was a London magazine.

"Hi." Guccione stood up and extended his right hand.

It was all Lyons could do not to stare. The shirt was unbut-toned nearly to the navel. Several gold chains and medallions hung from Guccione's neck. But it was the voice that clinched it. The swarthy but handsome Guccione spoke in a hushed, grav-elly voice and made no attempt to hide his Brooklyn patois. The Italian American had nothing to hide.

"My magazine is better than *Playboy*," Guccione boasted. "I'm gonna beat Hefner. I'm gonna beat him."

"Others have tried this before." Lyons was skeptical. He didn't want to sound too negative, but he couldn't quite believe Guccione was serious.

Guccione was. "We're outselling *Playboy* in France. In England, by three to one. Everyone's hungry for an alternative. They think *Playboy* is dated. There's room for another magazine and we can grab the younger audience in the States."

"You aren't the first to try this," Lyons repeated. "Just look at the market. *Playboy* sells five million copies a month. Then there are all the rest. I doubt any one of them sells more than two hundred thousand copies. And none of them gets any advertising. They're rags."

"A monopoly position like *Playboy*'s cannot last." Guccione had his mind made up. He didn't even seem to take in what Lyons was saying. "Sooner or later, every strong magazine runs into competition. Every number one has a number two. That's us."

Thumbing through a copy of the English edition, Lyons was impressed. The photographs were more tasteful than he'd expected, the paper better quality, the printing clean. At first glance, anyway, it seemed a cut above the rest of the pack snapping at *Playboy*'s heels. *Penthouse* could never hope to beat *Playboy* at its own game, Lyons thought to himself, but Guccione was right. There was room for a strong and profitable number two. And the only way Guccione could hope to get there was with an ad campaign designed to put *Penthouse* on an equal footing with *Playboy*, even though it wasn't. The propaganda would have to anticipate events as Guccione expected them to happen. But Lyons also knew that it was a dangerous strategy. The ad campaign could give *Penthouse* a shot at *Playboy*, but unless Guccione succeeded — and succeeded quickly — the campaign would become a liability, not an asset. That was the nature of propaganda: Lyons could convince the public that Guccione meant business, but only Guccione and *Penthouse* could deliver on the promise.

Guccione needed no convincing. The propaganda would convince everyone else. *Penthouse* needed a hard-hitting campaign; Lyons and Nadler & Larimer needed the work.

"It'll take two or three weeks, but I'll work flat-out on several dummy ads."

"That's great," Guccione answered. "But there's one more thing. We can't afford trade *and* consumer campaigns. The same ads will have to work for advertisers and the public."

Lyons tried not to look disappointed. "That won't be a problem," he said, thinking that it would. It meant, among other things, that there probably wasn't much cash for advertising in the *Penthouse* coffers. But Lyons figured, what the heck! Guccione was a far cry from the stodgy corporate clients he'd been used to dealing with at J. Walter Thompson, Benton & Bowles, and now, Nadler & Larimer.

"I'd like to come by and talk about how we intend to position ourselves with advertisers in the market." Keeton was talking; she had let Guccione talk about strategy. Now she wanted to talk tactics. As advertising director for *Penthouse* in England, she had definite ideas on how to get her message across in the States. She, Guccione, and Lyons agreed to meet again soon.

Keeton arrived alone at the Fuller Building the following Thursday morning for an 11:30 appointment with Lyons. He showed her around the office and introduced her to some of the other people at the agency who'd be working on the *Penthouse* presentation. They talked about how to separate *Penthouse* from the pack of *Playboy* imitators. Keeton kept stressing the magazine's international flavor; a distinctly European alternative, she said, would work for readers who had grown tired of *Playboy*'s red-blooded American appeal.

Lyons and Keeton scheduled another meeting for two weeks hence, May 1. By then, Lyons promised, Nadler & Larimer would have a full presentation on the boards. "Be sure to bring Bob along," he suggested. "I think he'll like it."

May 1 was a Thursday. It was an early-morning presentation. Guccione and Keeton arrived together at 8:30 on the dot. Perhaps because it was so early, Guccione wore a nondescript business suit. No gold chains, at least none in evidence. Lyons introduced Guccione to Robert Larimer, his boss and the agency president. Together with art director Irwin Goldberg and a handful of other agency personnel, they crammed into a small office the agency used as an impromptu conference room. Like *Penthouse*, Nadler & Larimer was barely four years old. It had to watch its pennies. It also had to try harder and take chances.

Larimer began the presentation. He laid in front of Guccione a stack of worksheets. The dummy ads were charcoal-penciled on large sheets of tissue paper. Larimer flipped from one to the next, each time shifting the top paper to the side, explaining the concept of each and then going on to the next one.

We're in trouble, Lyons thought to himself. Guccione hadn't uttered a word; he just kept watching and listening, his face impassive, aware that Lyons, next to him, was getting edgy. The presentation wasn't a strong one, Lyons reminded himself. But Larimer is holding the best for the last. If Guccione doesn't go for the one at the bottom of the stack, Lyons thought, we can write off the *Penthouse* account. Finally, Larimer got to the last sheet of tissue.

"Stop!" Guccione erupted. "That's the one. That's what I want. I don't need to see any more."

There were, of course, no more to be seen. Lyons had landed the account. "We're going rabbit hunting," read the slogan; Larimer himself had come up with that one. Goldberg had come up with the striking image of the *Playboy* bunny in a rifle's scope. Typed on a small piece of paper Scotch-taped to the dummy ad was the copy to run at the bottom of the page.

Larimer read it aloud. "If you catch a rabbit once, you can catch him again."

"Great," interjected Guccione. He liked what he saw. It was bold. "Great!"

"*Penthouse* is the magazine that caught him in England and France," continued Larimer, reading the copy aloud. "Our English edition outsells him three to one. Now the hunt is on in the rabbit's own backyard. Our American edition, edited in New York, will be on the stands August 12th."

"How soon can it run?" Guccione was enthusiastic.

"Soon," Lyons replied. "We have to plan it carefully."

Keeton had already told Lyons that he could have a budget of only $50,000 for the initial campaign — not much when a single full page in the *New York Times* was going for $10,000.

"You cannot shout in a small space," Lyons reminded Guccione and Keeton. He urged just a few big, splashy, attention-getting ads. The first would be the rabbit insignia in the cross hairs. Mechanicals on it could be ready within the week, and it could reach newspapers within a fortnight. Two more along similar lines could be ready and approved in a matter of weeks. By focusing the campaign on the *Times*, the *Chicago Tribune*, the *Los Angeles Times*, and *Advertising Age*, *Penthouse* could build awareness in the advertising and publishing communities. The rest would follow.

In less than an hour, the timetable for *Penthouse*'s opening salvo was in place. It was all geared to a clockwork campaign designed around the September issue of *Penthouse*, due on American newsstands August 12. The magazine would run three different full-page ads over a six-week stretch in major publications. The battle with *Playboy* was about to begin.

In politics, they'd call it dirty tricks. But in business, Guccione thought to himself, anything's fair. *Playboy* was entrenched and powerful and everywhere. It would take more than just an offensive strategy; *Penthouse*, after all, didn't have the wherewithal to match *Playboy*'s advertising and business spending dollar for dollar. Guccione knew he couldn't play the game on Hefner's financial terms. The terrain — the market for men's magazines — would be the same, but the ammunition had to be different. It had to be more explosive, and it had to be directed squarely at *Playboy*'s Achilles heel. But what was it? It was fine to put the bunny in cross hairs and tell the whole world about it. But the boast had to be more than a boast. Guccione would have to deliver on the promise. *Playboy*'s weak spot was clear: the magazine was becoming too staid, too conservative, not racy enough. American men were hungry for something stronger. Guccione's weapon had to be more raunch, more sex.

Robert Charles Joseph Edward Sabatini Guccione had been preparing to go up against *Playboy* for years, and he knew his enemy well. *Playboy* was a mix of sex and cartoons, and Guccione liked both. Even before *Playboy* had first hit the stands, Guccione was selling his own cartoons — cheap imitations of

> The preparation of total war must begin before the outbreak of overt hostilities.
> — Erich Ludendorff

Jules Feiffer's — to a fledgling weekly British paper called the *London American*. In 1958 he left New York, where he was barely making a living, and moved to London, where he worked full time for the weekly. The publication foundered, and as more and more of its staff quit, Guccione became editor and, eventually, managing director.

When the *London American* folded, Guccione was hooked on publishing. At thirty-two, he was out on the street peddling his cartoons again. But he also began selling pinup photos and back issues of American men's magazines, including *Playboy*, through the mail. He became obsessed with the potential for a home-grown competitor. British women and British authors, he figured, would lure British advertisers. Guccione took a daring gamble. The brochure he mailed to thousands of unsuspecting but prospective readers announced a new publication. The publisher himself shot the photos of partially clad women gracing the solicitation.

> For the first time in Britain, a magazine that separates the men from the boys . . . Penthouse is jam-packed with beautiful girls, controversial articles, intimate stories, and delectable lashings of bedside humor.

Guccione borrowed a few thousand dollars from his father to get *Penthouse* started. But he needed a lot more than that. The printer wouldn't start the presses rolling without payment up front. Deception, Guccione told himself. If readers thought that the magazine was bankrolled, the subscriptions would start rolling in — and *Penthouse* would happen. His deceptive tactics worked. The British government filed action against Guccione under Section 11 of the Post Office Act, which outlawed sending indecent materials through the mail. There was an outcry in Parliament. Fleet Street played the story for all it was worth. And with the added publicity, subscription fees began flooding Guccione's Chelsea flat.

For two weeks Guccione stayed inside, avoiding a civil summons, a summons Scotland Yard couldn't serve him forcibly. Associates passed page proofs of the not-yet-published magazine under the door, along with hundreds of subscriptions. Finally Guccione emerged. He had enough money in hand to pay the printer, stand trial, and cover his fine.

Guccione initially saw his magazine as a British version of *Playboy*. The articles, pictorials, and interviews would be similar. There would be a centerfold Pet of the Month. And cartoons, many drawn by Guccione himself, got prominent positioning. He'd even talked to friends about dubbing the new magazine *Playmate*, a working title he used until *Playboy*'s British solicitor objected. But he knew he couldn't afford a legal fight. *Playboy*, after all, held the high ground.

Guccione knew that Hefner would have an easier time defending his monopoly than Guccione would have attacking it. The *Playmate* name would have let Guccione trade on Hefner's success in Britain, but Guccione resigned himself to a tactical defeat — a small price to pay if he could keep *Playboy* unconcerned about the threat of an attack.

Penthouse hit newsstands in and around London in March 1965. Within days, the entire press run of 120,000 copies sold out. Now Guccione had to proceed carefully and deliberately. The instant success of *Penthouse* with British readers could have provoked a counterattack by *Playboy*, and Guccione still didn't have the resources to fight. Since his ultimate goal was to tackle *Playboy* in the States, it was essential not to get into a scrap with Hugh Hefner too soon.

Ironically, Guccione's first strategic decision toward launching *Penthouse* in America was to do the opposite: as best he could, he kept copies of *Penthouse* from reaching the States. The magazine wasn't yet ready to stand up to *Playboy*. And until it was, Guccione wanted no comparisons, invidious or otherwise. It was a costly decision for the still-struggling publisher, but he was willing to bide his time. Instead, he set his sights on the Continent. *Penthouse* quickly sold out on Paris newsstands. And by 1967, two years after its birth, *Penthouse* was readily available on American military bases outside the United States. Then Guccione decided it was time to go home.

Bob Guccione knew he didn't have the forces necessary to quickly cripple *Playboy* in the American market. Attacking the magazine on its British flank had been comparatively easy. Guccione suspected that Hefner wouldn't see *Penthouse* as anything other than an upstart local British imitator that would end up going out of business as several American imitators had. But once he'd made a decision to publish *Penthouse* in the States, Guccione knew he couldn't just hide from Hugh Hefner. And he knew he couldn't make it on his own. Guccione also knew he didn't have enough financing and that he needed a lot desperately if he was going to take *Penthouse* to America. Because of currency controls in Britain, all his profits on the magazine had to be kept there.

In the spring of 1968 Guccione spent a lot of time working out of his family's home in New Jersey. He first went to the banks, but they wouldn't play. Then he made the rounds on Wall Street. At first he refused even to meet with big private investors who wanted a large piece of equity in the company. Guccione was worried about undercutting his own power inside the company; with any partners on board, his hands would be tied. Rather than risk failing to come up with the cash, however, he eventually offered 10 percent of *Penthouse*'s stock in exchange for a cool $1 million. John Loeb of Loeb Rhodes considered a deal, but then pulled out. *Penthouse* might have a chance, Loeb figured, but it was a long shot. He knew Guccione didn't even have a distributor lined up; without a good one, the magazine would die on the stands.

Acutely aware of the problem, Guccione began to pour more of his energy into finding a reputable distributor. A dozen national distributors controlled the industry, some handling more than two hundred magazine titles at any one time. At first Guccione found no takers: his money was tied up in England, he hadn't found any outside financial help in the States, and *Penthouse* seemed to be just another unlikely upstart trying to crack *Playboy*'s monopoly.

With no alternative in sight, Guccione signed a deal with Kable News Company, a distributor that already handled a number of men's titles. But almost immediately he sensed trouble. Kable, several contacts warned him, had a nasty habit of acquiring many of the magazines it distributed. It was easy. If Kable advanced Guccione 60 percent of expected newsstand receipts, for instance, and *Penthouse* sold poorly, the publisher could end up owing Kable a huge amount of money. And if Guccione didn't have the financial backing, Kable could close him down — or insist on a majority stake in the company. It was SOP — standard operating procedure — for Kable. Guccione knew he needed an ally he could trust. *Penthouse* had to find another distributor.

"I've been giving a lot of thought to taking *Penthouse* back to the States." Bob Guccione was talking to Martin Levin in *Penthouse*'s cramped quarters just outside London. Guccione had first met Levin through Ed Ernest, the pen name of Ernest Edward Pustorino. Ernest had worked for fourteen years as editor-in-chief at Grosset & Dunlap, the publisher that made its name with a line of popular children's books, including the Hardy Boys, Nancy Drew, and Tom Swift series. He quit in the early sixties, moved to England to set up a small publishing business of his own, met Guccione, and became one of *Penthouse*'s first editors in London. In late 1966, when Guccione was unhappy with *Penthouse*'s U.K. distributor, Ernest called up Levin, who had been in charge of marketing for Grosset and later left to head up the Times Mirror Company's New York and international operations.

When he got the call from Ernest, Levin was under pressure to get out of Britain altogether. Times Mirror's main London subsidiary, the New English Library, was barely making money. He was under orders from Times Mirror headquarters in Los Angeles to turn the operation around or dump it. Levin decided to gamble, and it paid off. The New English Library began distributing *Penthouse* in England in January 1967. Within two years, Levin helped double the magazine's circulation to nearly half a million. The contract with Guccione transformed a marginal moneymaker into a flourishing enterprise.

Now, in December 1968, the same Martin Levin was sitting across from Guccione at *Penthouse* in London. "I've been giving a lot of thought to taking *Penthouse* back to the States," Guccione repeated. There's no use beating around the bush, he thought. Levin was in town to negotiate a renewal of the New

English Library's distribution contract, so Guccione held all the cards. "But I'm having problems," Guccione went on. "It's tough to line up a good distributor in the U.S."

"What does that have to do with us, Bob?" Levin knew what was coming.

"Well, it seems to me that you could help us in the States. You know a lot of people at some of the distribution companies, right?"

"Yeah."

"I'd be willing to renew this contract if you help me get started over there." Guccione was moving in for the kill. "This is a very profitable magazine for you. I presume you'd like to keep the contract."

Levin didn't flinch. Guccione's offer was clearly not negotiable.

"I'll do what I can. Let me get back to you."

The New English Library got a three-year contract for *Penthouse* in England, and Bob Guccione landed an American partner. Guccione had used the only thing he had — a profitable distribution contract in England — to win over an ally who would turn out to be a vital force in the attack on *Playboy* in the United States.

The Times Mirror Company lent both money and support. A ten-page contract obliged the Los Angeles publishing giant to lend Guccione $100,000 immediately, and another $150,000 in six months. The publishing conglomerate agreed to have its New American Library — also headed by Martin Levin — consult closely with Guccione on the American edition of *Penthouse*. Levin even had his staff in New York put together a comprehensive operating plan for *Penthouse*.

> *Where absolute superiority is not attainable, you must produce a relative one at the decisive point by making skillful use of what you have.*
>
> — Karl von Clausewitz

In return, Times Mirror's subsidiary got three things: a full-page ad in each American edition of *Penthouse* free of charge; a renewal for three years of its British distribution contract and first right of refusal to distribute any other publications Guccione might launch in Britain; and last but not least, a 2.5 percent cut of *Penthouse*'s net sales receipts above $42,000 for each American issue for the next six years.

The last provision represented a potential windfall for Times Mirror, and Levin knew it. If *Penthouse* took off, the deal could mean tens of millions of dollars to Times Mirror. But as Levin also knew, "net" sales receipts were as hard to police in publishing as they were in Hollywood. "Gross" proceeds were easy to track; it simply meant adding up all revenues at the box office or newsstand. To get the net proceeds, *Penthouse*'s own accountants would subtract all legitimate expenses from the gross proceeds; and typically in both the publishing and movie industries, the accountants were known for inflating their clients' costs in order to make the net look as small as possible, both for the Internal Revenue Service and for any investors with a stake in it. Times Mirror's cut of the proceeds, Levin would later admit, were easier negotiated than collected.

In February 1969 the Times Mirror contract was in the bag and Levin was becoming more and more involved with *Penthouse*. He took out a $250,000 life insurance policy on Guccione with Connecticut General to protect the company's investment. He had his financial staff run profit and cash flow projections for the magazine. He even had one of his employees, Christopher Shaw, scrounge around New York for back issues of *Playboy* to compile a complete list of advertisers who'd dropped out over the years, most of them because *Playboy*'s rates had risen almost exponentially. These "dropouts," Levin figured, would be prime candidates to head *Penthouse*'s inaugural roster of U.S. advertisers.

Levin also arranged to bail Guccione out of his distribution contract with Kable. When he and Ed Ernest were at Grosset & Dunlap, Levin had been in charge of several joint book publishing ventures with the Curtis Circulation Company. In 1969 Curtis was the largest magazine distributor in the country, with such major magazines as *Time, The New Yorker,* and *Sports Illustrated* in its stable. Curtis also owned two major names, *The Saturday Evening Post* and *Ladies' Home Journal.* Headquartered in Philadelphia, Curtis had a staff of two hundred field representatives blanketing the country, ensuring that its clients received preferential treatment from wholesalers and retailers. It was the perfect, respectable distributor for *Penthouse.*

There was only one problem. The president of Curtis, G. B. McCombs, didn't want anything to do with Guccione's magazine. Earlier Guccione had approached McCombs, who had turned him down flat. But Levin had worked frequently with McCombs on the joint ventures between Grosset and Curtis, and McCombs trusted him. At first McCombs still said no. Undaunted, Levin leaned harder and harder on his old colleague, battering away at how much money Curtis stood to make from *Penthouse.* Finally McCombs gave in; Curtis would take the account.

It remained somehow to buy out Guccione's contract with Kable. That proved easy. Levin personally negotiated the deal and handed over a $25,000 check drawn on the Times Mirror Company's account. It was made out to Kable's president, George Edwards, who in turn gave Levin his copy of the contract with Guccione. The deal was done. Edwards boasted that he'd made the deal of his life: $25,000 without lifting a finger or investing a penny.

From his spacious corner office in the Bankers Trust Building overlooking Park Avenue and the Waldorf-Astoria Hotel, Martin Levin continued deftly to open doors that had previously been shut to Bob Guccione. When a recalcitrant printer in Milwaukee at first seemed unwilling to get involved with Guccione, Levin flew to Wisconsin. Later he convinced Curtis to pay the printer's bills directly before remitting the receipts to Guccione. Another deal was done.

Levin was also putting together a team to run the American operation of *Penthouse.* From inside the Times Mirror organization, he recruited Mike Andrews to be circulation director. Andrews had held the same job at *Look, Family Circle,* and *The New Yorker,* where he had built up a close relationship with Curtis's line distributors.

Times Mirror staffers undertook a search for someone who could head up *Penthouse*'s advertising staff and go after *Playboy*'s accounts, past and present. Kathy Keeton still had responsibility for ad sales of *Penthouse* in Europe, and she was to assume some of the same responsibilities in New York with the title of president. But Guccione knew that he needed someone who knew his way around Madison Avenue and the big "men's" accounts.

One name came up frequently: Joe Coleman. A corpulent, slovenly man, Coleman had made something of a career working for — and more important, against — *Playboy.* He started selling space for *Playboy,* becoming ad manager for Hefner's ill-fated *Show Business Illustrated,* which folded in early 1962 after less than a year on the stands and $3 million in losses. Later Coleman headed the advertising staff at *Cavalier,* one of the better *Playboy* imitators, which had entered the fray in the mid 1960s. Convinced that *Playboy* was vulnerable, Coleman began consulting with *Penthouse* several months before its American appearance. Just before the first issue hit U.S. newsstands, he was on board full time.

The last key figure to join was Nils Shapiro, another veteran of Grosset & Dunlap. Shapiro had worked there for thirteen years in advertising and promotion. A tall, nervous man, he knew little about magazine publishing and had most recently been working at Clairol. But Levin and Ernest, his old colleagues, convinced him to sign on as associate publisher. And the publisher, Guccione himself, promised Shapiro a large degree of independence in managing the operation.

By June 1, just four months after Martin Levin began to orchestrate *Penthouse*'s advance into the American market, the magazine was just about ready to open for business. Guccione and Keeton planned to spend most of their time in London, where the editorial product would continue to be put together, but there was now a solid, experienced staff in New York. *Penthouse* had a distributor and a printer. It had a midtown Manhattan office at Times Mirror's East Coast headquarters, just a few floors away from the conglomerate's World Publishing Company, the largest publisher of Bibles in the world. And Guccione had a Madison Avenue advertising agency, Nadler & Larimer, which, within days, was going to begin telling America that *Penthouse* was out to beat *Playboy.*

Even Guccione knew that *Penthouse* was a long way from toppling *Playboy*. But it was no longer the time to hide, to back down. If *Penthouse* was to suc-

━━━━━━━━━━━━━━━━━━━━━

All warfare is based on deception. . . . When near, make it appear that you are far away; when far away, that you are near.

— Sun Tzu

━━━━━━━━━━━━━━━━━━━━━

ceed, Guccione would have to deceive not only *Playboy*, but its readers. The objective of *Penthouse*'s advertising campaign was to convince readers and advertisers that Guccione had the financial backing to sustain a prolonged attack on *Playboy*'s market. Despite the relationship with Times Mirror, Guccione knew he was still the underdog, and if the magazine didn't take off immediately on the newsstands, Times Mirror would probably try to pull the plug. The advertising campaign would have to convince everyone that *Penthouse* was "near," even though it was still a long distance from achieving its target. If the deception didn't work, the battle would be lost.

Over breakfast, in transit, and at the office, New Yorkers learned on one clear, warm morning in early June that a magazine called *Penthouse* was going "rabbit hunting." On a commuter train into Manhattan, Bill Lyons nervously watched his neighbors scan the ad. A few even talked about it. He felt like a proud father.

Nils Shapiro got to the office early that day. He was thrilled. The phone rang; it was a vice president of Kayser-Roth, a clothing manufacturer.

"I saw your ad," he told Shapiro. "It was terrific. Can you send someone over to see me?"

Could he? "Sure," Shapiro answered. "I'll have somebody call you this morning."

Kayser-Roth advertised its Esquire socks in *Penthouse*'s first American issue and was still a steady advertiser years later.

Penthouse's rabbit-hunting ad produced an enormous response. But when it came to selling space, the magazine's approach was wildly unpolished. Joe Coleman irritated a lot of potential advertisers with his cajoling, badgering, and bargaining. But at least he knew his way around. Keeton, on the other hand, didn't. Her miniskirts and patent leather boots turned off some clients. And Beverly Wardale, a handsome, fair-skinned Englishwoman who left the British sales staff of *Penthouse* to help launch the U.S. edition, rounded out a somewhat motley sales force.

Coleman, Keeton, and Wardale had an equally motley budget. Keeton lived at the home of Guccione's parents in New Jersey, and Wardale stayed with a family friend. They had no printed business cards and no formal presentations. Both women made it standard operating procedure to let their prospective advertisers, usually male, pick up the tab for business lunches. Both, on more than one occasion, found themselves stuck with a check they couldn't pay, forcing them to call the office and have someone send the money by messenger.

What they lacked in polish, the *Penthouse* crew made up for in bargains. The magazine's ad rates were dirt cheap: $1500 for a black-and-white page and $2200 for a four-color. *Playboy*'s rates, on the other hand, were ten times those figures, making it expensive for many advertisers who nonetheless wanted to reach an audience of young males.

"Who Bugs Bunny?" asked the second ad in the campaign. The line stood out in bold letters beneath a snarling *Playboy* bunny, predictably going on to answer the question with *"Penthouse* Does."

The third installment showed the same angry rabbit symbol above a series of expletive-denoting asterisks, stars, and exclamation marks. Below it: "Words can't describe how unhappy the rabbit is to see *Penthouse* in America. Or how pleased we are to be here."

Words couldn't describe what Hugh Hefner was feeling that day. The splashy ad in the *Chicago Tribune* was an affront. Hefner and his lieutenants had known of *Penthouse* for years. But success in Britain held no promise of success in the United States. Dozens of imitators had come and gone; even those still around could never aspire to more than a fraction of the five million copies *Playboy* would sell in June 1969. And none had more than a fraction of *Playboy*'s $25 million in annual advertising revenues.

Hefner was irritated when he saw Bob Guccione's ad, not because another competitor was after him, but because Guccione dared to compare *Penthouse* with *Playboy*. That was blasphemy.

The two months before *Penthouse*'s August 12 rollout were busy ones for Bob Guccione. He commuted between London and a single room in the Sheraton Hotel on Manhattan's West Side. In New York, he routinely worked eighteen hours a day, bolstered by a steady stream of cigarettes and coffee. Shades drawn, he worked while alert and slept when he was tired, oblivious to the time of day or night.

The same summer, Guccione was also spending a lot of time in London, busily preparing to open a Penthouse Club closely modeled on the Playboy clubs. With Alan Freedman, the talent agent who had introduced him to Kathy Keeton, Guccione had recently launched *Forum*, a *Reader's Digest*–sized monthly that carried scores of letters of sexual fantasy, "discovery," and experience. Another Guccione project, a glossy quarterly called *Lords*, folded after just four issues, unable to meet its astronomical production costs.

Guccione was determined not to see *Penthouse*'s American edition go the way of *Lords*. To make it a success, he knew it had to be a hit on newsstands. In retailing, the saying goes, success is a matter of location, location, and location. In publishing it's distribution, distribution, and distribution. The eye-catching ad campaign put together by Nadler & Larimer caught everyone's attention, and Guccione knew he could deliver a product, the magazine itself, that would rival *Playboy*'s. But *Penthouse*'s survival and ultimate success would hinge on getting the magazine in front of as many potential buyers as possible, and that meant undercutting *Playboy* among wholesalers and retailers. It wasn't good enough to be displayed with the other *Playboy* imitators. *Penthouse* had to be positioned alongside *Playboy* as a competitor, not an imitator.

Playboy sold nearly a third of its copies by subscription, but for the most part, men's magazines were still considered unsuitable for home mailing. Maintaining a full-fledged subscription department was a luxury that a smaller magazine could ill afford. Guccione decided to ignore subscriptions altogether, at least at the start. He placed the entire press run of the first four issues on newsstands.

Curtis Circulation was a key player in *Penthouse*'s newsstand strategy. Its contract with Guccione gave the distributor every reason to push a little harder for *Penthouse;* after all, it was receiving 8 percent of the cover price on each copy sold. On the day the magazine went on sale, Curtis would pay *Penthouse* 50 percent of each month's expected revenues. The balance was paid later, but not until Curtis had use of it for several weeks. It was especially lucrative for Curtis because it already had the structure in place to handle its two hundred other magazine titles. With the delivery trucks, accounting staff, and other elements already distributing the other magazines, Curtis's overhead was already covered, and new clients such as *Penthouse* were immediately profitable.

Curtis had another reason to market *Penthouse* aggressively. Despite McCombs's apprehension about distributing a men's magazine, Curtis needed the business. *The Saturday Evening Post* had folded. In just two years, the payroll at all of Curtis's subsidiaries had dwindled from six thousand to fifteen hundred employees. A year earlier, Curtis had signed up the little-known *National Enquirer* and had already helped boost circulation of the gossip tabloid.

Now Curtis was looking for another winner, and it unloaded its cannons. The distributor offered *Penthouse* to wholesalers at 40 percent off the cover price; *Playboy* was giving them only 36 percent. Retailers got 10 percent in the form of a retail display allowance, to assure good position. *Playboy* did the same in a few markets, but the *Penthouse* incentive was given nationwide. The tactic was critical: good display was absolutely essential for a new magazine that consumers didn't know well enough to ask for by name. And to keep *Penthouse* separate from the *Playboy* imitators, Curtis designed special magazine racks. They were configured so retailers could put both *Playboy* and *Penthouse* on the same rack. Curtis even supplied "blinders" — eight-and-a-half-by-eleven-inch pieces of cardboard to mask the covers of both magazines — to encourage retailers to use the display stand out front and bring the magazines out from under the counter.

The first issue of *Penthouse* appeared on American newsstands on schedule: August 12, 1969. The magazine's circulation director, Mike Andrews, had persuaded Guccione to underprice *Playboy*, which sold for a dollar a copy. *Penthouse* printed an ambitious 375,000 copies, each carrying a seventy-five-cent cover price.

The ninety-eight-page issue was tame, even by *Playboy's* standards. The Pet of the Month was a bosomy brunette named Evelyn Treacher, who managed to reveal as little as possible in the oblique photos of her breast and posterior. Several pages printed on olive-green craft paper, labeled "View from the Top," carried some American commentary and movie reviews. The only editorial element of note, engineered by the magazine's New York editorial director, Ed Ernest, was an article by the president of Notre Dame University, the Reverend Theodore M. Hesburgh. Hesburgh's piece was part of a symposium on "The Campus Convulsion," and Ernest had commissioned companion articles by two Columbia University students. The mere presence of Hesburgh's article, however, lent credibility to the magazine that was trying to compare itself to *Playboy*, a publication that had already become a forum for serious writers of fiction as well as nonfiction.

After *Penthouse's* flashy advertising sendoff, readers were amused at Guccione's uncharacteristically gracious comment about *Playboy* in the first American edition of *Penthouse*. Entitled "What About *Playboy?*" Guccione's valedictory said America was "big enough and lush enough to support two magazines of the same genre." Guccione noted *Playboy's* "position of absolute autocracy in the men's field." Finally, Guccione wrote audaciously for the publisher of a British magazine,

> *Playboy*, like all things quintessentially American, needs a competitor, and *Penthouse* is the only magazine around whose performance, quality and editorial temperament qualify it for the job.

Penthouse is not a parochial magazine, nor will it ever become simply reflective of the time and place in which we live. It is a fighter, a leader and an innovator, born not of the relatively placid *Playboy* epoch of the early '50s, but of the age of the social, moral and intellectual revolution of the '60s. . . . We have none of the sexual hangups of the lingering and fundamentally puritan tradition of *Playboy*. We report rather than preach [a reference to Hefner's tedious "*Playboy* Philosophy" series] and . . . the only *Penthouse* philosophy you're likely to encounter can be summed up in four immaculate and meaningful words: "To Each His Own."

The first U.S. issue of *Penthouse* sold some 235,000 copies. In one blow, *Penthouse* had become number two to *Playboy*.

Guccione had already attacked one of *Playboy*'s weak spots: the percentage it gave to wholesalers and retailers. Now Guccione knew he had to attack *Playboy* on another front: the product itself. Readers, after all, had to have an incentive to buy the lesser-known publication. Guccione had set *Penthouse* up to be compared with *Playboy*, but the editorial content still appeared to imitate *Playboy*. *Penthouse* had to offer readers something more. Guccione had to attack *Playboy*'s weakest flank, its editorial content, and he had to move quickly.

> *Necessity compels us to think of a way in which to conquer with numerically weaker forces. . . . If one is too weak to attack the whole, one should attack a section.*
>
> — Count Alfred Schlieffen

Vietnam, flower children, campus protests, the sexual revolution. *Penthouse* began publishing in the United States at a time of upheaval in the nation's mores. Obscenity and pornography laws were coming under attack, but even then, *Playboy* and its imitators refused to test the limits. Guccione recognized *Playboy*'s weak spot, its vulnerability. *Playboy*'s publisher craved respectability even as the magazine's readers were looking for a men's magazine that was sexier. Bob Guccione would give it to them. *Penthouse* would "heat up," in the industry jargon, even if it meant going into open conflict with local sheriffs and district attorneys around the country. Guccione believed the law was now on his side and that he could meet the Supreme Court's obscenity tests.

The "pubic wars" began. In 1969 pubic hair was taboo in men's magazines. To show it meant crossing the line into porn, whether in movies or print. Hugh Hefner had refused to cross that line; Guccione couldn't afford *not* to.

In February 1970, in his fifth U.S. issue, Guccione launched the attack. At the bottom of page 24, a side-view photograph of a young blonde showed only the barest glimpse of pubic hair. Guccione waited for the outcry, but it never came. No one seemed to notice. He would have to try again. This time there was no chance of missing the shots. In the April issue, several photos flaunted pubic hair, and Guccione didn't stop there. He published *Penthouse*'s first so-called love set, illustrations titled "Wild Gypsies," which featured a nude couple frolicking.

This time the censors noticed. In dozens of cities around the country, sheriffs impounded copies of *Penthouse*. But in the biggest markets, *Penthouse* remained on the newsstands. The attention in the press sent circulation into orbit. In the June issue of *Penthouse*, Guccione promised that the magazine wouldn't cave in. He planted a "Letter to the Editor" that asked when *Playboy* would follow *Penthouse*'s lead. That would take another six months. The growing boldness of *Penthouse*'s photo layouts caused a stir among editors at *Playboy*. At first Hugh Hefner adamantly opposed a shift to pubic hair. But by December, *Penthouse*'s gains in newsstand sales were worrisome. Hefner relented; for Christmas, *Playboy* readers could open to the magazine's first centerfold starring a black woman, pubic hair and all.

Bob is crazy, Martin Levin was thinking as he waited for Guccione to get off the phone. Two days earlier, the April issue had landed on Levin's desk. For months the Times Mirror executive had been sending Guccione notes and letters asking him to start paying his rent and fulfilling the rest of his contractual obligations to the company. Guccione had not paid a cent in rent during his year's stay at 110 East Fifty-ninth Street. He also hadn't made any 2.5 percent of net payments to Times Mirror, his landlord and partner. Now, with Guccione heating up *Penthouse*, Levin had had enough.

"Look Bob, this can't go on." Levin's friends and colleagues were beginning to question Times Mirror's involvement with this fellow across the desk. "It doesn't look good for us; we've got a reputation."

Guccione nodded. He knew it would come to this, so it was a matter of hammering out the best deal possible — for *Penthouse*.

"I'll tear up the contract if you'll pay everything you owe us," Levin offered. He knew he was giving up millions in potential revenues, and maybe even the New English Library's British distribution agreement with *Penthouse*. But there was no alternative. Times Mirror wanted out.

Guccione was secretly pleased. He had already been thinking of ways to deal Times Mirror out of its cut in future *Penthouse* revenues. Inadvertently, his strategy to attack *Playboy* with more explicit pictures was doing the trick. He agreed to Levin's deal. It remained for Guccione to find the money to buy his way out of the contract. He didn't have it, so he went to Curtis Circulation. Magazine distributors regularly handled hundreds of thousands of dollars in cash, and since Curtis received *Penthouse*'s receipts directly, there was little risk in its lending Guccione the money for the magazine, which by now had all the trappings of a long-term moneymaker for Curtis. By May Times Mirror was out of the picture, and Guccione had moved his magazine to drab quarters at 1560 Broadway, near Times Square. It would be home for nearly three years.

Bob Guccione was worried about his magazine's credibility. He didn't want it labeled pornography. The editorial quality of the magazine had to improve even as the pictorials got more and more explicit. April's daring issue contained "The Why of My Lai" by William Corson, a former Marine colonel and CIA agent who would become *Penthouse*'s Washington editor. In May George Mandel interviewed novelist Joseph Heller. Those pieces were followed by an exposé of American cults, an interview with political activist Allard Lowenstein, and in the December 1970 issue, the first of a two-part series by Corson. The subject was heroin, but what distinguished the series was the position Corson took, coming down hard on the dangers of the drug and proposing that the military napalm poppy fields around the world. The right-wing bias was unexpected from a publisher like Guccione, who took a beating from conservatives for his stand on explicit sexuality.

The shock tactics worked. The Corson series drew more attention to *Penthouse*. The January issue contained a coupon to mail to the *Penthouse* Heroin Action Campaign, expressing support for "the *Penthouse* declaration of war on heroin." In April Guccione published letters from half a dozen major political figures, among them Edmund Muskie, Jacob Javits, Howard Baker, and Charles Percy, all supporting *Penthouse*'s antiheroin position. The response helped secure the magazine's reputation as more than just a "skin" publication. In local court challenges to the distribution of *Penthouse* copies depicting pubic hair, the editorial product became a valuable element for the defense. Juries and judges had to assess the value of the magazine as a whole; it was clear that *Penthouse* was more than just pornography.

In the United States, Guccione was a relentless self-promoter. He appeared on radio talk shows, gave interviews to local or college newspapers, met with wholesalers and retailers, and even appeared on *What's My Line?* He did anything he could to attract attention to *Penthouse*.

Penthouse had a banner first year. Smirnoff Vodka, J&B Rare Scotch, Panasonic, and Jantzen clothing joined the roster of regular advertisers. In June 1970 *Penthouse* received its first readership profile from the Brand Rating Research Corporation. The news, as Nils Shapiro described it in a memo to the staff, was good. "The initial figures released [for age, income, and education of *Penthouse* readers] actually put us ahead of *Playboy* and *Esquire*," exulted Shapiro. "This is an incredible accomplishment. I urge you to make immediate use of it."

With its first anniversary issue in September, *Penthouse* cracked 400,000 in circulation, up 70 percent from its inaugural edition. By December the magazine had cleared the half-million mark. *Playboy* was still ten times larger, but the gap was closing.

If Bob Guccione was counting on complacency at *Playboy* headquarters in Chicago, he got it. Like most companies that hold virtual monopolies in their industries, *Playboy* was tied to the status quo. Even *Penthouse*'s impressive gains that first year weren't enough to set off the alarms. *Playboy*'s response was further tempered by Hugh Hefner himself; like other entrepreneurs, he was blind to many of his company's weak spots, and his autocratic style made it difficult for any of his lieutenants to push for a combative strategy that Hefner felt would sully his personal reputation. He wasn't ready to "get down in the gutter" just yet; he knew it was an alternative, but he didn't think *Penthouse* had made a big enough dent to justify a full-fledged return attack.

In fact, 1970 had been a great year for Hefner despite Guccione's arrival on the scene. *Playboy* picked up nearly 200,000 new readers in 1970, despite a recession that cut into advertising. The company earned $8 million after tax, its best profit ever. But the sybaritic Hefner was using the proceeds to transcend the magazine itself. He bought hotels in Chicago and Jamaica and began work on a $30 million resort in Great Gorge, New Jersey. He bought a DC-9 for $5.5 million and christened it the Big Bunny. Painted in white on the tail of the all-black plane was the distinctive rabbit-head logo, the same logo locked inside *Penthouse*'s cross hairs. Hefner and *Playboy* still seemed oblivious to the gains made by *Penthouse*.

The March 1971 issue of *Penthouse* ran the most daring cover to that date, a woman wearing a sheer top, her breasts clearly exposed. Some advertisers threatened to pull out. Liggett & Myers, one of *Penthouse*'s charter advertisers, had already pulled its cigarette ads when the content of some of the "Forum" letters got a little too hot for the company's taste. But Liggett left its ads for J&B Scotch and Bombay gin; few people connected them with the tobacco company.

"Screw the advertisers!" Guccione told a meeting of *Penthouse*'s ad salespeople. In March 1971 the publisher was more determined than ever to lessen *Penthouse*'s dependence on advertisers. Subscriptions were too expensive; *Penthouse* needed much bigger newsstand circulation, he decided, because larger readership figures would force advertisers to fall in line. There would always be problems with individual advertisers; even *Playboy* couldn't sign up many companies. But the only way to protect *Penthouse*'s editorial independence was to give readers what they wanted — and give advertisers those readers.

Inside *Penthouse* Guccione encountered resistance. Mike Andrews was a conservative circulation director. He placed great importance on the magazine's percentage of sale: the percentage sold of all distributed copies. Andrews was tightfisted with *Penthouse*, forcing Curtis and wholesalers to ensure a strong sale before he would hand out more copies. The policy kept *Penthouse* in demand and, Andrews felt, from overextending. A few consecutive months of high returns, Andrews repeatedly warned Guccione, could bankrupt the magazine.

Unconvinced, Guccione believed Andrews's circulation strategy was stunting *Penthouse*'s growth. Guccione thought the magazine appealed to a much wider audience that it wasn't reaching yet. For months Guccione and Andrews argued over the size of each press run, each time reaching a compromise, to Guccione's continual dissatisfaction.

As Guccione grew tired of trying to combat his own circulation director, he began to override the latter's press-run recommendations. And to Andrews's surprise, it didn't cut into the magazine's percentage of sale. "General" Guccione took *Penthouse* from a 618,000 sale in June 1971 to 722,000 in August.

In September *Penthouse* raised its cover price from seventy-five cents to a dollar and sold 870,000 copies. In November the number was nearing the one-million mark. Guccione had taken effective charge of circulation. He decided to gamble on a quantum leap in copies sold for the 178-page holiday issue. The December *Penthouse* carried a premium cover price of $1.50. The issue sold 300,000 copies more than the previous month —1,278,721, to be exact.

> *Battles are lost or won by generals, not by the rank and file.*
> — Ferdinand Foch

Guccione was elated. *Penthouse* had crossed an important

threshold in its attempt to grab readers from *Playboy*. With more than a million buyers, the magazine could no longer be considered just another imitator. Guccione knew that he needed to capitalize on the early momentum and gamble on consumers being willing to pick up just about as many copies as he'd make available. It was doubly important to keep the pressure on: he couldn't count on Hugh Hefner to remain complacent forever, and *Penthouse* had to make as much headway as possible before Hefner struck back. The fight was in the open, and Guccione wasn't shrinking from it. Before the year's end, it would take a distinctly personal turn.

Hugh Hefner and Bob Guccione met for the first and only time on December 31, 1971, at a New Year's Eve party at the Los Angeles home of financier and onetime fugitive Bernard Cornfeld. The meeting was cool and formal. Cornfeld introduced Hef and his girlfriend Barbi Benton to Guccione. Later that evening Cornfeld invited Guccione, who was staying at Cornfeld's home, to accompany him and a group of women friends to Hefner's mansion in Holmby Hills the next day for a screening of *A Clockwork Orange*, Stanley Kubrick's new film. Guccione agreed to go along. The next day, trouble. Hefner's secretary called Cornfeld to ask if he planned to bring his house guest to the screening. He did, Cornfeld said. The secretary then made it clear that Hefner didn't want Guccione in his home, but Cornfeld and his lady friends were still welcome. Irate at Hefner's pique, Cornfeld thought of not going. But Guccione prevailed on him not to change his plans. "Give him a message for me," Guccione instructed. "Tell him that the three years he has left before *Penthouse* beats him is down to two." That night Cornfeld passed on Hefner's reaction to the Guccione missive. It was, Cornfeld recounted gleefully, "Fuck you!"

Hefner's lack of politesse wasn't completely over worries about *Penthouse*. In fact, 1971 had been a big year for *Playboy*, too. Ad pages and revenues picked up and profits for the fiscal year topped $9 million. Despite *Penthouse*'s gains, *Playboy* was selling more than 6.5 million copies a month — more than five times *Penthouse*'s circulation.

For his part, Guccione was undeterred by the circulation gap.

Barely days after his chance brush with Hefner in Los Angeles, Guccione screened a new TV commercial in New York at the St. Regis Roof, a popular meeting spot for media and advertising groups. The thirty-second spot showed the *Playboy* bunny symbol in profile; beneath, it scrolled a list of *Penthouse* successes and projected successes. As each item hit the screen, a tear ran down the bunny's face. Advertisers were impressed; American Broadcasting Company wasn't. The ABC network refused to air the commercial, arguing that it was unfair and overly combative. Guccione went to the other networks; they, too, refused to carry it.

Determined to see the commercial air in prime time, Guccione ran a series of newspaper ads explaining the problem with the networks. Then he patched together a series of independent stations in major TV markets that agreed to carry the *Penthouse* commercial. His newspaper ads carried the local time and station to watch. One of the newspaper ads showed *Playboy*'s stylized rabbit, teary-eyed. As usual, the copy was right on target: "See a grown rabbit cry on TV."

Guccione knew it was only a matter of time before *Playboy* would respond. He was especially worried about one man, Robert Gutwillig. The two had known each other when *Penthouse* was using office space at Times Mirror's building in Manhattan. Gutwillig was first an executive for New American Library and later for World Books. He knew the *Penthouse* organization and had been impressed by Guccione's obsession with beating *Playboy*. So when Gutwillig left the Times Mirror organization in early 1970 to help *Playboy* launch a book club of its own, Guccione had good reason to be worried. Hefner didn't really know or understand his enemy. Now he could know him better.

Fortunately for Guccione, Hefner wouldn't even listen. Like Guccione, the *Playboy* founder was convinced that he knew best how to handle the enemy. Unlike Guccione, though, Hefner wasn't on the attack; inaction seemed the easiest course, gambling that Guccione would be unable to sustain the circulation and revenue gains that were scaring the rank and file at *Playboy*. Hefner saw the threat, but he didn't take it completely seriously. And he didn't fully use the intelligence he had in an employee who had once dealt with Guccione on a day-to-day basis. He dismissed Gutwillig's warnings, and in time the former Times Mirror executive was labeled a worrier — the house pessimist.

Gutwillig wasn't alone. *Playboy*'s assistant publisher, Richard Koff, realized early on the appeal of *Penthouse* to younger men. Together, he and Gutwillig went to Hefner with the idea of launching a second magazine, one that would compete more directly with *Penthouse*. *Playboy* was about to award licensing rights to French publisher Daniel Filipacchi, who already published a French imitator called *Lui*. As part of the deal, Filipacchi gave *Playboy* licensing rights to material from *Lui*, and the pictorial spreads in particular would be used to create a new magazine called *Oui*.

In theory, *Playboy*'s strategy should have worked like magic. *Playboy* would stick to its respectable image, while *Oui* would be even more daring than *Penthouse*, with a lot of the European flavor that Guccione liked to boast about. *Oui* would then become an experimental laboratory in which *Playboy* could test the market without any risk to its core readers and advertisers. In the process, Gutwillig had argued, the *Playboy* empire would stop Guccione dead in his tracks and gradually take circulation and ad revenues away from *Penthouse*. It was a classic pincer movement, designed to squeeze *Penthouse* on two flanks.

The first issue of *Oui* hit the newsstands in September. The cover showed a decidedly European, dark-haired woman sitting nude on a beach, her back to the camera, her head turned toward it, one breast partially exposed. One of the cover lines advertised "Bikes. Leather, Nazis, Flesh, Bestiality & the New Wave's Old Days." *Playboy* this wasn't.

Hugh Hefner gave *Oui* a big sendoff, with a print order of 800,000 copies. He matched *Penthouse*'s 40 percent discount to wholesalers, and ad rates were well below *Playboy*'s. Anyone who had doubts about the market was proved wrong: more than half a million copies of *Oui* were sold. But the magazine didn't actually take away from *Penthouse*'s circulation. Inside the *Playboy* organization, *Oui* was never taken very seriously. *Playboy*'s advertising director refused, with Hefner's okay, to offer advertisers combined, and discounted, ad rates for buying space in both magazines. *Oui*'s ad staff had to start from scratch, and the editorial side was in bigger trouble. Hefner refused to approve a single *Lui* cover for use in *Oui*. The new magazine's American editors balked at most of the racy material from *Lui*, and they used only one or two layouts a month from the French magazine. So producing *Oui* turned out to be far more expensive than Hefner had bargained for.

Privately, Guccione was worried. He knew that if *Oui*'s editors took full advantage of the material from *Lui*, the new magazine could be a formidable competitor for *Penthouse*. "But it won't work," Guccione assured one magazine interviewer, "because Hefner is doing it." He counted on *Oui* to reflect more of *Playboy* than of *Lui*. And if that was so, he reasoned, *Penthouse* wouldn't be hurt after all. Guccione was right. *Oui* never drew the advertising support it needed, and ad revenues peaked in 1974, two years after its inaugural issue, at a mere tenth of *Playboy*'s. In 1981 Hefner would sell the magazine, by then a forgotten part of *Playboy*'s empire.

As *Oui* was first hitting newsstands, however, it seemed that *Penthouse* could do no wrong. Undaunted by the threat of *Oui*, Bob Guccione had been bumping his press run each month, with no apparent impact on the percentage of sale. The August issue sold 1.8 million copies, and Guccione got ready to pass the two-million mark with September's third-anniversary publication, which was a landmark issue for several reasons. The magazine had survived. Jim Goode, a new editor, had lured Gore Vidal to write for *Penthouse*. The issue carried an interview with best-selling author and former madam Xaviera Hollander. And, above all, Guccione broke another barrier between men's magazines and pornography, with a pictorial featuring two women in a lesbian love scene. Guccione got what he wanted. The September issue generated controversy and sold 2.2 million copies.

From the outside, *Penthouse* looked stronger than ever. But inside, the cracks were showing. Ever the autocrat, Guccione was losing some of his best people, voluntarily or involuntarily. He demoted Ed Ernest from editor to a job running a small book publishing division. Jim Goode, a *Playboy* veteran, replaced Ernest. Nils Shapiro, who as treasurer had been instrumental in getting the magazine off the ground, quit after clashing repeatedly with Kathy Keeton. In his place, Guccione installed Irwin Billman, who had previously done the same job at Curtis Circulation and would earn a reputation over the next decade as Guccione's primary hatchet man.

Not long after Shapiro's departure, Mike Andrews quit. The circulation director was no longer making decisions, and Guccione usually overrode those he did make. Andrews's successor, Richard Smith, had his work cut out for him. A towering man who'd been circulation director at *Forum* magazine, Smith worked hard at a job Andrews had already begun — expanding the number of retail outlets that handled *Penthouse*.

The Southland Corporation, based in Dallas, was the main target. Through its chain of 7-Eleven convenience stores around the country, Southland controlled one of the most effective ways to reach young male magazine buyers. Andrews had traveled to Dallas on several occasions to try persuading Southland executives to sell *Penthouse* through their stores. About half the outlets were company owned, the rest franchised. By late 1972 most of the franchisees were carrying both *Playboy* and *Penthouse*. But company-owned 7-Elevens were allowed to sell only *Playboy*, even though in some areas, like Washington, D.C., franchise stores were selling roughly as many copies of *Penthouse* each month as *Playboy*s. Smith kept at it until Southland finally agreed to add *Penthouse* to its roster of magazines. The victory was critical; sales of *Penthouse* at the convenience stores would eventually account for as much as 20 percent of all the magazine's single-copy sales.

Penthouse's ad staff began to feel the magazine's growing acceptability. Ad revenues jumped 256 percent in 1972, and the magazine carried 85 more ad pages than in 1971. With its growing circulation, *Penthouse* consistently delivered to its advertisers large circulation bonuses — more copies sold than the minimum on which the ad rates were based.

In late 1972 Guccione redoubled his trade advertising efforts,

portraying *Playboy* as behind the times and unable to keep pace
with the younger, bolder *Penthouse*. An ad in the October 16
issue of the *New York Times* showed *Playboy*'s rabbit reading
Guccione's magazine. "*Penthouse* Envy," the ad declared. "Has
the aging playboy gone soft?" The ad went on, detailing some of
Penthouse's demographic advantages over its rival, and Guccione trotted out a new slogan: "*Penthouse* begins where *Playboy* leaves off."

The ad had a seamier side to it, though: Guccione's inclina-
tion for playing fast and loose with circulation numbers to present an inflated picture of *Penthouse*'s growth. It was a
dangerous penchant, especially considering the magazine's gen-
uine success. The text of the *New York Times* ad compared
Playboy's circulation with *Penthouse*'s press run. "After nineteen years, *Playboy* boasts of seven million worldwide circulation. The *Penthouse* worldwide print order for December is
four and a half million. After only three years in the United
States, *Penthouse* is the magazine of the Seventies."

Reading the "*Penthouse* Envy" ad, the uninitiated might have
thought print orders and circulation figures were comparable.
Far from it. *Playboy*'s September issue had sold more than seven
million in the United States alone; that same month, *Penthouse*
circulation hit a new high, but only at 2.25 million copies. Even
the huge December print run would result only in under three
million copies sold in the United States.

In January *Penthouse* made its bid for the big time. Guccione
raised the magazine's circulation guarantee from two to three
and a half million copies, promising to meet the new figure by
September, which was nine months away.

At *Playboy* headquarters in Chicago, executives were
stunned. If *Penthouse* managed to pull off its ambitious promise,
it would cement the upstart magazine's growing attraction
among advertisers, many of whom were adding *Penthouse* to
their media schedules, occasionally at the expense of ads in
Playboy. In a confidential memo to *Playboy*'s executive committee, Bob Gutwillig stressed the importance of acting immediately to injure *Penthouse*. "There is a hell of a lot that we can
and should do to hinder *Penthouse*'s profitable ascendance to

the 3,500,000 circulation guarantee," Gutwillig wrote. "Guccione has to suffer a real loss of face, credibility and income."

If ever *Playboy* had an opening, this was it. Despite his ambitious goals for *Penthouse*, Bob Guccione was boldly planning another new magazine, this one aimed at women. *VIVA* was to be racier than *Cosmopolitan* and higher-brow than the forthcoming *Playgirl.* Guccione did no market research: his colleague and lover, Kathy Keeton, was convinced that there was a market for a women's magazine with some of the same sensibilities as *Penthouse*, and Keeton herself would assume the title of publisher.

In a series of newspaper ads Guccione portrayed Keeton as "the kind of woman who reads *VIVA*." The ads failed to mention her background as an exotic dancer; they did, however, proclaim that the South African–born Keeton was one of America's highest paid women executives, earning $375,000 a year. The figure was pure fiction, a public relations stunt. But to Guccione, lying was all in the line of duty. He had become a master of propaganda and deception, juggling circulation and ad numbers and consistently painting a much stronger portrait of *Penthouse*'s finances than was ever the case. It remained a key ingredient of his business strategy, but before the year was out it would also get him into trouble.

After an unimpressive January showing of only 2.6 million in sales, *Penthouse* regained its momentum. Guccione steadily upped the print run, and readers steadily bought more copies. Circulation in February passed the three-million mark. Controversial interviews with Jesse Jackson and George C. Scott boosted sales further in April and May. And in June Guccione tested another limit: for the magazine's first Pet of the Year contest, the publisher picked five finalists and put their photos, bare breasts and all, on the magazine's cover. With Guccione's most daring cover to date, the issue sold 3,387,741 copies, giving Guccione just three issues to meet his September goal.

Penthouse now had momentum, and Guccione believed that the only thing that could slow down the growth in its circulation would be a full-scale assault by *Playboy*. Since that didn't seem to be happening, Guccione felt he could continue the same strategy. But suddenly the field of battle changed. The blow came not from the enemy, *Playboy*, but from the Supreme Court of the United States. In July the high court ruled on the landmark *Miller v. California* obscenity case. Local communities, the justices ruled, could apply their own standards when deciding whether something was, or was not, obscene.

> *There are in war no constant conditions.*
>
> — Sun Tzu

Playboy denounced the Supreme Court decision, but Hefner promised that he would keep the magazine in line with any local community standards, even if that meant toning it down considerably. The decision was a bigger blow to *Penthouse* because of its racier pictures and copy. Almost immediately, local authorities in Alabama, Georgia, Mississippi, and Virginia seized copies of the magazine. Guccione knew that if the Supreme Court had the last word, the entire foundation of his attack on *Playboy* — a "hotter" product — would crumble. *Penthouse* would have to go back to imitating *Playboy*, and that would destroy its chances of pulling even with Hefner's magazine in circulation. For the first time since launching *Penthouse* in America, Guccione found himself on the defensive. He could bide his time and do what *Playboy* was doing, or he could fight back, opening up a new front, this one against the decision of the judicial arm of the United States government, not just *Playboy*.

"We're making ourselves a target," Guccione swore to reporters. He was in his element. His dress was bizarrely appropriate for the occasion: white boots, brown leather trousers, a lace shirt open to the waist, the usual array of gold chains and rings. "There will be a lot of sheriffs waiting out there in the hinterlands to show me who's the boss. We intend to continue to do what we've been doing, and if the definition of that is pushing back the boundaries of permissiveness, then that's the way it's going to be."

Casting a defiant glare toward the TV cameras, Guccione went on to compare the censorship with Hitler's attempts to control the press in prewar Germany. Publishing nudity, Guccione contended, was no different from publishing stories about

Watergate. "What is at stake here," he said, "is that Americans can no longer select what they want to read or view. Somebody else is going to do the selecting for you. A government which couldn't control liquor, can't control drugs, and refuses to control guns now wants to control literature."

Apart from promising full legal support to every newsagent prosecuted for the sale of *Penthouse* magazines, Guccione announced he'd set up an agency to mail magazines and books to harassed areas on a cost-plus-postage basis. "If that means somebody in Nebraska can't get a copy of *Penthouse* and they write us, well, he'll get one."

The publicity blitz surrounding Guccione's challenge to local authorities pushed *Penthouse*'s circulation over the three-and-a-half-million level in August, one month ahead of schedule. And for the first time, the magazine's total number of advertising pages for a single issue topped those of *Playboy*. Guccione made the most of it. In full-page ads in the *New York Times* and *Advertising Age,* he was as subtle as Muhammad Ali. Below a comparison of numbers of ad pages sold by the two magazines, the *Penthouse* ad depicted its pet tortoise knocking out *Playboy*'s rabbit with a left jab. Guccione got his message across. In September 1973 *Penthouse* sold nearly four million copies, roughly 15 percent more than it had promised advertisers.

In 1972, *Penthouse*'s circulation was up 143 percent, *Playboy*'s only 10 percent. After the publicity surrounding Bob Guccione's attack on the *Miller v. California* decision, Hugh Hefner decided that *Playboy* could no longer ignore *Penthouse* when it came to dealing with advertisers. Pretending that *Penthouse* didn't exist was beginning to appear foolish. The two magazines were still far apart in both circulation and advertising revenues, but *Penthouse* was closing the gap much faster than the top brass at *Playboy* had believed possible.

On August 7, Richard Rozenzwaig, *Playboy*'s senior vice president and director of marketing, sent a memo to *Playboy* executives. The order, he made clear, was straight from Hefner. "Hef would like to change our policy on including *Penthouse* in future advertising promotional material," Rozenzwaig wrote.

"He feels that the best approach is to no longer ignore them. . . . By totally ignoring a publication which has reached such strength as they, we will only look jerky and lose credibility."

Two weeks later Hef said it himself. At a meeting of top executives, he urged *Playboy*'s ad reps to selectively confront advertisers with competitive data versus *Penthouse*, to give head-to-head demographic and cost comparisons to those advertisers who requested such data, or to those *Playboy* thought should be aware of them.

Given those gains, Hefner's new policy of acknowledging *Penthouse*'s existence didn't go far enough for everyone at *Playboy*. Dick Koff, the magazine's associate publisher, wrote a memo in which he called for *Playboy* and *Oui* to take off the gloves and begin battling Guccione on every front. "We have every reason to expect," wrote Koff, "that their sales will go beyond *Playboy*'s." The strategy that Koff outlined was twofold: *Playboy* should take the high road and put out a stronger editorial product, and *Oui* should fight *Penthouse* on the graphics front. "Get in there and fight as dirty as can be," he urged in his memo. "Discounts, deals, accept any product, fight tooth and nail for every page *Penthouse* has. . . . Promotion should be fiercely competitive and name *Penthouse* as the target every time." For his own part, Koff got *Playboy*'s advertising agency to draw up dummy ads comparing *Playboy* and *Penthouse*. But that went too far for Hefner, who found them out of hand.

In the fall of 1973, many *Playboy* advertisers had already added *Penthouse* to their schedules. But in November, the Brown Shoe Company canceled a four-color ad in the April issue of *Playboy* to place one in *Penthouse* instead. It was the first outright defection from *Playboy*'s advertising roster. It wouldn't be the last.

Hefner, meanwhile, was trying to find out more about his competitor. *Playboy*'s national distributor, Independent News Company, had undertaken a comparative study of *Penthouse* and *Playboy* circulation, examining figures from every wholesale and distribution outlet in the United States and Canada. The study accurately gauged *Playboy*'s sale for December 1973. But when the Audit Bureau of Circulation (ABC) came out with its report in March, it showed *Penthouse*'s December circulation exceeding Independent News's own best estimates by a whopping 600,000 copies. It wasn't lost on Hefner that the ABC numbers were based on reports supplied by Guccione himself. *Playboy* executives were elated. This could be the misstep they had been looking for. Guccione was known to play fast and loose with numbers in his ads. This time, they wouldn't let him get away with it.

Guccione was already making a big play of the ABC report for December. He took out ads in the *New York Times, Chicago Tribune,* and *Los Angeles Times* to spread the news. "*Penthouse* up 73.4%, *Playboy* down 9.3%." *Penthouse*'s tortoise logo was spraying the numbers, graffiti-style, on a wall. "It's all in the ABC statement," the ad's copy went on to say. "Check it out for yourself."

Hefner asked for a formal investigation by the ABC into *Penthouse*'s numbers. Almost a month later, on May 13, *Playboy* received confirmation of its doubts about *Penthouse*'s circulation claim. ABC Bulletin No. 74M57 recalled *Penthouse*'s previous statement for July to December 1973, substituting a revised statement. Not only had *Penthouse* overstated its December circulation by 613,416 copies, the investigation revealed, but November's sale had also been overreported by more than 256,000 copies. "The publisher states that the difference," the bulletin went on, "was due mainly to late shipments of increased allotments of copies to wholesale distributors, which resulted in some faulty estimates on the net sales."

Playboy had finally caught Guccione red-handed. Two days later a letter from John G. Kabler, advertising manager in the Midwest for *Oui,* was sent out to advertisers. He enclosed copies of the ABC bulletin and wrote:

It seems *Penthouse* did not meet their guaranteed circulation in November 1973 by 256,000 copies. In December, the *Penthouse* circulation was 613,000 under guarantee. For the six months ending December 31st, '73, they averaged 137,000 under what they guaranteed. This obviously means many advertisers were paying tremendous amounts of cash for circulation that was not even there. I hope you find this data interesting and informative.

Thirty-three advertisers got Kabler's letter. At least one of them immediately noticed that it contained a striking error — an error that would eventually backfire on *Playboy*.

Guccione was worried for weeks about how *Playboy* would respond to the revised ABC figures. But when he saw Kabler's memo to advertisers, he realized that *Penthouse* had the upper hand. In fact, the ABC had reported that *Penthouse*'s November and December circulation was less than what *Penthouse* had previously reported. It mentioned nothing about circulation guarantees. Indeed, the magazine had *exceeded* its guarantees for both months by wide margins, even using the revised statements. Kabler had misinterpreted the report. Five days later, he wrote the same advertisers to correct the mistake. It was too late.

> *Never interrupt an enemy while he is making a mistake.*
> — Napoleon Bonaparte

Penthouse had only a brief window of opportunity in which to take aim and fire. Guccione filed suit against *Playboy*, charging that Hefner was disseminating "false and fraudulent information" about *Penthouse* to advertisers and ad agencies. He demanded $40 million in damages. Overnight, *Playboy* was back on the defensive. The publicity surrounding *Penthouse*'s lawsuit obscured the magazine's misleading circulation numbers — a misstatement that *Playboy* had never openly taken shots at in the press. *Playboy* filed countercharges, but the damage had been done. *Penthouse* again looked like David to *Playboy*'s Goliath. The lawsuits dissolved into a legal morass that dragged on for the next six years. Ultimately a federal judge dismissed the case, stating that *Penthouse*'s charges were groundless.

Penthouse's overstatement of its November and December circulation was as innocent as Kabler's letter drawing attention to it. "It was a classic fuckup," circulation director Richard Smith later said. The publisher's statement was due by the end of January 1974. At the time, *Penthouse* had firm data only for July through October, and using the growth rate for that period to estimate circulation through the end of the year, the company came up with the ABC estimates. There were also delays in delivering the magazine, partly because of an injunction against the publication in December at the request of Groucho Marx, who was interviewed in that month's issue. Despite the mix-ups, though, advertisers got more than they paid for. *Penthouse* was guaranteeing a minimum sale of three and a half million copies; circulation actually averaged nearly four million during the last three months of the year.

Pubic hair, love sets, lesbian scenes, nude covers. Bob Guccione wasn't willing to rest on his laurels. In early 1974 he was going the whole hog. As *Playboy* itself began heating up its pictorial material, *Penthouse* went even further, offering readers a keyhole view: Pets fondling their bodies, Pets masturbating, Pets relishing threesomes. Soon the explicitness was complete: Guccione was treating readers to the "pink shot," a graphic, even gynecological view of women's genitalia. In erotic content, *Playboy* was left in the dust by Guccione's bare-it-all battle.

Guccione wasn't satisfied. Increased sexuality, he felt, was palatable only in the context of a steadily improving editorial package. The June issue contained an article by veteran journalist Harrison Salisbury, the first of many for the magazine, and *Penthouse* began earning the grudging respect of editors elsewhere. An eleven-part series called "The Vietnam Veteran" examined the plight of Vietnam vets in U.S. prisons for a variety of offenses. The series that followed took a sympathetic view of the vets' plight, perhaps the first journalistic effort of its kind in regard to the thousands of returning soldiers.

By all accounts, the idea of publishing a series on the veterans was Guccione's. He certainly went all out to see that it was done properly. Guccione turned over the idea to senior editor Joseph Spieler, whom he had hired away from the *New York Times*, and the initial article by Tim O'Brien was selected after several other writers' efforts had been rejected. The next month the series continued with an examination of Separation Program Numbers: three-digit numbers affixed to general and dishonorable discharges that went largely unnoticed, even by the vets who would be affected by them for life. The number labeled the less-than-honorable discharges as bed wetters, homosexuals, drug users, alcoholics, criminals, pathological liars, mental deficients: each category had a different set of numbers. *Penthouse* listed them and their meanings.

Future articles in the series would continue "serving" veterans, dealing with VA bureaucratic tangles, problems with the GI Bill, and the issue of amnesty. After the series was over, *Penthouse* initiated a Vietnam veteran adviser column that continued into the 1980s. The series made for good journalism. It was also a calculated decision by Guccione to capture hundreds of thousands of returning Viet vets. *Playboy* had long ago become a strong opponent of the war. Hefner could be the magazine of young liberals, Guccione decided, *Penthouse* the magazine of the returning veterans.

Playboy's editors and executives had other things on their minds as *Penthouse* embarked on its Vietnam series. On March 21, Hugh Hefner's personal secretary had been arrested outside *Playboy*'s Chicago mansion. Bobbie Arnstein was charged with distribution of cocaine; she had one gram of the substance in her purse at the time of her arrest. Later she admitted carrying half a pound of cocaine from Miami to Chicago for a friend, a drug dealer under surveillance by the federal drug enforcement agency.

Arnstein was vulnerable. Devastated by the death of her boyfriend Tom Lownes, the son of Hefner's top aide in London, Victor Lownes, in a car accident in which she was the driver, Arnstein was on the ragged edge. Shortly after her arrest, she attempted suicide. For months she remained under psychiatric treatment.

Hefner was upset. Arnstein had worked for *Playboy* for fourteen years, the last few for him personally. He supplied both emotional and legal support, but there seemed little he could do now; Arnstein would have to face trial. Besides, Hefner had a faltering corporation to worry about. *Playboy* ended its fiscal year for 1974 with disastrous results. Net earnings plummeted for the first time in memory; total revenues were up a fraction, but profits were down almost 50 percent. And earnings from the magazine itself were off by more than a third.

By the time the business press received advance copies of *Playboy*'s annual report on September 6, Wall Street had al-

ready shown what it thought of the company's performance and
the scandal that was enveloping Arnstein and, by association,
Hefner. *Playboy*'s stock closed below $3.00 a share for the first
time, and in the bleak months ahead, it would fall as low as
$2.00 — less than a tenth of its original value. In November
Hefner would refuse to show up at *Playboy*'s annual meeting.

Bobbie Arnstein was found guilty on October 30. Heeding a
psychiatrist's warning that a prison sentence could lead to her
suicide, the judge in the case sentenced Arnstein in late November to a conditional fifteen-year term. He ordered ninety days of
psychiatric observation, to be followed by resentencing and,
presumably, a lighter punishment. Until then, Hefner and the
rest of his *Playboy* empire hadn't been dragged into the Arnstein
case. On December 8, 1974, they were.

That morning the *Chicago Tribune* reported that federal
agents had all along been investigating Hefner and possible drug
abuse at his mansions in Chicago and Los Angeles. The revela-
tion shook the company. *Playboy*'s two outside directors resigned. Hefner's plans to reorganize top management were
stymied; it would look, he worried, like an admission of guilt.

Early in the morning of January 12, 1975, Bobbie Arnstein
registered at the Hotel Maryland, just two blocks from the
Playboy Building. She signed in under an assumed name, got
the key to room 1716, and took the elevator upstairs. Alone, she
swallowed an overdose of barbiturates. When the hotel manager
broke into the room late the same day, Arnstein was dead.

After Arnstein's suicide, Hefner began to reassert control
over the *Playboy* organization. During the final three months of
the year, the company posted its first quarterly loss, $365,000.
Hefner ordered an economy drive throughout the company and
took a 25 percent pay cut himself. As chairman, he had always
retained the title of chief executive officer. Now he demoted his
long-time lieutenant and former college roommate, Bob Preuss,
and assumed the title of chief operating officer as well.

In March Hefner took his campaign to the editorial side. At a
meeting of senior editors in his Los Angeles mansion, he urged
editors and photographers to throw away their hang-ups. *Playboy* would no longer waltz around the subject, he ordered; it

would get in the mud with *Penthouse* and beat Guccione at his own game. The magazine's covers and pictorials could go all the way. The staff was elated: Hefner the boss was on board, finally and officially.

The summer covers left little to the imagination. But October raised the roof. The cover showed two women in a lesbian love scene. "Sappho," read the cover line. "Stunning pictures of women in love." The pictures were tamer than most of the lesbian scenes Guccione doted on. But the cover story provoked a barrage of publicity, most of it negative. Several advertisers threatened to cancel. Howard Lederer, advertising director at *Playboy*, apologized and promised that things would get better. *Time* magazine got into the act with a piece entitled "Skin Trouble," railing against *Playboy* in particular for joining in the "war of the lower depths." *Playboy* editor Kretchmer denied it. "We still have the class magazine act of the men's magazine business," he told a *Time* reporter. "The answer is not more skin."

But the November issue made the October cover look tame by comparison. The cover promoted a feature called "More Sex in Cinema." But it was the cover image, again, that grabbed attention. There was Patricia Margot McClain, wearing an open blouse, panties, and spike-heeled shoes, her legs spread apart. Her skirt was hiked up over her waist; in her left hand, McClain held a box of popcorn, resting it on her thigh. The model's right hand delved into her panties. She was masturbating, the cover clearly implied, to the unseen movie in front of her.

Howard Lederer was furious, and so were dozens of *Playboy* advertisers. Lederer, who had been with the magazine since its beginning, threatened to quit. *Playboy* was jeopardizing $40 million worth of annual revenues, he told Hefner, and the raunch wasn't even working. Circulation was still falling, and the circulation department was warning that more covers like those of October and November could put the magazine behind blinders or, worse, back under the counter.

It was a somber Hefner who presided over the November editorial meeting in Los Angeles. In his mansion's richly paneled dining room, with *Playboy*'s top editors seated in blue, high-back chairs, Hefner made it official. "Gentlemen, we have lost our compass." To most of *Playboy*'s employees, it was Hefner who had lost his compass, fluctuating back and forth between hands-on management and letting the magazine drift, between hard-core and soft-core pictorials. Now, however, Hefner's audience knew exactly what their boss was getting at. "The magazine had lost sight of what it was meant to be. For the last few months, there's been very little difference at times between us and our imitators. It's time for that to end. We do not have to be another *Penthouse*. We can offer our readers a lot more than that. *Playboy* has to present the sensuality without the coarseness. We're going to make this a class act again."

To all intents and purposes, the pubic wars were over. Hefner was giving up on his strategy of fighting *Penthouse* with the same type of artillery Guccione had used to fight *Playboy*. *Penthouse* was coming off of its best year ever. In April 1975, for the first time ever, the magazine sold more copies on newsstands in the United States and Canada than *Playboy*. In part, its success was due to the pubic war Guccione had won so handily. Hotter books like *Hustler*, which entered the field in 1974, were taking the wars one step further, and Guccione, refusing to relinquish his niche in the mainstream men's magazine field, refused to match *Hustler*'s raunch. *Penthouse* would have to persist in upgrading its editorial product.

In 1975 the Vietnam series was beginning to win plaudits. *Penthouse* was nominated for a 1975 National Magazine Award for reporting excellence, along with *The New Yorker, Harper's, The Atlantic,* and *Business Week*. Guccione kept up the editorial push. An article in the March 1975 issue by Lowell Bergman and Jeff Gerth examined the mob's alleged ties to the $100 million La Costa resort in California. The story resulted in one of the nation's most publicized libel trials, eventually won by the defendant, Guccione. Harrison Salisbury returned to *Penthouse*'s pages in May with a blistering attack on the CIA's misadventures over the years. Cesar Chavez was interviewed in July, the same month that Anne and Paul Ehrlich wrote on world starvation. The list of serious fiction contributors grew longer: Philip Roth, John Irving, Paul Theroux. By 1976

Folio — a prestigious publication covering the magazine industry — said *Penthouse* was producing a better magazine than *Playboy*. Guccione adopted a new ad slogan: "*Penthouse*. More than just a pretty face." Brandeis University named Guccione its Publisher of the Year.

On April 9, 1976, Hugh Hefner turned fifty. Just one week earlier, *Playboy* sold the Big Bunny, its private airplane, for $4 million. Such luxuries were no longer affordable. Advertising director Howard Lederer resigned in June, and Bob Preuss also left the company. Through August and September, a hundred employees were fired, sixty-nine of them one crisp September morning. Gone were Dick Koff, public relations chief Lee Gottlieb, and two other corporate vice presidents. Hefner had hired a bright, soft-spoken Southerner and Presbyterian minister, Don Parker, as head of corporate planning to sort out what Parker would later call Management 101 problems. A Knight-Ridder executive, Derick Daniels, became president of Playboy Enterprises. And a high-powered ad salesman from Dow Jones & Company, Henry Marks, switched from the *Wall Street Journal* and *Barron's* to head *Playboy*'s advertising staff. Months later he cut *Playboy*'s circulation guarantee from 5.4 million to 4.5 million.

Guccione was poised for the final assault. He had never expected to destroy *Playboy*, although at times it looked as if he might. The drop in *Playboy*'s circulation guarantee was exactly what Bob Guccione had been waiting for. The hyperbole in his editor's note for the September 1977 issue was predictable. "*Penthouse* has surpassed *Playboy* to become the biggest selling magazine in the world," Guccione wrote. It was, of course, a lie. True, *Playboy*'s new circulation guarantee was lower than *Penthouse*'s actual sales the month before. But then, it was just a guarantee, and *Playboy* was still selling several hundred thousand more copies each month than *Penthouse*. Few ad execs on Madison Avenue would have been misled; *Playboy* refuted the charges in public, calling Guccione's statement "an attempt to deceive and mislead the advertiser." But the protest was lame. What mattered was that Guccione appeared to have won the war. All that remained was to tell the world about it, and tell Guccione did.

The new ad that morning in the *New York Times* reiterated Guccione's claim about passing *Playboy* in circulation. It reproduced *Penthouse*'s original "We're going rabbit hunting" graphics. Below it, the copy was succinct, playful, nasty — and completely faithful to Guccione. It read, in big, bold letters,

BANG! WE GOTCHA!

CHAPTER 4

Dogfight Over Deregulation

PEOPLE EXPRESS VS. THE AIRLINES

"WE HAVE the bomb ready to drop," Robert Cohn told a reporter by phone. The lawyer worked for Butler & Binion, a Washington firm that was representing People Express in its bid for rights to fly between the United States and the United Kingdom. People Express had received approval for its first overseas service from the U.S. Civil Aeronautics Board (CAB) less than eight weeks earlier, on April 1, 1983. Later the same month, British authorities had assured Cohn that there were "absolutely no questions" to be resolved before British approval. On the basis of those assurances, People Express proceeded to make the necessary preparations. Its reservation agents began booking passengers on the flight at the cut-rate carrier's customarily low prices: $149 one way for a coach seat. Fourteen employees had been dispatched to London to handle arrangements in England.

Burr and other staff members had flocked to the roof of the North Terminal to observe the arrival of the airline's first Boeing 747, only to be escorted off the roof by airport security. The exterior of the plane, purchased from ailing Braniff, had hastily been repainted a light beige, with a wide purple and red stripe halving the plane horizontally and the airline's trademark dual "people" profile emblazoned on the tail. The jumbo jet stood ready on the tarmac at Newark International Airport.

In a show of bravura that was characteristic of the upstart airline, People Express had publicly committed itself to flying out of Newark — destination Gatwick Airport, south of London — on Thursday, May 26. But with only twenty-four hours to go before Flight Two's inaugural takeoff, the new transatlantic service was in jeopardy. Negotiations between aviation authorities on both sides of the Atlantic and People Express were stalemated. British officials were balking at granting landing rights because of a dispute with Washington. U.S. antitrust officials were investigating the role of British Airways in the collapse of Laker Airways, People's predecessor in discount airline service. London wanted assurances, however, that British Airways would not be charged in court with helping to drive Laker out of business, and airline authorities in Washington were reluctant to make any promises pending final review by the U.S. Justice Department. People Express was caught in the middle.

The stakes were high and Bob Cohn knew it. Failure to fly would produce a barrage of bad publicity. From its inception, People Express had fought hard not to be labeled just another discount airline with shoddy service and broken promises. The transatlantic route wasn't expected to be very profitable, so its role for the young carrier was as a symbol, a symbol of People's somersault from its regional base to an international one. Having ballyhooed the new service in the media, People Express felt it had to deliver, even if it meant getting into a costly scrap with the British government, and perhaps with Washington too.

Backed into a corner, People Express was ready to drop its bomb. Cohn informed British authorities that he was on the verge of asking the CAB to halt all flights by British carriers to American destinations. Subject to White House approval, the CAB could order a halt immediately if People Express convinced it that the British government was acting in an anticompetitive manner. Cohn was convinced that he could.

The talks between British and American aviation officials in London ran into early morning, but Cohn was informed by a member of the CAB delegation that progress toward British approval was being made. The delegate was reluctant to go into more detail because the phone lines were unsecured, but he warned Cohn to stay by his phone. Negotiations would resume the next day, and if an agreement was reached, it would be done quickly. Cohn went to bed thinking there was a fifty-fifty chance that the British would cooperate. Hours later, it was official: Britain's Civil Aviation Authority had formally approved People Express's application for an operating permit to fly five round trips a week between Newark and Gatwick. Cohn reached Harold Pareti, People's chief operating officer, at home, awakening him at 6:00 A.M. with the news. Pareti, who had handled most of the original negotiations with British authorities, immediately telephoned his boss, the airline's principal founder and chief executive, Donald Burr. Burr's early-morning reply was "Let's get going."

The curt marching order issued from the study of a white clapboard house in suburban New Jersey couldn't conceal Burr's delight at the news. Early morning was Burr's favorite time of day. He liked to call it his thinking time. It was the solitary time he devoted each day to thinking ahead, a requisite, he felt, of strong leadership. Running, no matter what time of day, was another obsession of Burr's. He was accustomed to doing most of his problem solving on compulsory daily runs. Indeed, the most revolutionary aspects of People Express had gelled during the course of a run through downtown Houston on January 3, 1980, the day after Burr quit his job at another discount airline. "I had a lot of time and I did a lot of running," he later recalled. "I thought of a great many of the ideas that got translated into People Express: the whole business of fifty-cent cups of coffee and charging for baggage, the unbundled product, the horizontal structure — the whole design of People Express."

Now, three years later, Burr's brainchild was on the verge of becoming an international carrier. The scene at People Express's hangarlike terminal at Newark was chaotic. Dozens of reporters and TV cameramen jostled for space with the hundred passengers booked on the inaugural flight. Union Jacks hung from the rafters and big red, white, and blue flower bouquets lent an air of festivity to the otherwise dilapidated surroundings. On the second-floor observation deck, caterers were arranging huge platters of food for a VIP sendoff party. "Welcome aboard, pioneer!" exclaimed one flight attendant as passengers began boarding the jet. Just after 6:00 P.M. TV crews were allowed on board, as attendants served the passengers champagne — at no cost. At 7:15 the doors were shut, and the 747 taxied onto the runway. Rain and air traffic congestion prolonged departure, but finally, at 8:00 P.M. sharp, the plane lifted off to a round of cheers and applause.

With an uneventful touchdown early Saturday morning at Gatwick, People Express was flying an international route that many analysts said it couldn't crack. The airline was competing head-on with Pan Am, TWA, and other established giants of the industry on a major route. Although the London flights would take off only once a day, they represented a vital thrust in Burr's strategy. Having demonstrated that People Express could succeed on routes where there was little or no competition from other carriers, he had to prove that his airline could take away passengers from the giants on established routes as well.

Donald Burr had been fascinated by airplanes since childhood. His father, an MIT-educated engineer, would regularly take the family out for Sunday dinner at a Chinese restaurant, then stop at the local airfield to watch planes take off and land. The excursions would later constitute Burr's earliest recollection of being "inspired" by airplanes. "It was pretty exciting stuff for a little kid." Later, with his brother Myron, who became an air force colonel, Burr would hang around Braynard Field, the closest airport to his hometown of South Windsor, Connecticut. It was a hobby that became full-fledged when Burr attended Stanford University and was elected president of the Flying Club, a title that brought with it free flying lessons.

It was also at Stanford that Burr began to turn away from his long-time vocational ambition to become a Protestant minister. The church, he felt, no longer exerted the power it once had. His boundaries would be constrained, and he wouldn't be able to have much impact on the world. As a sophomore, Burr switched from English to economics. It seemed natural. He had always been in business, after all, from delivering newspapers when he was seven to selling encyclopedias while attending Stanford. When it came time to decide on graduate school, he opted for business instead of law. "I'd always sort of been in some sort of business activity," he later said. "Trying to create or deliver something of value was something I'd always done." Burr spent two years at Harvard Business School.

Armed with an M.B.A., he signed on as a securities analyst with National Aviation in 1965. The Manhattan-based investment firm specialized in airline and aerospace securities. It would give Burr a chance to work extensively with airline executives, tracking their companies for investors and lenders. It would also give the financial analyst who had once stared wide-eyed at planes taking off at Braynard Field a chance to work his way inside an industry that had always fascinated him.

It took eight years, but that chance finally came, in the form of a telephone call from another Harvard Business School alumnus, Francisco A. Lorenzo. A banker by trade, Frank Lorenzo had been plucked from a job at Chase Manhattan Bank to help save a small southern carrier, Texas International, from bankruptcy. More than a year into the job, Lorenzo had managed to line up new credits for the airline, in part through National Aviation. He was offering Burr the chance to help him run Texas Treetop, as the airline had unfortunately been nicknamed in the industry, as an executive vice president. If the airline prospered, Lorenzo suggested, Burr might one day get the presidency and the opportunity to run it on his own. Texas International was a risky venture. But Burr figured that, at the very least, it would provide him with a crash course in managing an airline, and that was what he wanted to do. He took the job.

For a while it was a match made in heaven. Don Burr and Frank Lorenzo became good friends, with Burr acting as best man at his boss's wedding and godfather to one of his children. For seven years he worked in Lorenzo's shadow, but Lorenzo took most of the credit for innovations introduced by Burr. Three years into his tenure, Burr launched a daring marketing campaign to boost load factors — the percentage of seats filled — on Texas International flights. Mr. Peanut, the ubiquitous mascot in the airline's new advertising, promised "Peanut Fares." The deeply discounted fares were available only on selected routes inside Texas, but they were a smash from the start. The concept was not entirely new to the industry. Dallas-based Southwest Airlines had pioneered low fares in 1971, and Braniff and Continental eventually followed suit. But with a combination of lower fares and meticulous concern for cost cutting, Burr quickly boosted revenues and put Texas International back in the black.

Lorenzo rewarded Burr in 1978, relinquishing his position as chief executive officer, but not as president. Restless and displeased with Lorenzo's reluctance to cede the title, Burr threatened to resign. Finally, in June 1979, Burr got the title, but by then he was disenchanted with Lorenzo. Despite committing much of the company's resources to an aggressive campaign to expand, Lorenzo had failed in two 1979 attempts to take over much larger airlines, National and Trans World. Over time Burr began to see that he and Lorenzo looked at the world differently. Burr also disapproved of Lorenzo's dictatorial management style. Lorenzo was a believer in strict hierarchy; Burr, on the other hand, felt that employees would perform better if they were given more freedom to make decisions and greater flexibility in their job responsibilities. "It became clear that he had to run [TI] his way and I had to do my own deal my way," Burr said. "We couldn't coexist for a further period of time." Burr was convinced that he'd never get a chance at Texas International to prove that he knew how to run the airline better than Lorenzo did.

Although dissatisfied with Lorenzo, Burr stayed at TI. He was intrigued by the revolution that was overtaking the airline industry. The Airline Deregulation Act, signed by President Jimmy Carter on October 14, 1978, legislated the end of CAB authority over domestic routes at the end of 1981, and over fares at the end of 1983. In one fell swoop, the domestic industry was being set free to compete on whatever routes and at whatever fares the market could sustain.

Deregulation was a new field of battle. Frank Lorenzo knew it. So did Burr. If Texas International could operate profitably inside Texas, they asked themselves, why not a low-fare airline that could compete nationally? Unfettered by the high costs inherent in the existing national carriers, Texas International had a chance. And if Lorenzo and Burr were tantalized by the opportunity, wouldn't others be, too? It was critical to stake out a claim in the emerging market, and to do it before anyone else did.

He who occupies the field of battle first and awaits his enemy is at ease; he who comes later to the scene and rushes into the fight is weary.

— Sun Tzu

Lorenzo figured he could stake that claim with Texas International, going "national" via acquisitions, hence the abortive attempts to take over National and TWA. But Burr saw in deregulation another opportunity. For nearly a year, he had talked on and off about leaving Texas International. Only his closest colleagues knew what he was thinking. A start-up company could provide Burr with the opportunity to design an airline that would command the lowest costs in the industry, and Burr knew that the lowest-cost carrier would eventually be able to make inroads into markets long dominated by national airlines.

So, after collecting his Christmas bonus for 1979, Don Burr resigned. It was a gamble. He had no job, no paycheck. What he did have was an unabashed ambition to prove to the entire airline industry, and Frank Lorenzo in particular, that there was a better way to run an airline. The next day two colleagues joined him: Gerald Gitner, Texas International's senior vice president for marketing and planning, and Melrose Dawsey, Burr's executive assistant, whose pending divorce convinced her that it was time to cut short a twelve-year career at TI and cast her lot with Burr and Gitner in a new venture. The Gang of Three, as they came to be known inside People Express, boasted a collective age of 102. Burr, at 39, was the undisputed ringleader. But from the start, Gitner, who was 35, and Dawsey, 32, were considered full partners in the small office set up at 7721 San Felipe in the

Galleria section of Houston. Burr covered most of the $1291 monthly rent himself.

People Express Airlines was incorporated that spring, soon after Burr completed his fastest-ever marathon, running the twenty-six mile course in just under three and a quarter hours. Chairman and CEO Burr invested $350,000 in the new venture, his entire savings. Gitner, who became president and chief operating officer, sold his house to come up with $175,000. Dawsey became an officer and director, pulling together $20,000. Each received stock in the new company.

The name was critical to the future of the airline. Burr came up with a play on the recently successful Federal Express airfreight venture, and people, employees as well as customers, who were the focus of the new airline. "People Express intends to create a working environment conducive to personal responsibility, accountability, and commitment," Burr wrote in the airline's original business plan. Promising a radically different type of company, Burr outlined for investors a horizontal management structure, nonunion employees, and a policy of personnel mobility that broke down the standard job classifications that characterized the airline industry.

As soon as the corporate papers were in order, Burr and Gitner began approaching investors, many of them venture capitalists who knew Burr from his days at National Aviation. But he had never met the man who took the quickest shine to People Express, Larry Lawrence, the head of FNCB Capital Corporation, Citibank's venture capital unit. FNCB had been among the earliest investors in Federal Express, and Lawrence was convinced that there were equally spectacular profits to be made in the airline business as a result of deregulation. The salient point, he warned Burr prophetically, was not to go directly up against the big carriers in the early days. The key to success had to be what Burr called the sofa trade — new flyers who would otherwise stay home or travel by car or bus.

On his fortieth birthday Burr received $200,000 from Citibank. With it he set out to hire the core staff that would become the fledgling airline's senior management. With only one exception, they were all alumni of Texas International. Robert

McAdoo joined in June as chief financial officer and controller. Harold (Hap) Pareti, who had been responsible for government relations at Texas International, came on board the following month. In August TI's director of personnel, Lori Dubose, arrived to oversee personnel and coordinate the hiring process. TI's director of facilities, Donald Hoydu, also joined in August, as did David McElroy, a former Flying Tiger engineer who was to oversee the yet-to-be-acquired fleet. All five became officers of the company and all drew the same salary as Burr and Gitner, $48,000 a year plus bonuses. Melrose Dawsey had agreed to work for half that salary.

Burr was firm from the start that all People Express employees have a stake in the company, and he asked each of the new officers to buy 50,000 shares of People Express stock at $1.00 a share. Each paid $15,000 in cash, the rest in promissory notes. It was a precedent for all future hirings, although the amounts and the promissory portions would vary according to the investment abilities of new employees. With the key staff in place, it was time to beat potential competitors to the punch. Burr was aware that Wall Street was awash with proposals for small commuter and regional airline start-ups, all seeking financing. It was essential that People Express position itself as a pioneer in the era of deregulation if it was to survive the onslaught of its prospective rivals.

People Express was the first new carrier to ask for certification by federal aviation authorities after deregulation. It didn't take Hap Pareti long to draft an application, filling page after page of yellow legal pads in one room, stopping only to hand them to Dawsey, who was typing them next door. Together, they took the two-hundred-page volume to a local photocopying shop, and on July 22, 1980, they filed the thick application in Washington. Then, for what seemed an eternity to both Burr and Pareti, the small staff worked around the clock, getting into the office at six in the morning and leaving at midnight — usually seven days a week — to prove to aviation authorities that they could operate an airline.

Although it seemed longer to Burr, federal authorities granted

Speed is the essence of war.
— Sun Tzu

the new carrier final certification to fly in record time — barely three months from the day Pareti filed the request. If the race went to the swift, People Express had taken a crucial lead in the new age of deregulation. But on that day Burr spent little time thinking about what certification meant; most of it was spent, by his own admission, at "the biggest party of our lives."

Even before CAB approval, Donald Burr and his senior officers had begun talking with potential investors about the $5 million or so needed to lease three planes and establish service. It quickly became apparent, however, that the carrier needed to make an even bigger splash. In the wake of Laker Airways' failure a year earlier, leasing just three planes would put in question People's financial backing and, by inference, its longevity.

Through a mutual acquaintance, Burr got in touch with a leading West Coast venture capitalist, William Hambrecht. The co-founder of Hambrecht & Quist, a San Francisco investment firm, Hambrecht had helped several high-tech firms go public, chief among them Apple Computer and Genentech. Burr knew that Hambrecht was primarily interested in start-ups in new industries; what he didn't know was that Hambrecht was also impressed with the opportunities provided by airline deregulation.

Hambrecht had represented federal authorities in the bankruptcy of a company that owned Air California, and in examining other regional carriers he had been particularly impressed with Texas International. Hambrecht also sat on the board of a company called Evans & Sutherland with Ted Walkowicz, who had been head of National Aviation when Burr joined it right out of Harvard. When, at an Evans board meeting, Walkowicz mentioned that Burr — widely credited with Texas International's turnaround — was looking for financing to start up a new airline, Hambrecht was intrigued. He began studying Burr's plans without actually approaching him.

Meanwhile, Walkowicz suggested to Burr that he get in touch with Hambrecht, with an eye to taking People Express public even before it started flying. With that, Burr began a relentless campaign to set up a meeting with Hambrecht, with Hambrecht holding him off until he could finish his own independent analysis of People's prospects.

In August 1980 the two met for lunch at the University Club, just off Fifth Avenue on Fifty-fourth Street in Manhattan. At first they simply exchanged Wall Street small talk. Forty-five minutes later, Hambrecht said he had to run off to another appointment. Panicked that he hadn't yet made his pitch, Burr quickly poured out his proposal. In return for a fat fee and possibly a stake in the company, he wanted Hambrecht & Quist to take the infant airline public, underwriting the sale of People Express shares.

Hambrecht asked only a few questions. How much money did the airline need? How long could People Express operate on the funds raised in a public offering? And most important, how much value did Burr think the shares should be sold for on Wall Street? Burr answered $5.00 a share, which meant that two thirds of the equity would go to the public. "He wanted to do it right," Hambrecht later stated. "He was planning for expansion and something big," not just a quick cash fix to pay for the start-up. It was the one major question outstanding for Hambrecht, and he got the answer he wanted.

To Burr's surprise, Hambrecht ended the meal with a handshake, agreeing to sell $25 million worth of People Express stock. He had done his homework, and he was impressed with the strategy Burr outlined. Hambrecht had already been approached by several West Coast operators interested in deregulation. He had turned them all down because none had the airline experience needed to operate a cut-rate airline profitably up against bigger carriers in the market. Burr, on the other hand, had put together an experienced team from Texas International that was used to running an airline on a shoestring budget. People Express was also planning a low-fare, high-frequency structure that the San Francisco banker had seen work at Pacific Southwest Airlines in California. Hambrecht was also impressed by Burr's "people" skills and his requirement that all employees of the new company be shareholders.

On November 6, 1980, barely weeks after it got thumbs-up from the CAB, People Express went public, selling three million shares at $8.50 apiece. After Hambrecht's fee and other costs, People Express would pocket $23.5 million dollars — enough to run the airline for three months even without any operating revenues. When the money came in two weeks later, the day before Thanksgiving, Don Burr invited his entire management team to his house for a barbecue to celebrate. They had plenty to give thanks for. The stock they had bought only months earlier was worth more than fifteen times as much as the founders had paid for it. Almost overnight, Burr's $350,000 investment was worth $6 million.

With financing in place, Burr and his team had to implement the proposal they had sold to investors. At its core was a three-stage offensive. First People Express would earn its wings on northeastern routes served primarily by local and regional carriers, providing a proving ground for the airline's organizational and fare policies without forcing a direct confrontation. During stage two the airline would compete selectively on major international and national routes. The routes would strengthen People's profile without the company dedicating so many resources that larger carriers would feel obliged to retaliate, conceivably putting People Express out of business. Finally, if all went well, the airline would expand from being primarily a northeastern carrier to a national one.

If Donald Burr knew where he wanted to take People Express, the most pressing business after the airline won certification was to develop stage one of the strategy, creating a network of routes in the Northeast. Other carriers served the region already, so People had to adopt a more cost-effective approach to serving passengers. What emerged was a "hub-and-spoke" patchwork of air routes, using Newark International Airport as the hub and operating all flights out of there. Then, instead of planes making several stops to discharge and pick up passengers, all flights would be direct out of the hub. So a traveler from Boston to Washington, for example, would have to travel via Newark. As a result, People Express would have to operate only one major airline terminal, with skeleton staffs on the ground in the other cities it serviced, immediately giving the airline a cost advantage over traditional airlines.

Burr knew from his experience at Texas International that keeping costs down was of primary importance if People

Express was going to appeal to the "sofa trade." He was convinced that, if airfares weren't so high, millions of Americans would fly more often instead of sitting home on the sofa. Thanks to deregulation, the floor had been pulled from under the airlines, which traditionally could count on regulated fares that ensured little competition — and guaranteed profits. With airlines free to cut fares, Burr was sure that if People Express could radically cut the cost of flying, it would lure passengers who had never even thought of taking a plane trip.

The choice of Newark as a base of operations seemed unconventional at first. Donald Burr had researched Dallas, Chicago, and San Francisco as hubs for People Express, but ruled out all of them. Dallas was scratched because of stiff competition from American Airlines, which had one of its two main hubs there, Chicago because of United, and San Francisco because the traffic volume wasn't heavy enough to sustain the rapid growth Burr already was targeting. The East Coast short-haul market, between major cities in the crowded northeastern corridor, held the greatest potential. Most of the larger carriers had stopped service, leaving the demand to small commuter airlines such as Piedmont or Allegheny (later USAir). New York was the logical hub to serve the market, but leasing space and facilities would be expensive. On its tight budget, People Express couldn't afford to operate out of La Guardia or JFK International.

Establishing the site of conflict so that it is advantageous is very important.

— Miyamoto Musashi

Burr had heard that Newark International Airport, thirteen miles southwest of Manhattan, had plenty of space available. On the strength of that information, People Express had filed for permission to serve twenty-seven cities, all east of the Mississippi, from Newark. But it wasn't until months later that Burr first set foot in the airport's North Terminal. A shell of a building that had been abandoned in 1973, it had two things going for it: the rent was cheap and People Express would have the terminal to itself. The latter was important, Burr figured, because passengers flying in on People Express would be less likely to switch airlines for ongoing flights if it involved the hassle of trekking to one of the newer terminals at the airport.

Trying to keep costs down, Burr had been shopping around for three or four secondhand planes with a line of credit set up by the Mercantile Bank of Dallas. In October he had seen a report in a trade paper that Lufthansa, the German airline, was trying to sell a fleet of used Boeing 737s. Hap Pareti flew to Frankfurt to negotiate a deal, ending up with seventeen planes for an average of $4.5 million each, less than a third what Boeing would have charged the airline for new ones. But the Dallas bank was unwilling to finance a much bigger aircraft deal, so Burr turned instead to a consortium led by the Bank of America and several major New Jersey bankers. With the prime rate hovering around 20 percent in late 1980, Burr also turned to Washington for help, and he got it. Pareti masterminded a lobbying effort to get Congress to amend a little-known federal program called the Government Guaranty of Equipment Loan Act of 1957. It had been set up to guarantee loans taken out by small commuter airlines, and the amendment widened coverage to newly created carriers in the wake of deregulation. Armed with a federal guarantee, People Express got its line of credit at 16⅞ percent, several points below prime. The airline would take delivery of the first three of a dozen Lufthansa planes, repainted to People's specifications at Lufthansa's expense, in March 1981.

As 1980 drew to a close, Burr began making arrangements for the move to Newark. It would be a major test of the corporate "ethic" Burr was relying on to make his new airline a success. In Texas the founders and early employees of People Express had become closely knit, and Burr hoped that the same spirit could survive in a larger company. The office on San Felipe had become home to fifteen managers, most of whom lunched together daily at one of the two nearby Mexican restaurants. Over the first few days of 1981, Burr and his colleagues moved into adjoining rooms at the Howard Johnson motel located directly across from Newark International. The raw January weather was far from comforting for the transplanted Texans, and the condition of their new offices at Newark didn't help. It took days just to remove debris from the North Terminal, but everyone pitched in. Despite the hard work and long hours — or perhaps because of it, Burr thought — the spirit of camaraderie was high.

At his new offices Burr began to put meat on the bare-bones fare strategy outlined to investors. People Express would compete with high-frequency flights at rock-bottom prices. The fares on most short-haul routes would be competitive with travel by bus or car, and the discounts would range between 40 percent and 60 percent below standard coach fares on rival carriers.

To offset low fares without going into the red, People Express would have to keep all its costs down. In addition to using the hub-and-spoke route network, People Express would be a no-frills airline. Passengers would pay $3.00 to check each bag, and snacks and beverages on board would be available for a charge. Burr had experimented briefly with no-frills food at Texas International, but the innovation hadn't sat well with many passengers. Indeed, the test had mushroomed into a major source of friction between Burr and Frank Lorenzo, who felt that TI's discount strategy would work only if travelers felt they were getting the same quality other airlines provided, but more cheaply. To a small extent, Burr knew, Lorenzo was probably right. It was always hard to withdraw frills from passengers who had become accustomed to them. Now, however, Burr was in the unique position of inaugurating a completely new airline, so when it came to no-frills policies, People Express was starting with a clean slate.

Costs would also be less than for other carriers because most tickets would be sold on board during the flights. The policy would create more work for flight attendants but let People save most of the money that traditional carriers turn over to travel agents in the form of ticket rebates.

If ticketing was something People Express could do more economically in-house, Burr knew, other services would be cheaper commissioned from outside. He decided to contract for aircraft and ramp maintenance as well as baggage handling. And in an overt gesture to stress that People Express was not aiming to become "just another airline," Burr refused to sign the standard interairline agreement on cooperation with other carriers on ticketing, baggage, and other services. People Express tickets could therefore not be exchanged for other airlines' tickets, and vice versa. The "fortress" strategy, signaled by its terminal at Newark, would pervade the entire operation.

The ultimate test of the People Express fortress would reside with the employees, and Burr was adamant about keeping labor costs down. That meant no labor unions in an industry where all but a handful of carriers had to negotiate with several unions. In the start-up phase, Burr knew that unions wouldn't be a problem; but over time, as the airline expanded, the pressures from organized labor would build. To avert unionization, he would give employees something that no union could get them, an unprecedented degree of freedom and flexibility on the job.

Monetary compensation, Burr believed, was less essential to the airline's employees than job satisfaction. To keep satisfaction high and unions out, employees of People Express would be owners, too. Thus evolved the People Express credo. New employees were required to buy at least one hundred shares of the airline at a deep discount; those who couldn't afford it were given interest-free loans by the company. More important, Burr worked out a horizontal management system, the antithesis of the highly structured environment he had overseen at Texas International. In short, everyone would be a manager. Every employee would be "cross utilized," occupying staff as well as line — flight-related — functions. Each one would have some contact with customers. Pilots became flight managers, alternating flight time with ground duties that could involve booking passengers one day or personnel recruitment the next. Stewards and stewardesses became customer service managers. Each individual would perform a rotating duty like marketing or scheduling, and hierarchy was kept to a minimum. The line managers reported to eight general managers who, in turn, reported to six managing officers. No one, including Burr, would have a secretary. And with no secretarial help, memos were out. People at People Express would have to talk to each other.

Burr's vision for employee relations was revolutionary, but it

It is not gold, but good soldiers, that insure success in war.
— Niccolò Machiavelli

was also hard-nosed business strategy: the absence of unions and strict job guidelines meant that People Express could operate with an average of fifty employees per aircraft, barely half the industry figure. Planes would fly an average of twelve hours a day, compared with eight at most airlines. Flight managers would get substantially less pay than pilots earned at established carriers, but Burr reasoned that they would derive more satisfaction with the variety of other duties, and anyway, they would be making almost as much as Burr and the other senior officers.

The prospect of job diversity was what had sold Gil Roberts on the company from the start. A veteran of thirteen years in the military, he was, at thirty-nine, too old, under union guidelines, to qualify as a starting pilot for a commercial carrier. Instead, he had gone back to work pushing paper for the Federal Aviation Administration. One set of papers that had crossed his desk in Washington was the volume drafted by Hap Pareti. Roberts quickly contacted Pareti to volunteer his services as a pilot. He was also intrigued at the prospect of learning how to run an airline. It was a chance of a lifetime, even at a salary that paled in comparison to what pilots his age were making at the larger airlines. Roberts was hired as the airline's first flight manager, and in his staff role, the former rodeo rider dealt with federal authorities to get the carrier's first planes certified. Less than four years later, he became chief operating officer of the entire airline.

Gil Roberts was at the controls of a Boeing 737 shortly after seven on Thursday morning, April 30, 1981. Just outside the airport perimeter, Melrose Dawsey was sitting on her bed at Howard Johnson's, writing out forty bonus checks to celebrate People Express's first day of service when she heard the engines roar overhead. She had missed the event she'd been working hard for more than a year to see. The tears began to well. Outside, on the North Terminal observation deck, Don Burr and the rest of the team watched the plane until it was no longer visible. "Please," Burr muttered under his breath, "let it make it back." When Roberts returned from his run to Norfolk, Virginia, dozens of reporters and New Jersey officials were on hand to celebrate. The new airline had completed its first round-trip journey.

Later that day, the two other planes in People Express's fleet made their maiden runs to Columbus, Ohio, and Buffalo. Over the next few months, People Express filled roughly 60 percent of all the seats it made available on those first three routes and the five new destinations added during the summer. Sixty percent represented the magic load factor that Burr estimated was necessary for the airline to break even on what appeared to be absurdly low fares. Passengers bound to Norfolk, for instance, paid $23 off-peak and $35 during peak hours, compared with the regular coach fare of $82. And the same People Express fares to Buffalo represented an even larger discount from the $99 one-way fare charged by other carriers on the Buffalo–New York area corridor.

By the end of the summer, People Express had taken delivery of several more Lufthansa jets, and the payroll had grown to cover more than five hundred employees. Burr was scouting for new destinations when, all of a sudden, his entire strategy was in jeopardy. No amount of planning or experience could have prepared the People Express team for what happened on August 3, 1981. The Professional Air Traffic Controllers Organization (PATCO) called a strike, and the federal controllers at Newark and airports around the country walked off the job.

As the air traffic controllers departed, the very existence of six-month-old People Express was placed in jeopardy. From his office window, Don Burr watched the Newark tarmac with growing trepidation as the strike dragged on. Day after day, 737s bearing the People Express colors taxied toward the runway, where they usually sat, burning fuel, before taxiing back for refueling. Few planes ever made it off the ground despite efforts on the part of FAA managers to staff the control tower and keep the airport operating as usual. Still, Burr believed the trouble was temporary. Then the Reagan administration threatened to fire all the striking controllers. As federal employees, the government reasoned, the controllers didn't have the right to strike. Within weeks the government began firing strikers, replacing most of them with on-duty military air controllers. Safety precautions forced the FAA to order a 50 percent cutback of flights at twenty-two major airports, including Newark, during peak morning and evening hours.

When the FAA announced later in August that the flight cut-backs would continue through April 1982, Burr realized for the first time that People Express might not make it after all. The major carriers were reporting losses of approximately $20 mil-lion a *day* because of the strike. For smaller carriers that de-pended on frequent flights and high load factors to make money, the cutbacks in takeoffs spelled disaster. Within weeks three re-gional carriers — Golden Gate Airlines, Air New England, and Swift Aire — were forced into bankruptcy. Burr was reluctant to say so in public, but he knew People Express would have to follow suit unless revenues rebounded quickly. The airline was scheduled to take delivery of three more 737s in October; failure to do so would result in the forfeiture of a $6.5 million deposit held by Lufthansa. That loss could, in turn, trigger problems with People Express's existing lines of credit, and the airline's bankers were already getting nervous about the impact of pro-longed traffic cutbacks. Without being allowed to add flights, People Express could only hope to boost revenues by raising its fares. If that happened, the airline would find it almost impossi-ble to compete with rival carriers on its routes.

As a result of the strike, People Express lost as much as $6 mil-lion between August and the end of September. "We were bleeding at a terrific rate," Burr reported. "It was gun-to-head time. We were going out of business." Burr petitioned the FAA for help, getting a quick lesson in deregulation. The federal agency told him that just as People Express was on its own to set fares, it was also on its own when times were bad. Then Donald Burr and Gerald Gitner flew to Germany for meetings with Lufthansa officials to ask for a delay in aircraft deliveries. The German airline was willing to be flexible about the schedule for the jets as long as People Express came up with a plan to ride out the financial trouble posed by the strike. On a plane heading home, Gitner, the co-founder and master scheduler who had de-vised People's original route strategy, came up with an alterna-tive that was as risky and dangerous as it was necessary. October would be a make-or-break month for the carrier because of mounting losses. Gitner knew that to do nothing would only lead to bankruptcy. His alternative strategy, if it worked, would allow the company to survive the strike; if it failed, it would bankrupt the company. As Burr recalled, it meant "betting the company a second time."

Arriving back in the United States, Gitner called the scheduling team to his house. That Sunday morning, arrayed around the Gitners' dinner table, the group plotted a new set of routes that would allow the company to move most of its takeoffs to off-peak hours. It would also mean a dramatic shift in People Express's hub-and-spoke strategy, however. Planes would take off before dawn from Newark and fly to airports not covered by the FAA cutbacks, mainly Buffalo and Syracuse. From there, instead of returning to Newark, the same planes would go on to a Florida destination. And the typical fare for passengers from the New York area to Florida, $69, would still be less than half the normal coach fare on the route.

The risks in the new strategy were substantial. People Express would have to pay for expanded services at several airports instead of handling most of the technical operations at Newark, and the higher costs wouldn't necessarily be offset by higher revenues. There was no proof that travelers would jump at the chance to fly, even on the cheap, to cities such as Sarasota and West Palm Beach, where People Express was allowed to land. The only plus going for the new plan was that it allowed People Express to keep its planes in the air without continually having to touch down at Newark International. As long as People Express could fill the seats, Gitner and Burr knew, the airline could hold on until the traffic restrictions at Newark were lifted.

He who knows the art of the direct and the indirect approach will be victorious.

— Sun Tzu

Going into the winter travel season, the strategy appeared in retrospect to be a stroke of genius. On October 25, 1981, the first plane left Newark at dawn for Buffalo en route to Sarasota. From the start, the planes flew 60 percent full, but within a month load factors were typically hovering around 85 percent of capacity. The "bypass" ploy remained more expensive to operate than People Express's hub-and-spoke service, but it allowed the airline to rebuild revenues, take delivery of the next three 737s, and reassure creditors and investors that the airline was no fly-by-night operation. Eventually south Florida would become a major destination and source of revenue for the airline, breaking up Eastern Air Lines' long-time near monopoly of the market.

With the airline flying once again at capacity on its revised schedule, Burr turned his attention to internal problems. It was clear that People Express would fill seats as long as the airline could operate profitably on low fares. Labor costs were a scant 20 percent of People's overall costs, compared with 37 percent at Eastern, for instance. To maintain that edge, People Express had to outperform other carriers, and to Burr that meant motivating a work force that now numbered more than six hundred "managers." Burr's charismatic manner and almost evangelical zeal had convinced the original team to join up. But increasingly, the personal touch wasn't enough; as Burr frequently complained, it was impossible to know each and every one of the newcomers on a first-name basis. His time was limited, but Burr continued to speak to each new group of trainees. He also set an example. If the lower echelons were asked to work fifty or sixty hours without overtime, Burr regularly put in more.

By December, with the PATCO strike over but People Express still struggling to recover from its effects, Burr called a meeting to formalize the company's six guiding precepts. But as others in the company were quick to point out, the list was essentially dictated by Burr himself over few objections from the other senior managers. At the top of the list was "growth and development of the individual." At the bottom, below such standards as providing the best air transportation, the highest quality mangement, setting a role model for others in the industry, and simplifying operations, came precept number 6, maximization of profit. To many outsiders, Burr seemed to have his priorities backward.

The newest recruits eagerly subscribed to Burr's corporate precepts, but one of his fellow founders did not. People's president, Gerry Gitner, had quit Texas International to help set up People Express because he believed that deregulation made the new airline viable, not because he was entranced with Burr's vision or management style. From the very start, Gitner was worried that Burr, preoccupied with designing a new corporate structure, wouldn't be sufficiently profit-oriented. The six precepts simply confirmed what Gitner had felt even before the move to Newark, that Burr's people experiment would be paid for in lower profits.

Gitner was also peeved at what he considered the hypocrisy of Burr's management style. He felt that Burr didn't practice what he preached. Despite the horizontal management structure that made managers of all employees, the important decisions were ultimately made by Burr himself with little regard for dissenting opinions, including Gitner's. "Don was a dictator," Gitner confided. "He runs the company his way and always has." It was a charge that regularly recurred within People's ranks in even more cruel incarnations. At one point the carping escalated into a campaign by disenchanted employees who put up Kool-Aid posters in staff lounges, the international "not allowed" symbol superimposed on a Kool-Aid packet. The reference was obvious. "I don't know," Gitner answered when asked how Burr got most of the employees to follow him. "How did Jim Jones get all those people to drink Kool-Aid?"

Don Burr hotly denied charges that he was fostering a personality cult at People Express, or that he was a dictator among top management. He saw his job as setting direction for the company, creating an environment. "Some people criticize that as being manipulative and so forth, and I say, yeah, it is manipulative," Burr said in his own defense. "But it's good manipulation, it's constructive manipulation." There could be disagreements on specific policies, he felt, but only within limits. "Don't go contrary to direction," he warned one manager. "If you don't go with the direction of this company, you ought to go elsewhere." The direction, of course, was set by Burr.

Gerry Gitner quickly tired of taking Burr's directions, and as his disagreements with Burr grew, he knew his tenure was limited. So when Pan American approached him in February 1982 to take a senior job in charge of the ailing carrier's finances, he jumped. To the outside world, the departure was amicable. Gitner confessed that his work at People Express was finished, and he was ready to take on the bigger challenge of reviving Pan Am. Burr gave no public hint of his perennial feud with his co-founder, because if it surfaced, People Express's stock would plunge, chopping hundreds of thousands of dollars off the paper profits piled up by both men.

In the first quarter after Gitner's departure, the company earned almost $3 million between April and June. Much of the internal criticism abated and, at least temporarily, the No Kool-Aid posters disappeared. Don Burr, it seemed, was right after all. People Express could emphasize the growth and development of its employees *and* maximize profits. Burr now went back on the offensive. So far, People Express had studiously avoided competing head-to-head with major carriers on their established routes until it had the financing to sustain a prolonged incursion into their territory. Yet the entire low-cost, low-fare strategy was designed for competition with the big airlines. They were saddled with high labor costs, far-flung networks, and "full-frills" service, as opposed to People's ability to break even on much lower passenger traffic.

The expansion into "national" routes, Donald Burr knew, had to be staggered. As it was, People Express was having a tough time instilling the airline's unique work ethic in a company that would grow to more than one thousand employees by the end of 1982. The first aggressive move forward was prompted, oddly enough, by Burr's former boss at Texas International, Frank Lorenzo. The Texas entrepreneur had responded to Burr's plans with an East Coast carrier of his own. Created in 1980 as a subsidiary of Texas International, New York Air inaugurated service in December of the same year, even before Burr and his colleagues made the move from Houston to Newark. Lorenzo's venture started out as a cut-rate, no-frills carrier, but the losses piled up. Even as People Express was breaking into the black, New York Air was losing money in mid 1982. To rebound, Lorenzo switched strategies. New York Air began offering below-coach fares with full-coach service, a clear pitch for business travelers. The new service began in May, and New York

Air promptly applied for landing rights at Washington, D.C.'s National Airport. Until then the National–La Guardia route had been virtually monopolized by Eastern Air Lines and its shuttle service. Now Lorenzo was taking a stab at the lucrative trade along the New York–Washington corridor.

Convinced that neither New York Air nor the Eastern Shuttle was drawing the soft trade because of fares and services catering specifically to business travelers, Burr decided to make Washington the first battleground with a major carrier — in this case, one major carrier and his former employer. Lorenzo had already been forced to change tack by staking out a position in the New York–Washington market, and Burr was attracted by the chance to prove that a well-run, no-frills airline with a superior management style could compete against Eastern.

In June Hap Pareti, Gitner's successor as president, negotiated with Washington's National Airport, paying a record $1.75 million for landing rights on the already crowded runways. Barely weeks after New York Air first touched down in Washington, People Express was packing Washington-bound passengers into its planes at Newark. The new ad campaign trumpeting People's low Washington fares said it all: "Fly Smart."

People's Washington flights filled up almost from the start, winning more than just new customers to the airline. Wall Street was taking notice, and Burr, with his background and contacts in the financial world, knew it was time to cash in on the interest. Once again he contacted Bill Hambrecht in San Francisco. Where the first issue of public stock had been shunned by the biggest New York investment firms, this time Hambrecht got Morgan Stanley & Co. to join it in underwriting a second offering. Morgan Stanley was one of the top three old-line investment firms on Wall Street, unlike the recently formed and San Francisco–based Hambrecht & Quist. Only one condition was stipulated by the staid financial firm, in tune with its conservative reputation on Wall Street. The prospectus for the offering had to put emphasis on the airline's low-cost strategy, not its experiment in employee democracy. Morgan Stanley, like Gerry Gitner, wasn't enamored of Burr's people strategy. Nevertheless, with the investment company's imprimatur, the offering of 2.47 million shares on August 19, 1982, was quickly over-subscribed at $12.25 a share. People Express netted just over $28 million from the sale, and even after the sale its stock continued to rise. The public perception, reflected on Wall Street, was that People Express could do no wrong. Internally, that approval bolstered spirits: after all, the average People's employee owned approximately $20,000 worth of stock.

People Express was getting ready for a major expansion phase, and Burr geared up to borrow more money to finance new planes. Simultaneously, Braniff was trying to work its way out of insolvency by selling twenty Boeing 727s at what Donald Burr considered fire-sale prices: $84 million for the 727s and the lease of one Boeing 747. To help finance the deal, he and Hap Pareti went back to the airline's principal creditors, arranging a new $22.5 million revolving credit line with the Bank of America and four New Jersey banks. On April 26, 1983, Morgan Stanley and Hambrecht & Quist issued another million new shares of stock in the airline — at more than $32 a share, fully $20 more than investors had paid just eight months earlier.

For Burr, People Express's reputation on Wall Street was a vindication of his management views, views not shared by such former colleagues as Frank Lorenzo and Gerry Gitner. The vindication also carried with it a very palpable benefit: the chairman's personal stake in the company was worth more than $22 million after the third stock issue in April. In addition, the rise in the stock price kept People's shareholder/employees happy.

Burr had insisted on the lease of Braniff's 747 in the deal for the 727s for good reason. He had already set his sights on London. The demise of Laker Airways and its cut-rate, no-frills service had led to broad-based airfare hikes across the Atlantic over the previous year. But despite warnings from some inside the company that expansion into the London market would force British Airways, Pan Am, and other big carriers to retaliate, Burr proceeded anyway. He saw the London route, with only one flight a day, as a limited offensive against two major U.S. carriers, TWA and Pan Am, and a move that would not force either to rethink their full-fare strategies.

After British officials approved its route request and Flight

Two took off for Gatwick, People Express was an international carrier. It quickly was filling 80 percent of its seats on the once-a-day flights, well above the average on transatlantic routes. But the load factor mattered less than the public relations. Although the few flights each week limited profits, Burr had served notice to the giants of the airline industry that People Express could go anywhere it wanted and still make money. It was also important internally to show the airline's expanding work force that People Express was building momentum. The London flights would provide a steppingstone to expanded service. Soon People Express would expand into markets west of the Mississippi, which at first it had carefully avoided.

In March 1984 Burr could report to shareholders that revenues were up 100 percent and profits were at ten times the level of the previous fiscal year.

In Burr's mind, it was no longer a question whether People Express could afford to grapple with the big guys. To build on the momentum along the East Coast, it had to. Once again, the first big guy on Burr's hit list was Frank Lorenzo. Texas Air had recently taken over troubled Continental Airlines in Houston. Almost immediately, Lorenzo's attempts to cut costs ran afoul of Continental's unions. When the mechanics' union went out on strike, Lorenzo swore he wouldn't give in to labor demands. Early on, Burr was convinced that a protracted and bitter struggle between Lorenzo, the tough-as-nails boss, and Continental's unionized work force was unavoidable. Based on that insight, Don Burr decided to take advantage of the turmoil.

The timing was perfect. On September 8 People Express announced that it would start flying between Newark and Houston. Lorenzo knew he couldn't afford to wait for a settlement with the union in the face of the danger of People's grabbing a share of the Houston market, which Continental would have a tough time winning back. Two weeks later Lorenzo told a packed press conference in New York City that Continental was filing for reorganization under the federal bankruptcy code. It was an unprecedented bid to break union contracts. Without it, Lorenzo stated, Continental would have gone bankrupt, pure and simple.

People's first passengers on the route paid only $99 one way from Newark for Houston's Hobby Airport, less than a third of the $320 charged by most of its rivals for regular coach seats. The airline's first foray into the West, in October 1983, went like clockwork. It was clear that Burr had devised a winning strategy that was unlikely to falter as long as larger airlines didn't compete with People Express on price. And as long as their costs were so much higher, Burr believed, they couldn't.

Burr's next strike was against Northwest Airlines, in the Minneapolis/St. Paul market. Despite Northwest's long stranglehold in the market, People Express began flying, with almost no notice, between Newark and the Twin Cities on June 1, 1984. Just fourteen days later, Burr invaded the heavily traveled transcontinental market with $125 flights to Los Angeles. And on August 22, Chicago, long the preserve of the nation's two biggest carriers, United and American. As service to Chicago got under way, People committed itself to taking delivery of twenty-five new Boeings. The expanded fleet would be necessary to service the new destinations — Detroit, Miami, Oakland, and Cleveland — that quickly followed.

Burr was insistent that new routes be opened up as quickly as the organization could handle them. To keep the big carriers on the defensive, People Express needed to strike as quickly as possible, with only enough notice necessary to generate passenger traffic in each local market that the airline added to its roster. Suddenly, People Express was a truly national airline.

Just as suddenly, the airline appeared to stumble, to some observers potentially fatally. The day Burr announced service to Chicago, Wall Street panicked. Airline stocks dived across the board. There were so many sell orders that trading was delayed by as much as two hours. People's attack on United and American was bound to solicit retaliation, Wall Street worried, and if the two largest domestic carriers felt obliged to play by People's rules, the rest of the industry would have to follow suit. Fare wars, investors figured, would destroy profits for all the airline companies, People Express among them.

Within days United and American came close to matching the Chicago fares on some, but not all, of their seats. On the Minneapolis route, Northwest retaliated with fares that actually undercut those offered by People. As long as Burr had refrained from trying to grab a share of their most lucrative markets, the big carriers had been reluctant to adopt lower fares to fill seats. Now People Express was a clearly focused threat to the traditional, high-cost airlines, and they responded the only way they could — by slashing fares.

As Wall Street had predicted, the ensuing fare wars cut sharply into every airline's operating revenues. For the first time in two years, People Express began piling up losses. By year's end the airline's high-flying stock had plummeted to as low as $8 a share, roughly the same price investors had paid before the airline took to the sky. It was less than a fourth the value Wall Street had placed on Burr's brainchild just a year and a half earlier. The seemingly endless rise in the "paper" wealth of People Express shareholders, chief among them the airline's employees, had come to an end. No one was more aware or affected by the airline's tumble on Wall Street than Burr, whose net worth had shrunk by millions.

The loss had a sobering effect on Burr. The entrepreneur whom *Inc.* magazine had profiled on its January 1984 cover as "That Daring Young Man and His Flying Machines" was in a tailspin, and Burr was intent on pulling out of it. The new buzz word at the North Terminal was *consolidation.* "In 1985 we intend to pull back and consolidate," said the chairman. "It's time for some fine-tuning at this airline."

People Express was already starting to pay dearly for a fleet — and a work force — that was growing too fast. The employee rolls had mushroomed to four thousand names from the two hundred fifty that had been there when the first flight lifted off the Newark tarmac. At the same time seat capacity had more than doubled in 1984 as Burr picked up nearly forty new planes. In the scramble to use them, load factors plummeted. While the airline had

> *The employment of too many forces in combat may be disadvantageous; for whatever superiority it may give in the first moment, we may have to pay dearly for in the next.*
>
> — Karl von Clausewitz

once been able to fill 80 percent of all its seats, the ratio had dropped to below 64 percent during the last three months of 1984. In January it slipped further. Passengers were filling

barely one out of every two seats in and out of Newark, despite
the airline's admitted need to fill three out of every four seats
just to break even. Admitted one senior official, "We just
slapped planes into markets."

Until the autumn of 1985, Burr was convinced that the airline
could expand nonstop by "growing" managers internally and
adding new routes all the time. But the setbacks and financial
losses incurred as a result of People's overexpansion forced Burr
to re-evaluate his position. To fine-tune the network, he ordered
an extensive review of routes, raising or lowering fares selectively where the market conditions permitted. Minneapolis was
cut back from seven to four flights a day. Fares to Los Angeles
and Oakland dropped to $99. In some markets People Express
hiked its fares by as much as 60 percent.

The tinkering in fares, though, would no longer be the responsibility of Hap Pareti. In early January he quit to start an
airline of his own with a hub of its own at Dulles Airport outside Washington, D.C. The departure was amicable, but it was
apparent that Pareti, like Gitner before him, had never enjoyed
playing second fiddle to Burr, even in a company that extolled
the merits of collective decision making. "I want to set the strategies for a company," Pareti admitted, "so I want to go out and
be a chief executive." Coming from People Express's president
and chief operating officer and one of Burr's earliest recruits, the
official statement was a not-so-subtle indictment of Burr's private, autocratic management style. It was blatantly at odds with
the public perception of People Express as a fundamentally egal-
itarian place to work.

Burr bridled at the charge. "This business that I run everything and every detail," he told outsiders, "is nonsense." As
proof, he pointed to the airline's $50 million annual advertising
budget. After setting up the marketing department in 1980, Burr
left its management to the "marketing guys." He would go for
months without even meeting with them, or, for that matter,
with People's ad agency. How many other chief executives, he
asked, would keep their hands off a $50 million expenditure item
in a company the size of People Express?

Urged by the editors of the *Wall Street Journal* to contribute to the newspaper's popular "Manager's Journal" column, Burr deflected criticism of his own management style. But he did acknowledge the growing disenchantment inside People Express over compensation now that the company's stock was no longer rising. "The biggest complaints I get from those who work here are that they want more pay," Burr wrote.

Undaunted, Burr was convinced that morale would rebound with the stock price, and for that, People Express needed to show Wall Street that it could get back into the black after losing an average $12 million a month on its operations in early 1985. Paradoxically, the quickest route to closing the gap was to raise prices. By March 1985 general fare increases averaging 10 percent were in place. An upturn in the economy led other airlines to boost prices as well, and People Express once again began filling more than 60 percent of its available seats, with even higher load factors on its winter routes to Florida and California.

Higher fares reduced People's losses, and the improvement was enough to convince at least some Wall Street investors that Don Burr could turn the airline's fortunes around. For six days at the end of March, Burr blitzed the boardrooms of key financial institutions around the country, among them the Bank of America in San Francisco and Allen & Co. in New York. Burr was looking for new funds, not only to maintain People's position in the new markets, but to continue the rapid expansion that had seemed so foolhardy barely months earlier. Economists were predicting a boom in air travel as the economy expanded, and Burr was worried that People Express would be hard put to cash in on the boom if it didn't expand. To do that, he needed new funds from Wall Street, and he got what he wanted, $33 million. The offering of convertible preferred debentures, at $25 for coupons carrying a 10 percent annual yield, was oversubscribed.

Three months later the airline was back in the black. With the delivery of seven more Boeing planes, People's fleet stabilized at seventy-two jets, making it the ninth largest airline in the United States and the biggest carrier of air travelers in and out of the New York area. During the summer the expansion continued, with People Express inaugurating service to several new domestic markets, including Atlanta, and in September, Brussels.

At least temporarily, the airline had survived its overexpansion. Despite internal dissent and the defection of Gerry Gitner, Hap Pareti, and several other original officers of the company, Don Burr was still at the controls. At a meeting of all shareholders in August 1985, he made the turnaround official and asked shareholders to vote themselves their first dividend. The five-cents-a-share quarterly dividend made headlines, but it obscured a much more important outcome of the meeting. In a series of votes on corporate by-laws, Burr pushed through several antitakeover measures aimed at keeping control of the company in the hands of the existing shareholders.

It was a far-sighted maneuver based on Burr's vision of where the airline industry was headed. People Express was in no immediate danger of being taken over. But as the larger carriers began to look for ways to cut costs, Burr expected his airline to become a likely target. By acquiring People Express, after all, a high-cost carrier could lower its average rate of carrying passengers virtually overnight. Even if it meant mounting a hostile takeover bid, Burr knew, the big airlines would find it much cheaper and quicker to take over People Express than it would be to break a union contract, as Lorenzo had done at Continental, or go about cutting costs the hard way.

But People Express hadn't ruled out becoming a predator itself. Burr became convinced that People Express needed to become a more truly national airline, with its presence west of the Mississippi as strong as the one east of it. The West would allow People Express to attain the "critical mass" essential to compete with other national airlines. Without such a major presence, Burr figured, People's rivals would outcompete by "cross subsidizing" their fares, using profits in the West to pay for losses incurred on eastern routes where they had to compete with lower fares.

The gateway to the West was Denver, and the biggest player in the market was Continental Airlines. As Don Burr began looking for an acquisition to give his airline a western base,

Frank Lorenzo was moving to lock up the Denver market for himself. On September 20, 1985, the chairman of Texas Air made a bid for control of Frontier Airlines. Like Continental, already part of Texas Air, Frontier was based in Denver. If the merger had gone through, therefore, Lorenzo would effectively have controlled the gateway.

Lorenzo's $20-a-share bid for Frontier met with immediate resistance among the airline's employees. Rather than face a repeat of the union-busting Continental debacle, Frontier's unions offered the airline's management more than $40 million in wage concessions. In return, the unions would get part ownership of the airline — and vote against any sale to Lorenzo. At the same time, however, Frontier began the search for a "white knight," Wall Street jargon for a company that would come into a takeover battle with a higher bid than the one already on the table from an unwanted suitor.

Donald Burr got the call from a Frontier lawyer one Monday morning, his first day at a tennis camp with his wife, Bridget. By noon he had made his decision to go after Frontier. Late in the week, Burr broke away from his vacation for two days of negotiations in Monterey, California, with Frontier's chairman, Joseph O'Gorman. He then flew to Denver for talks with union representatives, who were desperate to find an alternative to Lorenzo. Burr was an adamant opponent of union representation at People Express, but during the weekend back-and-forth, he promised to operate Frontier as a separate, unionized entity. In return for job guarantees for all four thousand employees for at least four years, the unions agreed to fulfill their promises of the wage and other concessions already made to Frontier's management.

Burr went into the talks with the unions with an ambivalent attitude. He wanted to secure Frontier — badly. Denver was a perfect hub for flights throughout the West, Burr figured, and Frontier had enough cash on hand to effectively reduce the $300 million price tag on the company by as much as two-thirds. Not inconsequentially, the acquisition, if it went through, would provide another payoff by stymying Lorenzo's plans to lock up the Denver market. But Burr was also aware of the cost. After steadfastly opposing any union presence at People Express, he would have to accept and deal with labor leaders at Frontier. A bitter pill to swallow, it was made only slightly easier by the unions' readiness to make good on the concessions.

When Frank Lorenzo got word that Frontier was seriously negotiating with Burr, he upped his offer to $22 a share. Hours later Frontier's board of directors met to consider a $24-a-share bid by People Express. With strong union support, the board voted unanimously in favor of a binding agreement with People Express, which was subject only to government approval. Admitting defeat, Lorenzo withdrew his bid.

Burr expected his own rank and file to object to the Frontier acquisition. It flew in the face of everything they had been told: that People Express would grow internally; that it would never allow unions inside the company. But the chilly reception never took place. When Burr walked into a Q and A session with employees at Newark headquarters right after announcing the Frontier acquisition, he anticipated rough questioning. None was forthcoming.

The acquisition went through without a snag. Less than five years after People Express first took flight, Burr was presiding over the fifth largest airline in the United States. The carrier was competing in every major market and against all the major airlines. The risk, Burr knew, was that People Express and Frontier just wouldn't mesh — union versus nonunion, West versus East, no-frills versus full-frills, and so on.

And mesh they didn't. Within weeks of taking control at Frontier, it became clear that huge losses were piling up. To minimize them, Burr ordered a drastic overhaul, cutting fares and copying People's no-frills service. With strong price competition in the Denver market already, fliers who had once stuck with Frontier because of its reputation for quality service no longer felt compelled to do so. Load factors dropped sharply in the spring of 1986, and Frontier continued losing $10 million a month. Far from bolstering profits, Frontier became a seemingly permanent drag on earnings at People Express. When it came time to report first-quarter results for the two airlines combined, Burr announced an unprecedented loss of $58 million.

Burr tried to offset some of the losses by raising fares on People flights, but quickly reversed course when bookings for the all-important summer tourist season dropped sharply. As the Frontier merger unraveled, Burr also became convinced that People could no longer afford to be a strictly no-frills airline. The airline needed a way to fill seats during those months that it couldn't count on vacation travelers. Airlines such as Lorenzo's Continental were proving that low-fare carriers could appeal to full-frills travelers as well, but People Express was at a disadvantage. It was doing nothing to appeal to business fliers, while overbooking and flight delays had earned the airline a reputation for unreliability. On May 1 Burr instituted the first of many changes designed to lure a new class of passenger, without losing the low-fare travelers who were People's main constituency. The airline created a frequent-flier program aimed primarily at business people. Crowded coach seats in the front of each plane were abandoned in favor of wide leather seats and a first-class section with free drinks, meals, and baggage service.

Burr hoped that, in time, the changes would lure a new class of passenger to People Express, but it was obvious that the airline couldn't wait that long. At the rate its Frontier subsidiary was losing money, People Express would be out of cash by September or October. The company, Burr knew, couldn't wait until then to try to find a solution. The only way for People Express to survive intact, or minus Frontier, was to find a buyer soon, while it could negotiate from a position of strength, knowing that it had more than $50 million in its coffers.

The first approach by a potential buyer came in mid May. Frank Lorenzo called John H. McArthur, dean of the Harvard Business School, who had recently joined the board of People Express. At first Burr balked at negotiating with his former boss, but McArthur prevailed and a series of meetings ensued, some in Manhattan, others at Burr's and Lorenzo's respective vacation homes on Martha's Vineyard and Nantucket. When word of the talks began to leak on Wall Street, Burr and Lorenzo were far from concluding a deal. So on June 23, the airline's principal investment bank, Morgan Stanley, announced that People Express was "exploring the possible sale of part, or under certain circumstances even all, of the company."

The statement touched off a frenzy in two places — on Wall Street and in airline board rooms. The price of People Express shares plummeted by nearly 50 percent in one day, on fears that the no-frills carrier was going out of business. The stock began bouncing back, however, when it became clear that several major airlines were indeed interested in all or part of the company. Representatives of Western Airlines, United, and Delta all expressed their interest to Morgan Stanley. But Lorenzo was clearly the most interested.

For Burr, a takeover, especially by Lorenzo, would be tantamount to an admission of defeat. It came down to numbers. Could People Express sell its Frontier subsidiary for enough cash to let the airline survive and, eventually, prosper? And if not, how much could Burr squeeze out of Lorenzo for the entire airline? If possible, Burr wanted to maintain People's autonomy. If not, he wanted to get the best deal he could.

The talks were interrupted only by Independence Day celebrations. Then on Sunday, July 6, Lorenzo's representatives made a bid of $9 a share, half in cash, half in notes, for People Express. Burr was not present at the meeting, and Texas Air gave him only two days to respond or risk the chance that Lorenzo would lower his bid. Returning that night from Martha's Vineyard, the People Express chairman decided to take that chance and allowed the deadline to pass. On Monday United Airlines offered to pay $146 million for Frontier.

The two offers were on the table when People's board of directors — among them John H. McArthur, a Morgan Stanley officer, and Bill Hambrecht — began meeting at six o'clock on Wednesday evening at Morgan Stanley's offices on the thirtieth floor of the Exxon building in midtown Manhattan. Union representatives from Frontier had made it clear to Burr that they would once again oppose any takeover by Lorenzo and block the merger in court if necessary. At the same time, Morgan Stanley officials and Burr's financial lieutenant, Bob McAdoo, trekked back and forth between the thirtieth floor and the floor below, where United representatives were on hand, to try to squeeze a better offer for Frontier. The to-and-fro continued through dawn on Thursday morning, when a Morgan official stopped one last time on the twenty-eighth floor, where Texas Air representatives were meeting. Unless Lorenzo upped his offer by 20 percent, they were told, People Express would sell to United. Texas Air refused to budge. The final vote was taken at six that morning, and it was unanimous: People Express would sell its Frontier subsidiary to United for the price the larger airline was offering. The vote allowed Burr to cut his monthly losses on Frontier while making a profit on the transaction. United was paying almost $50 million more than People Express had effectively paid for Frontier eight months earlier.

The vote was also a vote for survival. The airline had run into trouble, Burr conceded to colleagues on the board, because it tried to expand too quickly. Now, he promised, proceeds from the sale of Frontier would be used to buy People Express what it needed most: time. Time to remake the airline. To improve service. Time to attract business travelers. To complete construction in 1987 of a giant, automated air terminal in Newark.

But time was no longer on Burr's side. If the acquisition of Frontier was a "disaster," as he later admitted, so was the sale. Within weeks, unions representing both United and Frontier torpedoed the deal when United refused to give Frontier pilots pay equal to those at United. A $50 million sale of planes and landing slots at Denver's Stapleton Airport went through, but Frontier — and its operating losses — remained part of People Express. To end the cash outflow, Burr halted all Frontier operations and opened talks aimed at an honorable surrender.

His interlocutor was the man he left waiting at the merger table: Frank Lorenzo. In victory, the Texas Air boss was magnanimous. He agreed to buy all of People's operations, provided the acquisition made its way successfully through the months-long process of approval from government agencies and shareholders. Meanwhile, Burr would stay on for at least a year at the helm of People Express and attempt to remake the carrier into a full-frills, low-fare service that could eventually be merged with Lorenzo's Continental. Together with Lorenzo's purchase of Eastern Air Lines, the deal would make Texas Air the largest airline company in the free world. People Express would be part of that company, but it was Frank Lorenzo who would command the unrivaled airline network. Not Don Burr.

CHAPTER 5

Car Wars

GENERAL MOTORS VS. THE JAPANESE

WHEN EIJI TOYODA checked into the Waldorf-Astoria Hotel on March 1, 1982, he registered under a false name. It was a minor precaution, designed to drape a veil of secrecy over the exploratory discussions that had brought the chairman of Japan's largest automobile company, Toyota, to New York. When Toyoda arrived at Manhattan's exclusive Links Club on East Sixty-second Street early the same evening with an aide and interpreter, the climate of confidentiality persisted. Escorted to a private dining room, Toyoda came face to face for the first time with the powerful chairman of General Motors, Roger Smith, and two of Smith's deputies. During the meal the talk was general. Toyoda expressed his concern over mounting threats in Congress against Japanese imports. Smith expanded on his own opposition to import restrictions, but warned Toyoda that he was in a minority among Detroit auto executives. The two executives also went over their respective companies' recent financial performance, Toyoda downplaying his firm's record profits and Smith expressing optimism that the losses GM had incurred in 1980 were a thing of the past.

The conversation was low-key, slowed by the interpreter's repeated punctuation of the dialogue with translations into and out of Japanese. Then, as coffee was served, Smith got down to business. Hauling a stack of charts and briefing papers onto the dining table, Smith laid out the essentials of a far-reaching proposal, which, if accepted, would dramatically alter the American auto industry. He wanted GM and Toyota, archrivals and, respectively, the number one manufacturer and number one exporter in the world car market, to build passenger cars in the United States together. The venture would be without precedent and seemed to fly in the face of GM's strategy to "beat" the Japanese. But did it? Smith knew otherwise. To beat 'em, the automaker figured, GM would first have to join 'em.

Smith's presentation touched on the three key issues that preoccupied the Japanese executive. One was Toyota's preference for building cars in the United States without having to go it alone. Another was its goal of selling more cars in the American market without having to cut back exports from Japan. Finally, Toyota wanted to manage any joint operation itself. In each case, GM was eager to cooperate. Smith's words left Toyoda grinning.

As he concluded, Smith was blunt about his ambitions for the joint venture. It would allow General Motors to convert a former assembly plant to a modern facility operating under Japanese manufacturing systems. In turn, Smith said, it would give GM a firsthand look at the latest in Japanese automaking technology. The strategy stemmed from what Smith considered the insularity of the U.S. industry. "We thought we could lead and everybody would follow us," Smith later explained, recalling the rationale for joining forces with the Japanese. "So that's when I said, 'Let's go out and find out what everybody else knows.'" The proposed venture, however, was not merely an attempt to buy Japanese technology. It was to become the cornerstone of a new strategy in small cars aimed at pulling buyers not only out of "import" showrooms, including Toyota's, but away from domestic small cars built by Ford and Chrysler as well. What Smith *didn't* tell Toyota at their meeting was that he considered the joint venture a stopgap solution to GM's problems. The temporary action would give Smith and General Motors more time to create a strategic plan to compete directly with the Japanese.

As the dinner broke up around ten o'clock, Eiji Toyoda

agreed to appoint several senior executives in the Toyota organization to study the proposal and recommend whether to enter into full-fledged negotiations with GM. Within weeks it was clear that Toyoda had taken more than a passing interest in the proposal. Reports of the top-secret dinner and GM's joint-venture proposal quickly surfaced in the Japanese press. The leaks had come from inside Toyota headquarters, a typical ploy to smoke out any opposition from the Japanese government or the banks that owned most of Toyota's stock. The small office GM maintained in Tokyo kept a constant vigil on Japanese press reports about the pending deal. So did representatives of the other U.S. automakers. Despite denials by Toyota and GM that any deal was near conclusion, the negotiations that appeared to pick up where Ford's had left off became an open secret, and a subject of acrimony, in Detroit. As Smith admitted later, "A lot of people said we were consorting with the enemy."

The detailed proposal took Eiji Toyoda by surprise, even though his company had been talking about consorting with Ford, on a much smaller scale. Several months earlier the Japanese executive had, in fact, disbanded talks with GM's principal rival about a joint venture to build vans in the United States. The American company wanted to build minivans small enough not to compete with Ford's homegrown passenger cars. Toyota was interested in a new base of manufacturing in the United States but wanted to build midsize vans, for which there would be a larger market. Negotiations ground to a halt, and after pulling out the Japanese automaker began to make plans for manufacturing in America on its own. It also turned to General Motors.

Just before Christmas 1981, a Toyota executive had called on Roger Smith to broach the possibility of future cooperation between the two companies. Intrigued at the Japanese company's overture, GM's chairman sent Jack Smith, GM's director of worldwide product planning — and no relation to the chairman — to Tokyo for further discussions. In Japan the GM envoy found Toyota's ardor to have cooled. Instead of expressing interest in building vehicles jointly, as they had with Ford,

Toyota executives suggested that any joint venture be limited to manufacturing auto parts. Jack Smith left Toyota's headquarters disappointed that GM and Toyota weren't even on the same wavelength.

But back in Detroit, Roger Smith was undaunted by the inconclusive discussions and ordered a thorough review of all potential ventures between the American and Japanese companies, from auto parts up to and including a fifty-fifty automobile manufacturing operation. Unlike Ford, GM was willing to explore a joint venture to produce vehicles that would compete with models coming off its U.S. assembly lines. But to Roger Smith the alternative of *no* deal was unacceptable: GM couldn't expect to build small cars as cheaply as the Japanese unless the automaker could dramatically alter its manufacturing operation. By joining forces with Toyota to produce small cars for the balance of the 1980s, Smith hoped to buy the time he needed to redesign General Motors itself. And time was what Smith knew GM needed in order to compete effectively against Toyota and other Japanese automakers in the 1990s and beyond. Ford, he felt, had taken a short-term view in its talks with Toyota. GM had to ally itself with Toyota in the short run if it hoped to compete with that company in the long run.

Only after meeting regularly over a six-week period with Jack Smith and the planning staff to formulate several alternative proposals had the chairman of General Motors invited Eiji Toyoda to the dinner at the Links Club. When the time came to see the Japanese automaker, Roger Smith wanted the meeting to take place on home ground.

Roger Smith had once considered Toyota and other Japanese automakers the "enemy." When he took over as General Motors' tenth chairman in January 1981, the world's number one car manufacturer had lost more than $750 million in the preceding twelve months, its first annual loss in sixty years. To Smith and others in Detroit, the Japanese were the culprits. Capitalizing on a second upward spiral in world oil prices, they had exported small, fuel-efficient cars to the United States. In 1980, for the first time ever, Japan had also overtaken the United States in total car production. If Japan's automakers weren't the overt enemy, they were certainly taking their toll on Detroit. More than one in every four cars sold in the United States were now made in Japan, and several Japanese exporters, among them Mitsubishi, Subaru, Mazda, and Isuzu, were just beginning to expand their marketing efforts in the United States.

By 1981 high gasoline prices were cutting into sales of GM's large-car models, which traditionally led the industry and accounted for most of the company's profit. GM had been slow off the mark in automating its assembly lines. As a result, GM was building and selling its small cars at a hefty premium over the going rate for Japanese models, and at substantially lower fuel-economy levels. Indeed, earlier attempts to respond to the "Japanese challenge" had met with little success. GM's well-publicized X-cars were already suffering from a series of recalls that eventually would lead to a government suit against the company. And GM's best-selling small car, the Chevette, was five years old, a rear-wheel-drive model at a time when Americans were increasingly shopping for front-wheel-drive subcompacts.

Five months after moving into the chairman's walnut-paneled, fourteenth-floor suite atop the company's headquarters building in Detroit, Smith unveiled the J-car, the product of a $5 billion crash program undertaken in the mid seventies to build a series of models that would compete one on one with Honda's hot-selling Accord and similar imports. Yet, to save money, GM's designers had packed the J-car with components taken off the shelf from other models, and automotive writers blasted the new models as underpowered, overoptioned, and overpriced. Consumers apparently agreed. GM sold fewer than a quarter of the one million J-cars it had hoped to move out of showrooms in their first year on the market. The costly project also took its toll on GM's balance sheet. In just two years the company's long-term debt had quadrupled, while its working capital plunged to less than one-fifth the level of 1979. The J-car program had been an embarrassing setback, and a clear reminder that General Motors could no longer throw money at its problems.

Fairly or not, Roger Smith took the heat for GM's costly disaster. Virtually all the decisions on the J-car had been taken in the previous decade, first when Smith was in charge of GM's nonautomotive businesses, including the Frigidaire household appliance division, Terex construction equipment, and several defense-related businesses, and later when he was GM's top financial officer. Indeed, Smith had never held any direct operating role at a GM car division. The closest he came to making cars was during the summer of 1946, when he had installed brackets and roof insulation on a Chrysler assembly line to earn money for college.

In many ways Roger Smith, born July 12, 1925, was an unlikely captain for one of America's largest industries. At five feet nine inches, with a reddish complexion and high-pitched voice, he was anything but charismatic and had few of the outward qualities typically associated with leadership. Unprepossessing to an extreme, he was a poor public speaker who typically read from the same typed three-by-five-inch cards that he carried to keep track of his daily schedule. He eschewed the aides — he called them bagmen — and fancy trappings to which previous GM chairmen had become accustomed. And despite his almost legendary reputation as a cipher of accounting tables and financial statements, Smith rarely read books, even management tomes. His expressions, in public as well as private, were folksy and unassuming. Holy Toledo was his favorite.

Instinctively, Smith was a "company man," but he rarely took his work home. Unlike most of his fellow executives in the auto industry, Smith made best friends from outside big business, friends, neighbors, and former schoolmates who shared his passion for sport fishing, preferably Atlantic salmon, and hunting, stalking quail, deer, and wild turkey in northern Michigan. The executive who was chided by colleagues for dressing conservatively (button, rather than gold, cuffs) indulged in one extravagant hobby, vintage General Motors automobiles — a 1923 Buick touring car, a 1936 Cadillac convertible sedan, and his favorite, a mint-condition, blue-and-white 1959 Corvette.

Smith had grown up around the auto industry. His father, a banker and entrepreneur, was wiped out during the Depression. He later helped start and then sell a succession of businesses in and around Detroit. Roger worked part time in one of his fa-

ther's industrial tubing mills until he was fired when his father
worried that he wasn't paying enough attention to school. After
a stint in the U.S. Navy (1944–1946), including a tour of duty
in the South Pacific aboard the U.S.S. *Montpelier*, Smith
worked his summer at Chrysler before enrolling again at the
University of Michigan. He earned his M.B.A. from the university in 1949 and intended to move to California and the aviation
industry. On his father's advice, Smith agreed to apply for jobs
with the two biggest automakers. He was rejected by Ford, but
General Motors was more hospitable. Smith landed a job as an
accounting clerk for the company's overseas operations. Then,
for most of the sixties, he worked for GM in New York as an ac-
countant, gaining a reputation for hard work and his command
of details. He was also one of a small team of executives charged
with helping the company's legendary chairman, Alfred P.
Sloan, with his memoirs of the early days at General Motors.
The assignment gave Smith a firsthand look at the inner workings of GM's upper echelons, a glimpse of the organizational
structure designed by Sloan that had become a model for much
of corporate America. On March 2, 1970, when GM announced
a series of personnel changes, Smith's promotion to treasurer
went virtually unnoticed. A year later he became a vice president in charge of GM's financial staff. Then, in December 1971,
Smith was given his first direct operating role, in charge of
GM's nonautomotive subsidiaries. It was in that role that he
began developing the logistical and planning tools that were
previously anathema inside General Motors.

Roger Smith knew that most of his colleagues disliked the concept of strategic planning. So he did it without any fanfare,
quietly hiring half a dozen peo-
ple and installing them in a
small office in the basement of
one of the buildings housing
GM's Technical Center north
of Detroit. The corporate di-
rections group, as it was called, was headed by Michael Naylor,
a British engineer who had joined GM from Rolls-Royce in

*He who lacks foresight and un-
derestimates his enemy will surely
be captured by him.*
—Sun Tzu

1967. The rationale for the new team was clear: away from GM's core business, car manufacturing, Smith's brain trust team was free to develop a method for mapping out proposals for each of the nonautomotive sector's profit centers.

The principle was simple but surprisingly revolutionary inside GM. Each strategic business unit would have its own objective and profit responsibility. Senior management could therefore assess the strengths and weaknesses of the overall organization by tracking rates of return and other barometers for each unit, investing in those sectors that promised higher returns. Ultimately the planning method could be adapted to GM's car divisions as well, where Smith was convinced they were most needed. In the auto industry, after all, forward planning was like shooting a slow arrow at a moving target. It usually took four or five years to bring a new model from drawing board to the dealer's showroom, another five or six years in production, and the same models could be expected to stay on the road for ten years after that. If ever there was an industry that needed a crystal ball, it was autos, especially if Detroit was to mount a serious challenge to Japan's growing threat in the American market.

The tools Roger Smith developed with Naylor and his team for the nonautomotive sector weren't abstract models, either. Three years after setting up the group, Smith moved on to become an executive vice president in charge of GM's financial operations. But he took with him a dramatic proposal that came out of his planning exercises. Two of the company's business units, he told the board of directors, would continue to face trouble and should be sold because they would earn lower rates of return than GM's other units well into the future. Smith also pointed out that the sale of both units, Frigidaire refrigerators and Terex earth-moving equipment, would allow GM to concentrate its energies in the areas it knew best. Initially the company's directors were skeptical of the plan, but within five years agreed to sell both divisions.

Smith's reputation as a strategic planner and cost-conscious manager eventually won him the chairmanship of GM. But when Smith took over, strategic planning was the least of his worries. The top priority was to cut $3 billion in annual budget expenditures on salaries, benefits, and plant closures in order to get GM back into the black. The easiest route was a drastic downsizing of GM's worldwide labor force: one in every six employees lost jobs over the next twelve months, a loss of 115,000 jobs in all. The layoffs earned Smith the enmity of the unions from the outset, and the business media wasted no time characterizing GM's new boss as a less-than-visionary accountant. It was a reputation that would take Smith not months, but years, to live down.

GM's J-car made matters even worse. The company had gambled heavily on the luxury compact before flagging sales forced widespread layoffs that Smith had not even accounted for when the cost-reduction campaign began. But the failure of the J-car to make any real dent in Japanese imports did reinforce something that Smith already believed, that GM couldn't cure problems simply by spending money. To compete with the Japanese, he believed, American automakers would have to reduce the labor costs that were averaging $8.00 an hour more than what Toyota, Nissan, and Honda were paying in Japan. On a standard compact model, the wage discrepancy amounted to at least $500 per car in favor of Japanese automakers. To reduce that lead, GM's only two alternatives were to wring concessions from the United Auto Workers (UAW) in the form of lower wages and benefits and/or invest in automated assembly lines that would gradually reduce the labor man-hours required to produce each car.

In May 1981, the same month that GM launched its J-car, Japanese automakers, reluctantly accepting a deal worked out between Washington and Tokyo, began limiting their exports to the American market until at least 1984. They agreed to sell the same number of cars each year, with a promise to continue the limits one more year if the two countries agreed it was necessary to allow U.S. automakers more time to catch up with the Japanese export juggernaut. It quickly became apparent, however, that despite the restraints, GM's existing strategy to combat imports wasn't enough. Roger Smith knew that he had three, or at most four, years to put a new strategy in place. After that, Japan's car companies would go back on the export offensive in the U.S. market, and automakers like GM would no longer have time to catch up.

Smith also faced a tough decision about what to do with another new model targeted at Japanese competition, the S-car. On the drawing boards for several years, it was due out in 1984. A front-wheel-drive model, it was supposed to become GM's standard small car when the Chevette went out of production. Smith knew how important it was for GM to offer a full range of small cars to lure first-time buyers who would later trade up to larger vehicles. But when Smith ordered a reappraisal of what it would cost to build the S-car, it quickly became apparent that GM would have a tough time ever breaking even on selling the car against cheaper imports. A Japanese manufacturer, GM concluded after extensive research, would be able to make the S-car for $2000 less.

The appropriate response to Japan's edge was to kill the project, even though GM had spent millions of dollars on it. The death of the S-car left the auto company with a gaping hole in its line of small cars and a major incentive to develop what would eventually come to be called an Asian strategy. Put simply, Smith decided to break

> *When you know the enemy's plans, it will be easy to gain victory by means of an appropriate response.*
>
> —Miyamoto Musashi

with convention and procure small cars where he could get them cheapest, in Japan.

In August of the same year, even as he was being lambasted for massive layoffs, Smith announced that GM was buying 5 percent of a Japanese manufacturer, Suzuki. In exchange, Suzuki would gear up to sell GM 80,000 subcompacts a year after the export controls were lifted in 1984 or 1985. After that, GM would sell the subcompacts, later dubbed the Sprint, through Chevrolet dealerships. At the same time, GM began negotiating with another Japanese automaker, Isuzu, in which it already owned a 34 percent stake. Nine months later, in May 1982, Isuzu agreed to supply GM with as many as 200,000 cars a year.

And not long afterward, GM signed a similar deal with an even lower-cost exporter, South Korea's Daewoo Motors.

The deals themselves were not revolutionary. Chrysler had been importing the Mitsubishi-built Colt and selling it through Dodge dealers since 1970. GM had briefly imported an Isuzu model, selling it as the Opel, the name of its German subsidiary. But in each prior case the imported models were specialty extensions of each automaker's product line. Now, with the Suzuki and Isuzu deals, GM was planning to use Japanese-made cars as its principal entries in one whole segment of the market, subcompacts.

The Suzuki deal was predictably suspect within the industry. Other automakers perceived a major shift in the way GM was going to "source" its small cars. The UAW interpreted the deal as handing jobs to the Japanese at the same time that Smith was putting Americans out of work. Even with that, the company reported only a $333 million profit for 1981, a far cry from the billions it was used to making for its shareholders each year. The UAW knew Smith would be under heavy pressure to go beyond layoffs in order to cut costs, targeting paychecks, not just jobs.

For his part, Smith knew he would have few opportunities to reduce the labor costs that were essentially fixed by union contract. Going into 1982, a golden opportunity was at hand. The UAW contract would expire in September, and the resulting provisions would to a large extent determine whether GM was going to continue to face much higher labor costs than the Japanese or bring them more into line, allowing GM to compete head-on with imports in the future. At least temporarily, Smith would have to focus his attack on an enemy closer to home — labor costs — and he had to do it quickly. It was clear on both sides that Smith held most of the cards. Smith knew it, too.

Rather than wait for the normal negotiating sessions to roll around, Smith took the lead. In January he invited UAW president Douglas Fraser to early talks aimed at settling on a new contract even before the old one was due to expire in September. Smith believed the UAW's members would be willing to accept a reduction in wages and benefits rather than risk pushing GM into more plant closures and the consequent lay-offs. By raising the prospect of an early deal, Smith knew that the UAW would perceive it as a way to keep separate its bar-gaining rounds with GM and Ford, whose labor contracts would also be up in Sep-

Take advantage of the enemy's unpreparedness; travel by unex-pected routes and strike where he has taken no precautions.
                                    —Sun Tzu

tember. If the union had to deal with both at the same time, the pressure to settle would be greater.

Thus, Fraser agreed to the talks but promptly refused to go along with Smith's proposal that the union accept a pay cut. Then, with the prospect of months of negotiations prior to the September contract renewal, Smith decided to play hardball. On the first day of the talks, the company announced that any savings from the requested pay cuts would be used to reduce sticker prices on GM cars. Smith also threatened to step up the pace of automation on GM assembly lines drastically if the union refused to agree to the cuts, which raised a red flag to union officials and workers who had already felt the loss of jobs from the introduction of robots and computers. Smith was going for broke. Even if the negotiations failed now, he reckoned, GM's demands would force the next in line for talks with the UAW, Ford, to make similarly demanding overtures. Either way, the UAW would have to make major concessions, even if the union didn't go all the way.

But the tactic backfired in the marketplace. By going public with his demands, Smith raised the possibility of cuts in sticker prices if the UAW agreed to accept a cut in pay. As a result, many buyers decided to wait before buying, and auto sales fell by a whopping 38 percent during the first ten days after the an-nouncement. The move also pushed the UAW into a corner, and it came as no surprise when the union broke off talks, accusing Smith of unfair practices.

The UAW opted to hammer out a deal with Ford first, but as Smith had expected, Ford used the hard-line GM position to push demands that were only slightly less onerous. In the end,

Ford autoworkers agreed to a pay freeze and fewer days off, so-called givebacks, and Roger Smith agreed to the same terms for GM's new thirty-month contract. Although it fell short of the outright pay cuts Smith had been seeking, the contract represented an important turning point for the industry, putting a lid on the escalating labor costs that had kept Detroit at a competitive disadvantage vis-à-vis Japanese automakers. It was unlikely that Ford could have pushed through a pay freeze if GM had not previously staked out an even stronger bargaining position with the UAW.

Negotiating the new GM contract did not put an end to the rancor between Smith and the union, however. For months Smith had been talking with GM's board of directors about shaking up the company's management style, making it more aggressive by basing the earnings of its top managers on the company's performance. Under the new scheme, officers would get smaller annual salary increases, but as part of the plan the GM board would lower the amount of profits GM had to make before some six thousand executives could start receiving bonuses. Board discussion of the new bonus guidelines had begun in 1981, but the proxy statement containing the provisions was sent to GM shareholders the following April, the date stipulated by Securities and Exchange Commission guidelines.

Unfortunately for Smith, the timing couldn't have been worse. The proxy statement was made public on April 16, 1982, the same day the UAW had picked to sign the new labor contract. A furor ensued, because Smith appeared to be squeezing GM's blue-collar workers while handing out bonuses to white-collar managers. In fact, GM had not earned enough money the previous year to unlock bonuses under either the old or the revised plan. Still, the UAW's Fraser was furious; he demanded a meeting with Smith and other top GM executives. After eleven hours of bitter argument, Fraser signed the new contract, but only after Smith agreed to delay putting the new bonus plan for GM executives into effect until the end of the labor pact.

Smith's apparent insensitivity in dealing with the UAW provoked a barrage of bad press, most of it aimed squarely at Smith himself. The *Detroit Free Press* nominated the bonus plan as the "Dumbest Move of the Year" in the auto industry. The influential *Automotive News* said it showed that Smith and other executives lived and worked "far, far away from the real world." *Newsweek* magazine asked simply, "Has GM, under chairman Roger Smith, lost its management touch?" But talking to one of the magazine's reporters, Smith was unrepentant. "If you say I'm tough, I'd say, yeah. And I'll tell you, *times* are tough." Sixteen months into his tenure, Roger Smith had made his somewhat questionable mark on GM. The layoffs were draconian, and the pay freeze and givebacks didn't appear to be temporary.

Still, GM's otherwise mild-mannered chairman wasn't about to let the criticism derail his strategy for dealing with Japanese imports. His Japan strategy had begun to take shape at the secret dinner with Toyota's chairman, and in the wake of an agreement with the UAW little more than three months old, Smith ordered his own negotiators to put the heat on Toyota to hammer out the details of a joint manufacturing venture in the United States. Despite its deals to import small cars from Suzuki and Isuzu, GM was getting only a fraction of the models it needed to fill out its small-car line at Chevy dealers, and Smith figured that GM needed a total of one million compacts and subcompacts a year. Because of the export restraints, GM could not procure the extra cars from Japan, especially since Japanese carmakers were keen to sell all the cars they were allowed to sell through their own U.S. dealerships. Short of resurrecting the S-car, joint manufacturing was the only feasible way to plug the gap in GM's line of small cars. GM would have to make up the shortfall in small cars with a Japanese model built in America. If the deal with Toyota fell through, Smith had already drawn up a contingency plan to assemble an Isuzu model in the United States with American parts. Isuzu couldn't offer GM the advanced manufacturing know-how at which Toyota excelled, but at least Isuzu gave GM an option in its search for small cars. In the talks between Toyota and GM, Smith made sure that the Japanese executives knew he had another suitor in the wings.

The negotiations dragged on for months, but by the end of 1982 the venture began to take final shape. GM would be an equal joint partner and sell the 200,000 cars initially built at a disused GM plant in Fremont, California, as a new addition to Chevrolet's small-car line. As production expanded, Toyota would eventually be allowed to sell some of the cars rolling off the Fremont assembly line under its own name through Toyota dealers. It would have cost GM at least $1 billion to develop a new car on its own. By going the joint-venture route and letting Toyota take the lead, GM would have to put up only a relatively modest $100 million, including the plant. Toyota also got a good deal: the U.S. car would be based on a model Toyota was already selling in Japan, so development and design costs were minimal. The Fremont facility meant that Toyota would not have to spend the $400 million or so Nissan and Honda were spending to build their own plants in the United States. At the same time, Toyota would be getting its feet wet in dealing with U.S. parts suppliers and American autoworkers, a necessary prelude to any future plans to build cars on its own in the American market.

On February 14, 1983, almost one year after Roger Smith and Eiji Toyoda met, they announced simultaneously in Detroit and Tokyo that their two companies had agreed in principle to build cars jointly in the American market. Three days later, they both flew to Fremont to forge what many in the U.S. auto industry were calling an unholy alliance between an American automaker and its principal foreign competitor.

Almost immediately, the alliance drew heavy fire. Chrysler chairman Lee Iacocca bitterly accused GM and Toyota of "collusion" that would result in the loss of American jobs. The attack stung Smith. After all, it was Chrysler that had pioneered the sale of Japanese small cars in the American market under an American logo. Several years earlier Chrysler had begun importing cars built by Mitsubishi Motors, selling them as Dodge and Plymouth models through Chrysler dealerships.

The venture also drew barbs from the UAW leadership, even though GM and Toyota moved quickly to soothe fears that they were trying to make the new facility a nonunion shop. Toyota agreed to let the UAW organize workers at the Fremont plant, most of whom would be rehired from the ranks of those laid off when the plant was closed. Toyota also offered job security to employees as long as the joint venture was in operation. In return, the union promised a separate contract with fewer work rules and job categories than those stipulated in its new contract with GM. The concessions would give Toyota more flexibility in the way it used workers on the assembly line and provide GM with a test site for work rules that it hoped to introduce eventually at its other plants. The UAW also agreed to a pay scale that worked out to a 15 percent lower labor cost than the one in effect at other GM plants.

The joint venture was incorporated as NUMMI — New United Motor Manufacturing Inc. In April 1984, Toyota and General Motors got final approval from the Federal Trade Commission to proceed, on the condition that the joint venture not last longer than twelve years. In any given year, furthermore, GM agreed not to sell more than 250,000 cars from the plant, an apparent effort to guarantee that two of the world's three largest automakers (the other was Ford) not engage in the collusion that Lee Iacocca had evoked. Eight months later Chevrolet Novas were rolling off the Fremont assembly line on schedule and at a substantially lower cost per car than for comparable domestic models produced by Ford or Chrysler.

The Toyota venture meant that Chevrolet dealerships would have a well-rounded line of small cars in much less time than it would have taken GM to go it alone: the mini Sprint from Suzuki, the somewhat larger Spectrum imported from Isuzu, and the higher-end Nova built with Toyota in Fremont. Although GM didn't stand to make as much profit on the Japanese models as it did on its larger cars, it wouldn't lose money the way Ford did in building its main subcompact, the Escort, or the way it would have done if Smith hadn't decided to kill the S-car.

As Roger Smith saw it, the joint venture had one other overriding benefit for GM. It would give GM managers assigned to three-year stints at the Fremont plant a chance to survey the enemy up close, observing firsthand the technology and management style that had contributed to Toyota's overwhelming success in the export market. The new work rules forged in the separate contract with the UAW, Smith believed, would prove to be the thin end of the wedge, setting a precedent for all of GM's factories and providing the automaker with a test site for radically different production procedures that were to become the cornerstone of a small-car venture for the 1990s that had already begun taking shape inside GM's highest councils.

Roger Smith was not interested only in changing the way General Motors worked on the factory floor. Management had to change, too, if the company was going to become as flexible and open to change as Smith wanted his autoworkers to be. Six weeks after announcing the agreement with Toyota, Smith opened GM's annual management conference at the Greenbrier Hotel in White Sulphur Springs, West Virginia. For the nine hundred executives gathered at the stately conference center, Smith had a message. He wanted a cross section of managers to rewrite GM's corporate mission. Not just talk about it, he said, but put something down on paper, a blueprint that could be used as a reference point for future decisions about GM's direction. Smith also gave them a sense of what he wanted to see in the "mission" statement, his "three Rs": risk, responsibility, reward. In handling the task of redrafting GM's mission, Smith made it clear to everyone in the Greenbrier's ballroom that he wanted to push decision making and the responsibility for those decisions further down the organization, to get more people involved in the process.

The deliberations, Smith believed, represented a rite of passage for GM. The company that its pioneering chairman Alfred Sloan smugly said was in the business of making money, not cars, all but repudiated the notion. The new mission explicitly put quality before profit. The soul-searching and argument that went into the new statement didn't disappear when Smith left the convention site. Almost immediately, middle-level managers began suggesting new products, new ways of manufacturing. Several months after the meeting, the head of GM's engineering department sent Smith a bold plan to develop a "factory of the future" at a steering-gear plant in Saginaw, Michigan. The plant, as conceived by the engineers, would use the latest computer technology and become a prototype for all of GM's future plants. Smith gave the plan immediate, unqualified support. It represented, after all, what his new management plan was all about. He wanted the company to rethink the way it did business with an eye to remaining the top auto manufacturer well into the future. To Smith, that was the only way to meet the Japanese challenge.

To prove he meant business, Smith gave the green light to another project in the wake of the Greenbrier meeting. Called Project Saturn, it was first conceived as simply a method to develop a "car of the future." It was named for the late 1950s U.S. space project aimed at catching up with the Soviet Union's early lead in the space race with Sputnik. GM's Saturn project was also aimed at catching up — with the Japanese. Smith knew that GM couldn't count on selling Japanese models forever to fill out its line of small cars. In the short run, American labor costs, and the way GM ran its factories, made it virtually impossible to close the gap between Japanese and U.S. automakers in its cost of building a typical small car. General Motors had already adopted some of the more obvious Japanese production techniques, including "quality circles," which broke workers into teams that would regularly discuss ways to improve the manufacturing process and come up with suggestions for management; and the *kanban* system of inventory controls, which reduced the time and cost of securing components in the manufacturing process by coordinating the delivery of parts from suppliers "just in time" (the literal translation of *kanban*) for their use on the assembly line. But Smith was convinced that GM couldn't catch up in piecemeal fashion. The world's largest automaker needed a giant leap forward, a technological leap ahead of the Japanese, to "repossess" the American market.

The idea for Saturn came from GM's engineering department. Traditionally, new models were designed, then handed to the manufacturing operation for production. With Saturn, GM engineers hoped to marry design and manufacturing, creating new models that would be cheaper to make. The method used for casting the engine block, for instance, could cut out 40 percent of the machining needed to finish the blocks. And by designing models with fewer parts, GM's manufacturing operation would cut the cost of materials and handling. The car that GM's engineers envisaged would have an aluminum engine and get sixty miles per gallon, and on-board computers would regulate everything from engine performance to suspension, all at a price tag comparable to $6000 in the mid 1980s.

Smith seized on the engineers' plan for Saturn but didn't stop there. It became the centerpiece of a much more ambitious experiment in manufacturing procedures, corporate organization, and labor relations. Apart from the new approach to design engineering, Smith wanted Saturn to become the prototype for a totally new kind of automobile company. "The car isn't important," he said. "The important thing about Saturn is to show we can do it with Buick, Olds, Pontiac, Chevrolet, and Cadillac later on." Smith was hoping that Saturn would become the tail that wagged the GM dog, pioneering new management, manufacturing, design, and marketing techniques that would create a model for the entire corporation. In the process, he hoped to turn GM into a more competitive, technology-intensive automaker in the 1990s, giving it an edge over Japanese automakers, including its new partner, Toyota.

To do that, Smith wanted to create an entirely new company to design and manufacture the Saturn, selling it through a completely new network of dealerships. Smith hated the torrent of paper that GM's management system involved, so the Saturn — the first new brand name since GM introduced Chevrolet in 1918 — would be made by a company run on computers, not red tape. The goal was that a customer could order a Saturn by entering what he or she wanted into a computer at a Saturn dealer. The order would be logged simultaneously at the plant and with suppliers, who would then arrange to supply the necessary parts just in time for assembly. The paperless system meant that customers would be able to take delivery, even of customized models, within days or weeks instead of months, saving GM and its suppliers the cost of maintaining high inventories. Customers would get the cars and options they wanted, not just what was available on the dealer's lot. The objective, as Smith saw it, was to bring GM closer to its customers, a radical departure in an industry that frequently considered dealers to be its customers.

Even before the Saturn project was announced in November 1983, Smith asked his planning staff to assess the alternative of selling the Saturn through Sears, Roebuck, instead of the existing dealer network, in order to lower the typical 33 percent markup on sticker prices. But Smith knew such a move would probably spark a rebellion among current General Motors dealers. He also considered selling the model through Chevrolet dealerships alongside other GM small cars, but ruled that out too. He opted instead for a new network of Saturn showrooms culled from GM and independent dealers with the strongest records of customer service. They would also have to be well financed and willing to invest in the new computerized technology that Smith was counting on to link every dealer lot with GM headquarters and the assembly line.

As Smith saw it, the Saturn plant would also provide a model for labor relations in the auto industry. There would be few job titles or work rules. Saturn autoworkers would perform an even wider array of tasks than those who were working for GM's alliance with Toyota. Union members would be paid a salary, not an hourly wage, and would earn less in base pay than other auto workers. But they would also earn bonuses based on productivity. As a result, productive workers could earn more than their counterparts at old-line auto companies, including GM itself.

The absence of job categories would also allow GM to do away with the traditional assembly line in favor of "modular" manufacturing. Cars would move from workstation to workstation, where teams of workers would perform a group of tasks interchangeably. Whole sections of the Saturn, such as doors and dashboards, would be assembled separately and then added to the car as a whole unit. Each of the teams of workers would be able to perform a variety of tasks, and the car wouldn't move on until the team was sure everything was done right, eliminating the need for separate quality inspectors and repair staffs. Best of all, modular assembly would require less space, fewer workers, and many more robots, helping to cut by more than 50 percent the cost of labor going into the final assembly of each Saturn and bringing those costs in line with the lowest among Japanese automakers.

Roger Smith set no target year for the model's introduction

when he announced the Saturn project in November 1983, but he vowed to drive the first one out of the factory before retiring in 1990. By refusing to set a specific date, he explained, GM was handing its Saturn developers a clean sheet of paper, allowing them to start from scratch rather than forcing them to use the technology and parts already going into GM cars. Success, Smith admitted, would not come cheaply: an estimated $5 billion would be spent before the first model rolled out of the plant. But when it did, he pledged, Saturn would be the harbinger of a revolution in the way the rest of GM's divisions designed, built, and sold their cars.

The rest of the industry downplayed the importance of the Saturn project. Rival auto executives dismissed it as an exercise in public relations. Others saw in Saturn an attempt to build a car in the 1990s to compete with Japanese models already coming off assembly lines in 1983. But Smith was willing to suffer the brickbats; the payoff of the Saturn project was still years away.

Roger Smith made it clear that he wasn't going to wait for Saturn to reshape General Motors. Two months after unveiling the Saturn project, he announced a massive reorganization of the entire corporation. Designed to help make the company more entrepreneurial and adaptive to market conditions, it was the culmination of a long series of corporate reviews dating back to Smith's first foray into corporate strategy at GM's nonautomotive division. More recently, however, the catalyst for the wide-ranging change was the 1982 UAW contract and the uproar surrounding GM's white-collar bonus proposal. The reviews had convinced Smith that the company was no longer the model of a modern major corporation it had been during the days of Alfred Sloan. It had become increasingly centralized, with almost every decision made at the top, on the fourteenth floor of GM's headquarters. Decisions then filtered down to line managers through vast levels of bureaucracy. At times, Smith worried, GM seemed to produce more meetings and memos than cars. In the fall of 1982, he had hired the consulting firm McKinsey & Co. to review the GM structure that stood virtually unchanged since the

1950s. Interviewing five hundred executives up and down GM's corporate ladder, McKinsey worked for the next eighteen months with a team of GM planners to come up with a proposal for reshaping the organization.

GM's big problem, Smith concluded from the McKinsey report, was that it had become averse to risk, too bureaucratic, and centralized. McKinsey's suggestion was to reorganize the core business of the company by splitting it into two pieces. Smith agreed and consolidated the five car divisions and GM's Canadian subsidiary into two groups, one for small cars, the other for large. The two divisions responsible for manufacturing, Fisher Body and GM Assembly, were merged into each of the new groups. As a result, the small-car group would consolidate, under one roof, all operations from design through manufacturing for Chevrolet, Pontiac, and Canada. Similarly, all Buick, Oldsmobile, and Cadillac operations would be handled by the big-car group. By the separation Smith hoped to reduce white-collar staff and duplicate operations, as well as give senior management in each group wide-ranging control over everything from parts procurement to marketing strategies, pushing the authority closer to the factory floor and dealer showrooms.

In making McKinsey & Co.'s recommendations his own, Smith was also trying to respond to criticism that GM cars were starting to look too much alike. Centralized design and engineering helped reduce costs by allowing various car divisions to assemble many of the same parts, but GM paid the price in Chevrolet and Buick models, for instance, that looked virtually identical except for the trim. With two separate groups, each would operate independently and, presumably, offer dealers and buyers a wider array of new models, with little if any duplication between the two groups.

But inside GM's own managerial ranks, Smith's reorganization quickly ran into trouble. For thousands of executives and engineers, the changes had a palpable, immediate, and chaotic effect — a game of musical chairs, desks, offices, even buildings. Many executives also feared that the changes would take away their power, or their jobs. One manufacturing manager, Smith learned, responded to the reorganization by calling in his foremen and telling them they could run the factory on their own, without his help, from then on. An alarmed foreman wrote Smith about the stonewalling, prompting Smith to call the manager on the carpet and begin a series of meetings with white-collar personnel throughout the company to explain that the reorganization was supposed to get everyone working closer together, not create new barriers. "The easy thing is moving the boxes around on the organization chart," Smith told managers in one pep talk. "The hard part is changing the system."

A new management style wasn't all that was needed to make the Saturn project and GM reorganization work. Smith knew that GM had to integrate the incredible flow of information from one part of the company to another, enhancing communications throughout the corporation. GM had already made great strides in computer-aided design and engineering, but at the time the reorganization was announced

Communications are the most important single element in strategy.

—Admiral Alfred Thayer Mahan

in January 1984, the automaker still operated some 360 computer systems that, for the most part, couldn't communicate with each other. Yet if GM was ever going to bring its costs in line with those of its Japanese rivals, computers and robots would have to become the company's backbone. So Smith went scouting to buy companies that had the knowledge GM lacked.

The search began against the backdrop of another controversy over management pay. In April 1984, GM's board of directors awarded senior managers huge bonuses based on a record profit of $3.7 billion in 1983. Smith alone got almost $1 million. The bonus awards, Smith announced, made up for low pay increases in previous years when the company wasn't doing as well, and he defended them as just rewards for management's role in turning around the company's fortunes. To the press and the unions, though, the rationale was suspect. After all, the limits on Japanese imports were probably as responsible as anything else for the turnaround at GM. And what GM had taken out of its workers' overalls in the 1982 contract, the UAW believed, Smith was now putting back — into his own pocket.

The fuss persisted, but Smith knew it would be even more damaging to the company if he tried to withhold the awards. As it was, GM was finally settling into the reorganization that had caused a lot of consternation and fear inside management. Now executives were being rewarded for their cooperation, and any sign of Smith's buckling to UAW pressure or public opinion would have hurt his credibility with the people who ran the company day to day. Smith was resolved to ride out the criticism. He knew that the spotlight would soon shift to a major acquisition that would reshape GM and confirm its push into high technology.

That push began over steaks at a New York restaurant in October 1983. Eight executives were on hand, four each from General Motors and the Wall Street investment firm Salomon Brothers, but the conversation was mainly between Roger Smith and Salomon's chairman, John Gutfreund. Smith laid down the challenge. Armed with plenty of cash, GM was looking for a major acquisition that would complement its automaking. Smith told Gutfreund that he was unwilling to mount a hostile bid. He also felt GM's best chances were to target a publicly traded firm held largely by institutional investors who would be impressed with GM's financial and technological clout to make a merger work. Two months later Gutfreund got back to Smith with a list of twelve potential targets. After analyzing the list, Smith told Gutfreund he was interested in one that didn't exactly fit his preconditions, Electronic Data Systems. EDS was an unlikely candidate, he worried, because most of the stock was held by its founder, Texas billionaire H. Ross Perot. But if Perot could be swayed, Smith felt that EDS would make a great fit for GM's future.

The ball was then in Gutfreund's court. In April 1984 the Salomon chairman phoned Perot and said he had a proposition that would interest him. Perot asked whether Gutfreund could make a meeting the next day; Gutfreund replied yes and made the trip to Houston himself, an indication to Perot of how important the deal was to GM. Perot didn't want to sell but realized that if GM was looking for a partner, EDS might be able to sell Smith on a major data-processing project. Perot agreed to meet with Smith the following week. "I was going to Detroit not to sell," Perot said later, "but to figure out how to get them to be a customer." On April 10, Perot and Smith spent the entire day together, with Smith showing the Texas businessman around GM's proving grounds, its huge headquarters, and the GM Technical Center. The sheer size of GM's data needs and the scope of what Smith was talking about for the future intrigued Perot. It was as if a civil engineer were offered the chance to build, as Perot put it, "the Golden Gate Bridge, the Panama Canal, the Empire State Building, the Eiffel Tower, and if he had any energy left over, a couple of pyramids." But Perot was still interested only in landing GM as a customer, not an owner.

It took several months to change Perot's mind. Smith's main argument was that to do the job effectively, GM would essentially have to turn over ten thousand of its employees to work closely with EDS, giving EDS complete access to every internal secret and operating procedure on which GM was based. "We couldn't do that," Smith told Perot at one meeting, "if you're just a supplier." To reassure its chairman, Perot offered to sell GM between 15 percent and 20 percent of his company. Smith declined, saying it had to be all or nothing if EDS was going to play such a pivotal role in the reshaping of General Motors to make cheaper, more advanced cars in the 1990s. Finally Perot relented. On June 28, 1984, he agreed to sell EDS to GM for $2.5 billion, much of it going to Perot himself. The price was thirty-three times the company's projected 1984 earnings, a steep premium by Wall Street standards, but Smith figured that a long-term supplier contract might have ended up costing even more.

Smith got personally involved in structuring the financing for the deal and managed to keep the cash outlay to a minimum. According to one Wall Street analyst, GM was able to chalk up $1 billion in tax savings in its accounting treatment of EDS's assets. General Motors created a new Class E stock that was so attractive to Perot and other EDS shareholders that Smith was able to pay $500 million of the purchase price by simply issuing corporate paper. As a result, GM's out-of-pocket expenses for

EDS came to barely $1 billion. The deal left Perot with a hefty chunk of GM stock and the one thing he wanted most of all — as a member of the board of directors, he would have a continuing say in the way GM was run.

The financial deal was designed to keep EDS employees on the payroll. Dividends on Class E stock would be based solely on the earnings of EDS, which were bound to grow sharply just from the new business at GM. The automaker was already spending billions of dollars a year on data processing, with much of the business now to be funneled to EDS. Smith also arranged to give original holders of Class E stock a bonus in the form of a promissory note that guaranteed a minimum 16 percent annual compounded rate of return on the stock for seven years after the acquisition. Since most of Perot's employees owned EDS stock, the Class E shares were so attractive that most were willing to take the new GM stock. As a result, EDS employees had a strong incentive to stay with EDS even after it became part of GM, bringing some of their more entrepreneurial spirit to the giant GM bureaucracy that Smith was trying to transform into a more dynamic, risk-taking enterprise.

One month after announcing the EDS deal, Roger Smith faced a major challenge to his relentless attack on labor costs. On July 23, 1984, negotiations began on a new contract between GM and the UAW to replace the one signed in 1982. The threat was real. The UAW's newly elected president, Owen Bieber, was expected to take an aggressive stand in his first major contract negotiation since taking over the union's helm. And GM autoworkers wanted a stake in the huge profits the company was reporting, hoping to win back some of the wages and benefits conceded in the 1982 contract that helped put GM back on its feet. "Restore and More in '84" had become the slogan adopted by some of the more adamant union workers. However, as the negotiations began, the union position seemed to have changed. Bieber and the UAW official in charge of dealing with GM, Don Ephlin, insisted that pay was not the issue. They ruled out any more givebacks, but would settle for modest increments in hourly wage rates. What they really wanted was job security.

GM had already cut 120,000 jobs from its domestic payroll from 1978 through 1983, and a secret company document obtained by a UAW local indicated that Smith wanted to cut as many as 120,000 more jobs over the next three years. So Bieber and Ephlin set out to protect the jobs of workers already on the payroll, even at the expense of no real boost in their take-home pay.

Specifically, the UAW wanted to limit overtime, increase the amount of time off, and restrict GM's ability to "outsource" — buy parts or cars from domestic or foreign suppliers, including the Japanese. Yet outsourcing had become a major element in Smith's strategy to tide General Motors over until the automaker could bring down its costs as a result of reorganization, the EDS acquisition, and the Saturn project. GM needed Japanese subcompacts to fill out its small-car line for at least four or five years, and the company was trying to shift more of its parts to outside manufacturers covered by union contracts that were less onerous than GM's. While Ford, for instance, put an average 85 of its own labor hours into each of its cars, GM had become so vertically integrated before Smith's reorganization that it was putting 135 labor-hours into comparable cars, tacking millions of dollars on to its labor costs.

Smith decided not to play a personal role in the contract negotiations as he had done in 1982. There was still resentment in union ranks over his heavy-handed threats and the bonus plan for management. But he gave his negotiators clear orders not to agree to any deal that would prevent GM from getting more of its parts or small cars from outside suppliers. Going into the talks, Smith was worried about the impact a UAW strike might have on GM's recovering finances, but he was also unwilling to settle on a new contract that would cripple GM's long-term strategy for competing with the Japanese. He was convinced that GM was in a strong position to avert a strike, for political reasons. The UAW was a staunch supporter of Democratic presidential candidate Walter Mondale, who stood to lose public support if his union constituency was perceived to be asking for more pay at a time when their jobs were being protected by import controls that were adding thousands of dollars to the cost of imported Japanese models.

Bieber and Ephlin held their own trump cards, including the largest strike fund ever (a whopping $558 million) and the knowledge that GM's inventories of large cars were running dangerously low. But the UAW negotiators were also aware of "the Mondale factor." So when they called a strike, it covered only thirteen plants and fewer than one in five of GM's 350,000 workers. The strike was also short — it took only six days to come to terms on a tentative contract.

Smith refused to call management the winner, but he clearly got what he was after: the right to automate, cut the labor force, and buy parts or cars on the outside as GM saw fit. In exchange, the union got a $1 billion fund that would guarantee pay over the next six years for workers whose jobs were lost as a result of technological advances or outsourcing. More important for Smith, the new contract allowed GM to assign any worker paid out of the fund to any job, without regard to seniority and work rules. The UAW had gone along with similar moves in organizing workers at GM's joint venture with Toyota, but this was the first crack in rigid job guidelines at other GM plants. The contract was a turning point, as Roger Smith saw it. Labor was increasingly going to become a part of the solution, not of the problem.

The second part of the solution, Smith believed, had to be automation. GM's freedom to scale back the work force would have been an empty victory unless the automaker could manufacture its cars with fewer workers. To do so, GM needed to put more robots on the assembly line, and Smith felt that robotics technology was crucial enough to the company that it should have its own in-house research and development program to keep one step ahead of other automakers.

General Motors had taken its first major step into robotics in June two years earlier, creating a joint venture with an affiliate of Japan's largest computer firm, Fujitsu. General Motors Fanuc (GMF) began by supplying the automaker with many of its assembly-line robots, later branching out to make robots for other industries. By 1984 it had become the largest U.S. manufacturer of industrial robots, with almost 50 percent of the market. But

Roger Smith didn't want to stop there. He aimed to make GM a leader in advanced robot technology as well, because, for all its strengths, GMF was mainly in the business of building robots using existing technology. If GM was to put more of the manufacturing process in the "hands" of robots, it would have to develop much more sophisticated machines that would "see" and "understand" what they were doing. It would also have to tie them all together and automate the entire process through computer systems. EDS would be instrumental in integrating GM's robot operations, but GM was still falling short in the field of basic research to create the next generation of assembly-line robots. So less than six weeks after announcing the EDS deal, GM stunned the industry again, with a clear-cut demonstration that the automaker wouldn't rely solely on big acquisitions to get the technology and know-how it needed.

As the search began for a takeover in the robotics field, GM quickly learned that there was no single company dominating the business that it could go out and buy, as it had EDS. The emerging industry called for a different strategy, with GM investing smaller amounts in a range of companies working on competing technologies. Consequently, in early August 1984, Smith announced that GM was buying minority stakes in four robot-vision companies. Like his Japan strategy, it was a considered attack on the "not-invented-here" syndrome that still characterized GM, except that this time GM didn't have to turn to the Japanese. American companies were on the cutting edge of vision research, creating robots that could artificially see what they were working on. GM spread its cash to support research among the four competing companies. In return, the automaker would have access to any breakthrough at one or another robot company. The decision to invest $50 million in several research projects allowed GM to hedge its bets and spread its risks. The stakes were high. For a company that was eager to automate as much as possible, "seeing" robots would hold the key to future automation. Robots could check the quality of welds, for in-

> *He who understands how to use both large and small forces will be victorious.*
>
> —Sun Tzu

stance, or determine by sight whether it was working on a sedan rather than a station wagon and perform an appropriate task. In other words, a breakthrough in vision technology would allow GM to assign a wider range of jobs to machines, and those machines would be able to do the jobs with greater precision and quality than most present workers could.

For the same reasons, Smith had also invested $3 million of GM money for a 13 percent stake in a small artificial-intelligence firm called Teknowledge. If vision technology could eventually let GM robots "see," Teknowledge was working on even more advanced skills that would let them "think." The company was focusing its research on "machine intelligence," a form of reasoning that, for instance, would allow a computer to work on a problem or make deductions based on a set of factors without continual input from humans. In many ways more complex than vision technology, artificial intelligence could eventually be used throughout GM, and once again, Smith didn't want the automaker's efforts in the field confined solely to GM's in-house endeavors.

Diversification had become a major ingredient in Roger Smith's strategic mix, but he was adamant that the array of new businesses had to relate directly to General Motors' core, making automobiles and selling them to consumers. The investments in robotics and artificial intelligence were aimed at helping GM make better, cheaper cars. At the same time, Smith was exploring ways to expand GM's relationship with its customers as more than just a manufacturer. The new relationship with dealers was one way, finance another. The company's financing subsidiary, General Motors Acceptance Corporation (GMAC), was already one of the largest lenders in the country, making approximately $1 billion a year in profit on loans to buyers of GM automobiles. But with GM gradually trying to shift some of its assets out of cars into other areas, non–auto financing was a clear option. In 1984 Smith began looking for an acquisition to expand the range of GMAC services. Early the following year he found one, the mortgage-processing operations of Norwest Corporation. The fit was almost perfect. The Norwest activities were virtually risk free, since the company was a "servicing" agent in handling the administration of mortgage loans. GMAC would therefore earn money whether loans were paid back or not, a big change from its business in auto loans. The Norwest operations would also be a first tentative step into a wider range of financial services that Smith knew were a natural fit for the company. Eventually, GM's former treasurer believed, the automaker would be servicing homeowners' mortgages, selling them a car, financing the auto, selling them car and home insurance, and providing other financial services such as credit cards and money-market accounts, which GMAC was already underwriting for GM dealers. And the entire system, Smith predicted, would be run as efficiently as any in the industry, with help from the information systems put in place by EDS.

The acquisition spree was meant to do more than just streamline or modernize the way General Motors made its cars. It was also part of a wider agenda to diversify the company into related fields that would help the automaker ride out the inevitable "down" years that characterized the American car market. Between EDS, robotics, and the expansion of GMAC in early 1985, Roger Smith was well on his way to making nonautomotive operations as much as one third of GM's business by his retirement date. But he was also worried about the make-up of that third and felt that General Motors still lacked a key ingredient — a major role in international satellite communications and defense contracting.

Ford was already well positioned in both those markets through its aerospace subsidiary. Smith wanted to tie together GM's worldwide data operations — and challenge Ford in the process. GM was expecting to spend billions of dollars on a worldwide communications system designed by EDS, and Smith saw no reason why GM couldn't be the one to build the satellites itself. He was also seeking to tap into the systems engineering expertise that characterized most defense manufacturers. GM, Smith recognized, was good at designing individual car parts, but it had made relatively few advances in designing whole systems at one time, for example, integrating the engine and transmission more closely or controlling more car functions electronically.

As early as 1982, Smith had approached the satellite industry's largest organization, Hughes Aircraft, about a buyout; Hughes had declined. Then, when John Gutfreund of Salomon Brothers drew up his list of potential targets in early 1984, one of the twelve was another defense contractor. After deciding to go after EDS first, Roger Smith chose to defer a defense acquisition. But not for long. Later the same year, the pressure on Hughes began to build. The high-technology company was 100 percent owned by the Howard Hughes Medical Institute, and the charity was under pressure from the Internal Revenue Service, which claimed that the institute was not giving away enough of Hughes Aircraft's profits to charity. Smith had been tracking Hughes's tax problems closely and knew it was only a matter of time before the medical institute would have to reorganize the company completely or sell it.

The institute put Hughes Aircraft up for sale in early 1985. GM wasn't the only participant in the highest-bidder-takes-all process organized by the Wall Street investment firm Morgan Stanley. Ford and Boeing also made it into the final round of bidding. But GM, after upping its original ante by almost half a billion dollars, took the prize. On June 5, 1985, Morgan Stanley announced that GM had agreed to pay $5 billion in cash and stock for Hughes. Smith had once again managed to structure the financial deal in such a way as to minimize the amount of cash GM would have to pay out. The medical institute would get $2.7 billion in cash, with the remainder to be paid in a new Class H stock similar to the Class E shares issued to EDS stockholders, with dividends tied to earnings at Hughes rather than GM as a whole.

Smith was also convinced that GM would make a big difference to operating earnings at Hughes. For years it had been left to its own devices by the medical institute, with little incentive to maximize profits because of the institute's tax-exempt status. By adapting GM's manufacturing know-how to the running of Hughes' day-to-day operations, Smith anticipated a sharp jump in profitability. GM's manufacturing expertise, including robotics, would also buttress Hughes in an area where it was lacking. Most of its missiles and other products were put together one at a time, with little attention to cost-saving production techniques developed by mass-market manufacturers such as GM. And stronger production technology would contribute to heightened quality control, an important factor in bidding on Pentagon contracts. For GM, those defense deals would be critical. Smith was counting on the highly profitable, long-term contracts to bolster GM's earnings while the automaker was spending heavily on reconstructing its car business.

The acquisition of Hughes wasn't, on the surface, a particularly cost-effective way to compete with the likes of Toyota or Nissan. But it was a vital addition to General Motors' strategic arsenal. To catch up with the Japanese, Smith knew, GM needed to do more than spend money on designing new cars. The automaker had to gain a technological advantage that no Japanese automaker would be able to match. It was a competitive edge that EDS and Hughes, as well as Saturn within the company, were expected to give GM.

To GM-watchers who had all but written off Roger Smith as an uninspired leader when he took over in 1980, the acquisition of Hughes appeared to be a brilliant maneuver. Halfway through his expected ten-year tenure as chairman and chief executive officer, Smith had radically transformed the company in a manner that was not yet totally apparent to buyers of GM cars. For almost forty years, Roger Smith had worked inside one mammoth corporate bureaucracy. Now he was openly talking of taking risks and giving subordinates a greater say in decision making. His business philosophy had more in common with his entrepreneur-father's rather than Alfred Sloan's. The executive who on taking office cautiously warned reporters that he didn't foresee any great changes ahead for GM had quickly become a tireless promoter of change. The apparently timid "number-cruncher" at one time vilified for his cold attention to the bottom line had succeeded in reshaping the values of a giant organization to reflect his own concern for quality over profit. And the man who inherited a $750 million loss had succeeded in racking up $5 billion in profits during the first three years of his chairmanship at GM.

But as Smith knew all along, the real impact of GM's reorganization and high-tech strategy would only start to be felt in 1986. The automaker would take at least that much time to absorb the companies that Smith had bought. The acquisitions themselves underscored where GM was headed, each strengthening the automaker's core business but also developing new, stand-alone businesses to counter the cyclical nature of the car market. The GMF robotics venture would give General Motors an edge in automating its factories of the future, allowing the company to become the largest robot manufacturer in the United States. EDS would streamline and computerize the company from top to bottom, making GM a major competitor in the computer software and services market, too. Hughes Aircraft would provide the satellite and systems-engineering needs of the international automakers, positioning GM among America's largest electronics giants and defense contractors. And the succession of small investments in robotics and artificial-intelligence companies would give the large corporation a stake in the technology advances Smith knew were possible only in a thoroughly entrepreneurial environment.

If at times he seemed like a juggler keeping all of GM's new balls in the air at once, it was characteristic of Roger Smith that he disliked the circus atmosphere surrounding GM's most publicized decision: where to locate the jewel in the automaker's new crown, the Saturn project. For months following Smith's Saturn announcement, governors and industrial officials from thirty-eight states made pilgrimages to GM's Detroit headquarters, offering sites, tax incentives, and more. Some towns sent bouquets of roses to key GM executives working on Saturn. Youngstown and Chicago took out billboards along Detroit highways to lobby for the new plant and the twenty thousand jobs it was expected to create. Thousands of Clevelanders mailed in "We Want Saturn" coupons. Then the jockeying was over. On July 29, 1985, GM announced that it had picked a two-thousand-acre tract of farmland thirty miles south of Nashville, Tennessee.

Tax incentives didn't make a difference: the state didn't offer any. Nor was Tennessee's largely nonunionized labor force a factor, because Smith had all along included UAW officials in the planning stages for Saturn and a labor pact was already in place. In weighing their decision, Smith and Saturn executives were more impressed with Tennessee's pioneering move into incentive payments for teachers in local schools, a sign that the state was committed to improving local education and providing strong training programs for Saturn employees. General Motors also picked Spring Hill over one thousand other sites because of its central location, with twenty-four-hour freight-delivery time to three of every four Americans.

For Roger Smith there was another reason for selecting Spring Hill. The entire thrust of the Saturn project was to put GM into a position where it would be able to compete with high-tech Japanese automakers in the 1990s, erasing the cost and quality advantages they had enjoyed for more than a decade. In Spring Hill, Smith saw a chance to prove what he had maintained all along, that GM could compete successfully with the Japanese. The world wouldn't have to look beyond Tennessee to make the comparison because the Saturn plant was located just forty miles southeast of Nissan's spanking-new assembly plant in Smyrna.

The Nissan plant represented the advance guard of a new onslaught in the American market. Hampered by continuing export restraints, Japanese automakers were not only building more cars in the United States, they were building a different kind of car. Bigger. More luxurious. More expensive. In short, the kind of cars that represented the backbone of GM's business and most of its profits. By 1986 *Japanese* was no longer synonymous with *cheap* in dealer showrooms.

As Smith realized, GM couldn't wait for Saturn to deal with the rising tide of higher-priced Japanese cars being made in, or exported to, America. In the three years to 1987, General Motors would spend more than $15 billion to redesign or replace almost all its midsize, large, and prestige cars. In any given segment of the market, GM would offer two models while its competitors offered only one. The crash program included a major spending effort on state-of-the-art technology. GM spent $600 million, for instance, on its Hamtramck assembly plant near Detroit; by early 1986, Cadillacs, Oldsmobiles, and Buicks were rolling off automated assembly lines installed on the site of the old Dodge main plant. And GM had begun its most expensive single car project ever, earmarking as much as $7 billion for a medium-sized car code-named the GM-10 for the late eighties.

The measure of Roger Smith's strategy, however, wouldn't be the amount of money General Motors was spending on new cars. Despite the growing success of Japanese models, GM had managed to perpetuate its dominant share of the American car market. Its willingness to adopt Japanese technology and work rules, and even Japanese cars, ensured that GM was in a strong position to maintain that share well into the future. Not content to defend its market from the Japanese, General Motors had gone on the offensive to deal with new technology, the unions, design — even its own management. Not content to redesign cars, Roger Smith had redesigned the entire company.

CHAPTER 6

The Battle Against Ma Bell

MCI VS. AT&T

Eᴅ ɢᴀʟʟᴀɢʜᴇʀ trekked through the nondescript doorway at 437 Madison Avenue, walked into the offices of Ally & Gargano just before nine in the morning, poured himself a cup of piping black coffee, and sat down at his desk to scan the *New York Times*. It was Wednesday, July 18, 1979. Outside, the morning was already turning into one of those hot, stifling, muggy Manhattan summer days. Gallagher flipped to the business section and began riffling pages for Phil Dougherty's advertising column, the bible for ad execs, sprinkled with gossip, insider stories, tips, leads on potential new clients, and the like. Before finding the ad page, though, Gallagher did a double take. There, on the front of the Business Day section, was a familiar face, that of Bill McGowan, Gallagher's roommate at Harvard Business School twenty-five years earlier!

The photograph in the *Times* made McGowan look older than Gallagher remembered him. Once close friends, the former roommates hadn't seen each other in ten years. After Harvard both had moved to New York. But when Gallagher settled into a series of jobs on Madison Avenue, McGowan took the entrepreneurial route, setting up a series of new ventures, most of them in electronics, although he also dabbled in Manhattan real estate. They lost touch as work demands pulled them apart. Now, as he examined the photo and accompanying article, Ed Gallagher smiled. McGowan was glaring, even scowling, into the camera lens, his severity a fitting counterpoint to the upbeat tone of the article itself. Gallagher remembered McGowan as a free-wheeling, pranksterish fellow Irishman with a biting wit and an infectious grin. Beneath the photo the *Times* had run the headline MCI V. BELL: FROM COURT INTO THE MARKETPLACE. Gallagher had never even heard of MCI, the telecommunications company McGowan was running as chairman, chief executive, and principal shareholder.

The story was flattering. Six months earlier, McGowan had won a crucial court battle against the American Telephone & Telegraph Company (AT&T). The U.S. district court judge had ruled that MCI could offer long-distance telephone service to business customers. The decision was unprecedented. Long-distance service was a one-company industry, and the one company was AT&T. Unexpectedly, the article went on, Ma Bell's monopoly appeared to be crumbling, and McGowan's MCI was first in line to pick up the pieces. Investors apparently believed MCI could do it. The chart accompanying the article showed that MCI's stock price had jumped from $2.00 a share in early 1977 to more than $6.00 a share just two and a half years later.

"Dear Bill," began the letter Gallagher addressed to his former buddy that afternoon.

> I was delighted to see your picture and story of MCI vs. Grandma Bell in the recent issue of the *New York Times*. This seems a long way from our early days together in New York. By way of coincidence, I am your friendly, hard-working Executive Vice President at Ally & Gargano, which has done some exciting work in helping new ideas grow to be very big, very successful ideas. Not the least of which is helping establish Federal Express, which was and still is an exciting new concept that benefited from Ally & Gargano advertising programs. Perhaps MCI could also benefit from this kind of communication expertise. Perhaps I could give you a call to see if we can help from a business standpoint, and also to say hello. Best wishes.

He signed it Ed.

Gallagher was a new kid on the block at Ally & Gargano.

After running his own small mergers-and-acquisitions business, Gallagher had worked for two of the biggest agencies on Madison Avenue, Compton and McCann-Erickson. Just one month before spotting McGowan in the *Times*, Gallagher had joined ten-year-old Ally & Gargano as chief operating officer, running the agency's day-to-day operations for Amil Gargano, its chief executive. The agency's client list was impressive: Saab, Fiat, Pan Am, Oil of Olay, and, by far the biggest, Federal Express. But in the summer of 1979, Ally & Gargano was still small by New York standards, with only thirty-five employees and less than $25 million a year in revenue billings.

To McGowan, smallness was a plus. Ally & Gargano was one of the few agencies on Madison Avenue that *didn't* do work for AT&T. McGowan knew that that would be an important advantage as MCI continued to put the heat on Bell. Because MCI couldn't afford a megabucks campaign from the very start — its creditors were constantly reviewing the company's books for telltale signs that MCI might be overextending itself in the fight with AT&T — it would probably not be well served by a large agency that would be getting only a fraction of its billings from the Ma Bell rival.

A week after Ed Gallagher's letter arrived, Bill McGowan invited his ex-roommate down to MCI's headquarters in Washington. As Gallagher had suspected, MCI didn't have an advertising agency. If Ally & Gargano could come up with a fresh, strong approach to help in the marketing battle for Ma Bell's long-distance business customers, McGowan promised, Gallagher would land the account. After several meetings with Gallagher in the ensuing few months, McGowan asked for a formal presentation. He was ready to talk turkey.

Gallagher and Amil Gargano flew to Washington in early November to make the presentation to McGowan and a handful of senior MCI executives. There had been no time for consumer research, so Gargano focused instead on the parallels between MCI and Federal Express. Federal had entered the package-delivery business that was dominated by the U.S. Postal Service and United Parcel Service. MCI, for its part, was taking on the biggest regulated monopoly of them all, AT&T. Like MCI, Federal Express was serving fewer than a dozen major cities when its advertising campaign "broke," capitalizing on the use of TV in particular to speed the rollout of its service into smaller markets around the country. Furthermore, both Federal Express and MCI were selling primarily to businesses, but they were starting to look for individual clients as well. Finally, MCI didn't have much to spend. But then, neither had Federal, which started advertising five years earlier with a budget of only $150,000 a year. Yet by late 1979, Federal Express had become a household name, and its humorous and engaging commercials were among the most recognized on American television. Most convincingly, the campaign had helped generate more than a doubling in Federal Express revenues every year since it began.

If Ally & Gargano could do it once, the agency could do it again, this time with a propaganda campaign foreshadowing MCI's David-and-Goliath battle with AT&T. That was the pitch Gargano and Gallagher sprang on McGowan, and the MCI chief was impressed. He

> *Good propaganda must anticipate real events.*
> —Erich Ludendorff

liked the humor and irreverence that characterized much of Ally & Gargano's work. MCI was already engaged in a similar battle that centered on business customers, the same ones targeted by Federal Express. But soon, McGowan believed, AT&T's monopoly over residential long-distance service would crumble too. It was only a matter of time, but the ad agency had to have a handle on how to pitch individual customers with something more than the promise of cheaper phone rates. Humor was critical; poking fun at Ma Bell would work better than trying to compete on its own crusty terms.

McGowan asked the admen to proceed with preliminary consumer research. The objective was to find those who were most likely to use MCI and the most effective way to reach them. The results of the survey would then determine what sort of advertising strategy MCI should adopt. Usually such research would be paid for by an agency as part of the normal bidding process for new accounts. But McGowan wasn't soliciting bids from

other agencies, primarily because of his long-time friendship
with Gallagher. He wanted MCI to pay as it went. To finance
the research, the phone company would retain Ally & Gargano
for $25,000 a month, a sum that would be counted against future
commissions, if there were any. As a result, McGowan felt, MCI
wouldn't feel obliged to go through with an ad campaign just
because Ally & Gargano had gone to a lot of trouble and expense
on the research side. This way, the ad agency could count on
making at least some money on the account. And MCI would
keep its options open.

Bill McGowan had every reason to be cautious. For more than
a decade, MCI had managed to irk AT&T with its incursion
into regional markets with phone services that linked corporate
customers, in some cases bypassing Bell lines altogether. Now,
after years of litigation, McGowan had the go-ahead to offer a
full-fledged alternative to Ma Bell's long-distance service.
Quietly, as McGowan had confidentially explained to Gallagher,
MCI was exploring the possibility of offering discount long-distance phone service to residential customers. But McGowan
knew that Ma Bell wouldn't sit idly by without a challenge.

AT&T had gone to court to stop a wide array of alleged
abuses: to prevent people from hooking up answering machines
to their phones; to prevent the use of phones made by any company other than Bell's Western Electric subsidiary; even, in-
credibly, to prevent the sale of private vinyl covers for Bell
System telephone books. The reason was always the same. Such
incursions would harm the most advanced telephone network in
the world.

The giant had also fought MCI's incursion into the business
market every step of the way, and it would battle tooth and nail
to keep the fight from spilling over into the home marketplace.
McGowan knew that MCI could cut long-distance phone bills
by 20, 30, or even 50 percent from what AT&T was charging
individual callers. Yet the entire economics of the Bell System
was based on relatively high long-distance rates that subsidized
"universal" phone service — a phone in every home, no matter
where. "Going public" now, with a sharp-edged advertising
campaign, would be interpreted as an all-out declaration of war,

and McGowan knew that MCI had to expect massive retaliation. AT&T had already proved that it could be vindictive toward any enemy that threatened to undermine its monopoly. From its very inception, MCI had been doing precisely that.

The company was forced to battle AT&T from its very inception. Microwave Communications, Inc. (MCI), was the brainchild of John D. Goeken, a radio-equipment salesman. Goeken sold General Electric mobile two-way radios in Joliet, Illinois, just outside Chicago's suburban perimeter. In the early 1960s he became interested in microwave technology, a way to transmit voice, pictures, or data over long distances with relatively little power. Microwaves travel through the air much like radio waves, only on a much higher frequency. That means the wavelength is shorter, usually less than one foot, compared with a radio wavelength of about a quarter of a mile. As a result, microwave signals can carry more information but don't travel as far as radio waves, and they can't pass over or around obstructions such as hills, buildings, or even trees. In fact, the signal is so concentrated that towers have to be set up every thirty miles or so to relay the signal so that even the curvature of the earth doesn't interrupt the microwaves between point A and point B.

Goeken saw a major boom for his radio sales in the new technology. He figured that if he erected a series of microwave transmitters on towers between Chicago and St. Louis, truck drivers traveling between those cities would be able to talk to their home bases from hundreds of miles away over the same GE two-way radios that otherwise worked only when the operators were within a few miles of each other. Goeken would not only sell more radios; he would be able to charge the trucking companies and other business users for access to the relay system.

In December 1963 the thirty-one-year-old Goeken and three partners set up MCI and petitioned the Federal Communications Commission (FCC) for permission to build a microwave relay system between the two midwestern cities. The FCC sat on Goeken's request for more than four years, until a hearing examiner gave MCI the go signal in the autumn of 1967. AT&T

filed an appeal that put the case squarely in the hands of the
FCC's full board of commissioners. It wasn't until nearly two
years later, on August 14, 1969, that the board split in MCI's
favor, voting 4 to 3 to let John Goeken build his relay towers
between Chicago and St. Louis.

By the time MCI got the FCC okay, Goeken had picked up a
new partner. When an original investor in the company passed
away in 1967, one of the deceased's lawyers called on a business
acquaintance, Bill McGowan, for help in assessing the value of
the estate's MCI shares. When Bill McGowan first got a look at
the company's books, the situation seemed hopeless. MCI was
$30,000 in debt and didn't have enough credit to build even a
fraction of the relay system Goeken was trying to get the FCC
to approve. The biggest problem, McGowan realized, was Goeken himself. Despite his considerable talents as an inventor,
technician, and salesman, Goeken knew little about lobbying in
Washington and perhaps less about how to manage a company
once it was off the ground. Yet to make a go of it, MCI needed
both, badly.

At the time, Bill McGowan was looking for a new venture. The
son of a railroad union organizer, he grew up in Pennsylvania
coal country. He did three years as a noncommissioned officer in
the U.S. Army, then put himself through four years at King's
College in his hometown of Wilkes-Barre by working between
terms at the local railyard. He went on to Harvard Business
School, where he finished near the top of his class. Despite
offers from several major corporations, the scrappy Irish Catho-
lic took his first full-time job as an East Coast aide to Hollywood
producer Mike Todd. During the next two years he learned to
wheel and deal with Wall Street money men interested in financing the Todd-AO 70mm film-projection system. He also
drummed up backing for Todd's movies, among them the musical *Oklahoma!*, on which McGowan won mention in the credits
as an associate producer.

After his stint with Todd, McGowan set up on his own as a
management consultant and small-time investor. By the mid
sixties he was starting and managing several small electrical
ventures. One that he bought and rebuilt from the brink of

bankruptcy was the Ultrasonic Corporation, a firm that made ultrasonic devices used in space and missile testing. It also developed a device to keep sharks away from pilots who landed in the drink. When sharks refused to cooperate and attacked the machine itself in a demonstration for U.S. Air Force brass, McGowan resorted to his quick Irish wit, suggesting that Uncle Sam might be interested in acquiring a high-tech shark aphrodisiac instead.

Business per se paled as an aphrodisiac after McGowan turned around Ultrasonic. So he sold the company and decided to retire — at age thirty-nine. The fun had gone out of going in and out of a series of small companies, and he remained reluctant to go to work for a much larger corporation. He was a confirmed bachelor, and the adventurer in him surfaced. He traveled around the world in both directions with his brother, a Jesuit priest.

If Bill McGowan was an adventurer by nature, he was also a gambler, in more ways than one. An inveterate casinogoer, he was banned from more than one Las Vegas gaming establishment because of his penchant for racking up nonstop winnings. Now he was going to place his biggest bet of all. McGowan's retirement lasted only a few months. On his return from Europe he took on the task of assessing John Goeken's books. What he found convinced him that MCI had the potential to become something bigger than even Goeken had conceived.

McGowan offered Goeken $50,000 for a half stake in MCI. With the alternative prospect of bankruptcy looming on the horizon, Goeken accepted. He also agreed to cede the chairmanship and let McGowan move MCI's corporate headquarters to Washington, D.C. Given MCI's track record so far, the biggest obstacle to growth was almost certain to come from regulatory agencies that tightly controlled virtually every aspect of the telecommunications industry. McGowan knew that most of his time would have to be spent lobbying the FCC, other regulatory agencies, the Justice Department, Capitol Hill, and perhaps even AT&T through the courts. By basing MCI in Washington, he would be in the thick of things.

The timing of the move came on the heels of the first real

crack in the Bell System's hitherto unchallenged monopoly. In 1968 the FCC effectively vetoed that monopoly as far as the phone equipment industry was concerned. The case was brought by Tom Carter, the inventor of a device he called the Carterphone. The invention allowed mobile two-way radio users to patch into the phone system so that they could talk with anyone. It was especially useful for workers in the field who needed to talk with headquarters but were miles from any phone. AT&T threatened to disconnect anyone found using the device. Carter filed an antitrust suit and won. The Carterphone was quickly outdated, but its legacy was permanent. Henceforth AT&T customers would be able to hook up any phone equipment they wanted.

The Carterphone case set a precedent that McGowan believed could be used to advantage in challenging AT&T on services as well as equipment. From the very beginning, Goeken had seen only limited uses for his microwave relay system. McGowan set his sights higher. MCI, he believed, could provide companies with cut-rate communications between their headquarters and branch offices much more cheaply than AT&T, GTE, or Western Union. MCI would give companies access to their own private phone lines, lines the companies could use day and night for phone calls and data transmission.

The key to expansion, of course, was the microwave network itself, and that meant putting up relay towers all over the country. By the time the FCC gave final approval to the Chicago–St. Louis system in August of 1969, McGowan was already laying the groundwork for a more comprehensive nationwide network. Such a refinement would require an amendment to the original application. Fearful that further dealings with the FCC regulatory board would cause years of delay, McGowan went another route. MCI began setting up separate companies, seventeen in all. Twelve would be MCI subsidiaries, while the remaining five would be affiliates in which MCI would own a significant portion of the equity. As each company filed its new application with the FCC, it included a request to set up microwave-relay systems on specified routes, the first for a line between Chicago and New York modeled on the Chicago–St. Louis plan.

Construction of the original route began in January 1971, and by the beginning of 1972 the $4 million network of forty-four relay towers was in operation. Continental Can, Greyhound, and Kraft signed up with MCI to communicate between St. Louis and the Windy City. Nearly ten years after John Goeken first got the idea, MCI's microwave relay system was finally off and running. Now the daunting task of turning one midwestern route into a nationwide telecommunications network, and battling AT&T every inch of the way, fell to Bill McGowan. It was a task he would relish. McGowan the corporate renegade. The adventurer. The gambler.

The battle with AT&T would be expensive, and McGowan knew it. All told, MCI envisioned an 11,600-mile network of microwave stations. Between 1969 and 1972, to defray costs before and during construction of the original route, McGowan had made money one of his top priorities. He raised more than $100 million in venture capital from the likes of Allen & Co. in New York and the Rothschilds in London. He thrived on taking maximum advantage of the Wall Street skills he'd first developed working for Mike Todd: the all-night negotiating sessions, the ability to juggle numbers and sell investors on the promise of profits for even an untested venture. "They only have two emotions," McGowan later quipped to a reporter, talking, not unadmiringly, about Wall Street financiers in general. "Fear and greed."

McGowan was greedy too, and for good reason. MCI would need all the funds it could get as the FCC began to approve permits on new microwave routes. He considered bringing in new venture-capital investors, but thought better of it. MCI could get more cash while parting with less stock than venture-capital backers usually required by listing the company on the stock market. So on June 22, 1972, McGowan took the company public. The renamed MCI Telecommunications Corporation sold 3.3 million shares of common stock at $10 a share, netting MCI a cool $30 million after commissions to the underwriter. Independently, a major supplier of construction services, Bechtel Corporation, paid $2.7 million for a stake in MCI. The new capital was supplemented by a $64 million line of credit with a consortium of banks led by the First National Bank of Chicago. The loans weren't free and clear. MCI's major equipment suppliers, notably L. M. Ericsson of Sweden, the General Electric Company of Britain, CIT-Alcatel of France, and North American Rockwell, had to guarantee half the amount if and when MCI drew on the line of credit. Even then, the banks were taking few chances: they charged MCI a steep 3.75 percentage points over the prime rate and got the company to swear off paying dividends to shareholders of common stock until 1975.

As long as MCI could get by without drawing on the $64 million credit line, the terms would be no problem. For McGowan, that meant using up every cent from the stock issue first. Then, if extra funds were necessary to fuel continued expansion, MCI would bite the bullet and assume the financial burden of paying high interest on the loans.

Near the end of 1972, as the FCC began to speed up approval of route applications, McGowan began to consolidate, buying out minority holders in the affiliated regional companies in return for stock in MCI Telecommunications. MCI could then set about building its nationwide relay system without the administrative ruse that each application had been filed by a separate company. But the nationwide market McGowan was targeting justified the ruse. MCI was going after a large chunk of the $1 billion that companies were spending each year on phone lines installed by AT&T to link far-flung corporate operations.

Ma Bell had the immense advantage of holding a virtual monopoly, and AT&T executives were intent on preserving it. Inside company headquarters at 195 Broadway in lower Manhattan, the giant corporation's high command wasted no time responding to MCI. On May 8,

---

To preserve is easier than to acquire.

—Karl von Clausewitz

1972, the Bell System held its annual Presidents' Conference in Key Largo, Florida. MCI was Ma Bell's enemy number one. Several of AT&T's corporate customers on the Chicago–St. Louis route had switched to MCI to take advantage of long-distance charges that were as much as 30 percent less than Bell's. And staff economists calculated that more than 40 percent of MCI's business that first year came from businesses that had switched from using AT&T's *standard* long-distance service, not the intracompany lines that MCI was offering. Now McGowan was openly talking about providing a standard long-distance service. Consequently, the discussion among the top executives of all the Bell operating companies quickly centered on MCI. Behind closed doors in the meeting, AT&T chairman John DeButts was unequivocal about where he stood: "We don't welcome competition." The talk gradually turned to ways in which AT&T could hamper expansion of the MCI network, including a refusal to hook up MCI customers to local phone systems, as well as equal pricing of similar intracompany phone lines, taking away MCI's estimated 30 percent cost advantage over AT&T. The president of Illinois Bell (and later AT&T chairman) Charles Brown favored waiting to see how MCI developed before launching a major counterattack. But others weren't so sanguine. John Van Sinderen, the president of Bell's Connecticut affiliate, plumped for a pre-emptive strike: "Shouldn't we act now rather than wait until they have a going business, which regulators might not permit us to dislodge?" He went on to answer the question himself. "If we're going to do this, we have to do it *now!*" Brown seemed to concur, despite his earlier doubts. "We can preserve a large amount of vulnerable revenue if we choke off [competition] now," he admitted. "I think you have to hit the nail on the head."

After four days of intense discussion, AT&T's master strategists ended their Key Largo meeting by setting themselves a deadline of September 1, less than four months away, to come up with an overall plan. They were out to cripple MCI. None suspected that notes taken at their Florida conclave would reach enemy eyes years later.

The word was out: AT&T intended to stop McGowan. AT&T chairman DeButts himself publicly called for the FCC to revise its position on free entry into the market for intracompany phone lines. "MCI has captured over 80 percent of Bell System point-to-point services," he argued in one vitriolic speech. "That would *seem* to indicate that MCI is a pretty stiff competitor." But, he went on to say, MCI was charging unfairly low rates on the route, and "that, I submit, is not competition." DeButts also predicted that MCI and other private-line suppliers would siphon off more than \$220 million in revenues between 1973 and 1975.

Off the record, AT&T was gearing up to crush MCI even without the help of the FCC in Washington, and it had plenty of opportunities at its disposal to do so. Local phone companies could refuse to connect MCI customers to the low-cost network or allocate antiquated switching equipment to handle MCI connections. AT&T could oblige MCI to divulge the names of its customers, then contact the same corporations to dissuade them from signing up with its rival by promising better service or lower rates. To varying extents, the Bell operating companies began implementing all three strategies in a staggered fashion that made it difficult to discern whether the moves were part of an AT&T master plan or simply a haphazard, informal overreaction to the inroads MCI was making into their monopoly.

McGowan realized what AT&T was up to, and furious, he responded the only way he could, going public with his suspicions. On July 30, 1973, he told a Senate judiciary subcommittee that AT&T, in direct breach of antitrust law, was trying to put MCI out of business. McGowan also offered the senators a novel solution: break up Ma Bell. Thus began MCI's vigorous counteroffensive and

A swift and vigorous assumption of the offensive, the flashing sword of vengeance, is the most brilliant point in the defensive.
—Karl von Clausewitz

the face-to-face, almost daily confrontation that would pit MCI against AT&T well into the next decade.

Bill McGowan's first move was to file suit in Philadelphia. In early November the scrapper asked the federal district court to force AT&T to hook up customers of MCI's intracompany phone lines to their local phone lines, hookups that the Bell System regional companies were denying they had to provide. MCI needed to show the court that customers would benefit from a decision in MCI's favor, despite AT&T's contention that the change would not be in the public interest. For that, McGowan needed allies, existing as well as potential clients for the long-distance service and equipment suppliers who had in many cases been shut out of the telecommunications market by

AT&T's practice of manufacturing its own equipment. To drum up support, McGowan sent a five-page letter and copies of previous FCC orders to more than two thousand businesses around the country, only some of them MCI customers. For the first time, MCI was seriously expanding its lobbying effort beyond Washington.

Ironically, MCI's lobbying effort landed the company's most important ally to that date, the Justice Department. McGowan had been continuously feeding the department's antitrust lawyers with information on AT&T's activities in the private-line market. And in early December 1973, U.S. attorneys in New York walked into 195 Broadway and served AT&T with subpoenas for documents going as far back as 1967 that related to the company's private-line pricing and contracting policies. Ostensibly, Justice's inquiry was being carried out independently of MCI's charges against Ma Bell. But the inquiry clearly had an impact on MCI's legal complaints. Only days later, on New Year's Eve, a Philadelphia judge granted MCI's request for an injunction requiring AT&T to provide the local hookups that MCI was seeking in the same manner as it would for its own subsidiaries.

It was the break that Bill McGowan was looking for. Flush with victory, he broadened his offensive. Trying to piggyback on the Justice Department's antitrust probe of Ma Bell, MCI filed an antitrust suit of its own against AT&T in March 1974. In it McGowan charged that AT&T was "monopolizing the business and data-communications market in violation of the Sherman Antitrust Act." An AT&T spokesman responded by calling the suit "ridiculous," and Ma Bell filed an antitrust claim of its own, against MCI. In the suit AT&T charged that MCI had submitted "sham tariffs and pleadings before the FCC," "opposed tariffs and applications" unreasonably and without cause, and had filed "unreasonably low" rates that didn't meet the cost of providing service. AT&T's charges were filed on April Fools' Day 1974, a date which, as a company spokesman retorted, was "the only explanation we have for AT&T's claim."

MCI seemed to be on a roll, but not for long. On April 15 a federal circuit court overturned the earlier ruling that forced

AT&T to hook up MCI customers to the phone system. The appeals court contended that the decision should have been made by the FCC, not a court of law. The very next day, AT&T began to disconnect MCI customers, pulling the plug on at least nine major corporations, some of them in midconversation. But AT&T's rough justice would be short-lived. On April 23 the FCC delivered its unequivocal verdict: AT&T's subsidiaries had to furnish the local phone hookups to MCI and other competitors on a nondiscriminatory basis and on "reasonable terms and conditions." The federal agency also gave Bell ten days to "cease and desist from engaging in any conduct which results in a denial of, or unreasonable delay in, establishing physical connections with MCI and other specialized common carriers." In other words, AT&T had to stop disconnecting MCI customers, and it had to reconnect those it had already cut off. The FCC also said it would begin a general investigation of Bell's interconnection rates, which would thereafter have to be authorized by the FCC, rather than by state authorities over whom the regional Bell companies held greater sway. AT&T appealed the ruling but lost. "AT&T has never exactly welcomed competition," McGowan wrote in a letter to shareholders in August, "and I do not expect that completely amicable relations will come soon."

AT&T was furious with the FCC decision. It was clear that the Bell regional companies couldn't undercut MCI simply by refusing or delaying hookups. So in June AT&T adopted a new strategy to compete on price. It put into effect its so-called Hi-Lo tariff for intracompany lines, effectively lowering its rates on many routes served by MCI. Bell also asked the FCC for greater flexibility in the future to modify the rates on its regular long-distance services.

The tariff change forced Bill McGowan to retaliate in kind. About the time of the company's second annual shareholder meeting, in September 1974, MCI filed a revision of its tariffs with the FCC, primarily as a response to the lower rates Bell was charging. MCI's petition to the FCC also included a proposed change in the way customers would tap into the MCI net-

work, creating a service called Execunet. It would allow callers
to dial a local seven-digit number that connected them with the
MCI network; then the caller would dial a five-digit identification code. Once the MCI computer matched up the I.D. code
with the customer's account number, the caller could simply
dial the area code and phone number. The service would work
only between cities served by MCI, but the innovation was far-
reaching. MCI could use its microwave network to let customers
call long distance without subscribing to its intracompany service. The FCC approved the plan, and MCI inaugurated Execunet in January 1975.

McGowan saw the decision for what it was, a landmark, or
what he told fellow executives was the "first day of the rest of
our life." For the first time, MCI customers would be able to
place long-distance calls over the MCI microwave network not
just to other offices of the same company but to anyone located
in the markets MCI served. The FCC had broadened the front
on which MCI could challenge AT&T's monopoly.

Years later some FCC officials claimed that they didn't fully
understand what MCI was proposing. Staff members were
under the impression that MCI was simply trying to provide
customers of its intracompany lines with an easier way to dial
into the network. But AT&T knew what MCI was up to. The
upstart was trying to supply an alternative long-distance phone
service for corporate customers, and Bell was determined to see
it outlawed. The following April AT&T lobbyists set up a demonstration of the Execunet service for FCC commissioners in
Washington. Using an identification code borrowed from a
friendly Washington law firm, someone from AT&T used Execunet to call the weather report in Chicago. The demonstration
had its desired effect. Shortly thereafter, the FCC sent AT&T's
letter of complaint to McGowan and asked him for comments
before the federal agency decided on a course of action.

McGowan's argument was straightforward. Execunet, he
claimed, was simply another form of corporate service that allowed customers to dial inside as well as outside their own companies. But the FCC was unmoved. On July 2 the agency withdrew its previous authorization. Once MCI's greatest ally, the

FCC was now in the enemy camp. McGowan had only one place to go to appeal the order, the U.S. Court of Appeals. He stated that the FCC could not reject Execunet without first holding hearings on the subject, and the appeals court agreed. Later that month it ordered the FCC to hold a full-scale hearing; meantime, it authorized MCI to continue selling the long-distance service.

The decision in MCI's favor came at a critical time in negotiations to shore up the company's finances. In fiscal 1975 the company lost nearly $28 million, almost every cent it had earned in revenues. Of the loss, more than $15 million went to the banks to pay interest on MCI's huge debt. As of late May the company had drawn down its entire $64 million credit line, as well as an additional $8 million that its consortium of lenders was willing to provide. Bill McGowan was dividing his time between lobbying the FCC and trying to find new sources of financing to keep MCI's expansion on schedule. As long as the company could still operate Execunet, new investors would be willing to talk. The banks, however, were also worried about AT&T's new pricing strategy that threatened to cut into MCI's profit margins. But in January 1976, eighteen months after AT&T put the new rates into effect, the FCC declared that the tariffs were illegal. At the time, MCI had a negative net worth of $30 million, and its principal lenders got McGowan to replace Stanley Scheinman, the firm's chief financial officer, with Wayne English, who had held the same post at Hallmark. English's task when he joined MCI in February was to negotiate new financing arrangements and, eventually, raise more money in the stock market to let MCI expand its long-distance network. But even as MCI's profit margins were endangered by it, English's task was made easier when AT&T raised its tariffs on intracompany lines. He coaxed the banks, mainly Riggs Bank, into supplying an additional $16 million in loans under a revised credit agreement.

Meanwhile, MCI was in for trouble that would make the banks skittish about lending the money. The Execunet hearings were delayed again and again, and when they were finally held, in May 1976, the FCC again ruled against MCI. The agency acknowledged that it had never expressly defined the boundaries of microwave transmission services, but it did say that it never meant for MCI or anyone else to offer dial-up, long-distance telephone services. That was the exclusive preserve of AT&T.

By early summer Wayne English was again negotiating with creditors, and the FCC's decision was no help. After the previous year's losses, MCI's lenders had agreed to let the company suspend its interest payments until the end of August. But as of September 1, MCI would have to start paying interest in full to all five banks in the consortium: First Chicago, First National Bank of Boston, Continental Illinois, Citibank, and Manufacturers Hanover Trust. In the midst of the fight over Execunet, MCI's revenues were no longer growing fast enough to allow the company to resume those interest payments, and the FCC's decision made it virtually impossible to issue more shares on the stock market, given the heightened risks involved.

So Bill McGowan and Wayne English turned to private investors, including Martin Silverman, the owner of North American Leasing Corporation in New York. Silverman agreed to invest $3 million in MCI to help the company meet its deadline to resume interest payments. With that, English went back to the banks with a request for new loans. At first they acquiesced. But one creditor, First Boston, got cold feet and refused to go along with the plan. Since the terms of the credit line stipulated that any changes had to be endorsed unanimously, it looked as if the entire arrangement was about to collapse.

The only way out was to find someone to replace First Boston and the $12 million worth of loans from the bank carried on MCI's books. In late July English met again with Silverman and asked him to put up the entire amount in exchange for notes as well as warrants on MCI stock. One day before the expiration of MCI's interest-deferral agreement, with Silverman's investment in hand, Wayne English flew to Boston and settled the company's account with the bank.

Almost immediately MCI began work on a public stock issue that McGowan hoped would raise $30 million or so to reduce some of its debts and continue investing in new microwave relay systems. Unfortunately, MCI was forced to hold back its stock offering when Wall Street took one of its worst dives in years.

MCI's shares fell from around $5.50 to $3.25, reducing the company's market value by more than 40 percent in less than four weeks.

McGowan then decided to use the appeals process that AT&T had used so effectively to thwart MCI. He filed an appeal to the FCC's decision with the U.S. Court of Appeals in Washington, and while the case began making its way up a busy court docket, MCI continued to sell its Execunet service. It was an important ingredient in McGowan's strategy. He knew that the longer MCI was able to offer the long-distance service, the more difficult it would be for the FCC or AT&T to kill it. MCI continued to rally support in the marketplace. Every new customer who could save money by using Execunet was a potential ally. And despite continued court battles over its position as a competitor to AT&T's long-distance service, Execunet was good for business. Revenues jumped from $2.8 million its first year in operation to over $28 million the second year. By late 1976 the long-distance service accounted for nearly half of all MCI revenues — and an even bigger share of the company's profits.

In October, pending a final decision on the legality of Execunet, the court ordered MCI to stop selling the service to new customers, although the company could continue supplying it to ten thousand or so existing subscribers. Then MCI had to find jobs for its three hundred Execunet salespeople. Only one hundred were reassigned to new jobs inside the company; the rest were dismissed or placed in jobs outside the company. It was the first real blow to morale inside a company that had grown by leaps and bounds, with little regard to the pitfalls in expanding the work force as fast as it had. For McGowan the layoffs were also an acute reminder that, for better or worse, MCI's fate resided with the courts and regulatory agencies. He doubted that the final court ruling would ax Execunet, but there were no guarantees.

Fortunately for MCI, Bill McGowan was right. It took nearly six months for the Second Circuit Court of Appeals in Washington to hear oral arguments in the Execunet case and another three months for a final verdict. But when that verdict was handed down, it was a stinging attack — *on the FCC!* The court claimed that the FCC's original 1971 MCI decision had left the door open for services like Execunet. The court also claimed that the FCC could not redefine the rules of the game unless it could prove that the Execunet service was *not* in the public interest. "The Commission must be ever mindful," the court went on, "that, just as it is not free to create competition for competition's sake, it is not free to propagate monopoly for monopoly's sake. The ultimate test of industry structure in the [communications] field must be the public interest, not the private financial interests of those who have until now enjoyed the fruits of a de facto monopoly."

The FCC was stung by the rebuke to its authority and quickly appealed the case to the Supreme Court. Again the wheels of justice ground slowly, and MCI was still banned from selling the service. When the high court finally weighed in with a decision six months later, it was anticlimactic: the nine justices declined to hear the appeal. On January 17, 1978, MCI was openly and legally allowed to offer a long-distance phone service that competed directly with Ma Bell's. It was a major victory for McGowan, setting a precedent for future incursions into Bell territory.

The Supreme Court decision prompted a switch in AT&T strategy. On the very day the high court refused to hear the FCC's appeal, Bell executives announced that they were under no obligation to provide the local hookups needed to let customers tap into the MCI network from their own phones. The FCC, also angered by the Supreme Court decision, agreed, even though AT&T had previously been ordered to provide MCI with access to its local interconnections for private-line customers. Clearly, AT&T was adopting a strategy of delay and harassment, and the FCC was complying. Once again McGowan took them to court, and once again the U.S. Court of Appeals in Washington overruled the FCC, calling AT&T's position "strikingly unfair." Wrote the court: "AT&T's refusal, with the approval of the Commission, to provide interconnections to MCI does not simply raise questions of fairness vis-à-vis MCI. It also raises questions as to the propriety of allowing [AT&T] to renounce a position and obligation which they had assumed throughout the course of the Execunet proceedings." In other words, AT&T had objected to the Execunet service itself, not connecting local users, which its subsidiaries had been doing all along for other MCI customers. Now the court would not allow AT&T to argue that it was under no obligation to offer the interconnections on the same basis that had already been established under the law.

MCI was not about to waste time after the court's decision. McGowan was aware that other companies, such as ITT, were ready to enter the market once the courts confirmed their right to compete with AT&T. So MCI had to capitalize on its head start in the industry by quickly expanding its network. To do that, McGowan asked the FCC for authority to expand Execunet beyond the eighteen cities already on its network. Boosting the service to thirty cities, McGowan believed, would result in revenues from the long-distance phone service going from $2.5 million to $7.5 million a month. However, what it had not been able to win in court, AT&T tried to achieve by charging prohibitive rates for the local hookups it was obliged to provide MCI's customers. The new rates — filed for the approval of the FCC, itself unhappy at MCI's success in court against it — represented a tripling of existing rates for the crucial connections. Before deciding his next move, McGowan ordered an internal study of the impact the higher connection rates would have on MCI's operating costs. The study found that if the FCC approved AT&T's request, Execunet might no longer be an economical way to call long distance.

With those results in hand, Bill McGowan launched an all-out campaign to head off FCC approval, even though he knew it would be difficult. The federal agency remained staunchly in AT&T's camp. But the White House intervened. President Jimmy Carter's special adviser for telecommunications policy, Henry Geller, proposed that some sort of "rough justice" be worked out at a negotiating table with all parties concerned. The FCC relented, and the talks began in September 1978. On hand were representatives of AT&T, MCI, and more recent entrants in the long-distance race like ITT and Sprint, neither of which had even a fraction of the network MCI had built.

McGowan knew that the negotiations among AT&T, the

FCC, and the "alternative" long-distance carriers were proceeding smoothly and an agreement was just around the corner, even though it would be a temporary settlement. MCI's stock bottomed out in mid November and crept back up to a fraction under $4.00 a share by December 1. With the cash from Riggs Bank rapidly dwindling, both McGowan and English knew they couldn't wait until after a settlement to issue new stock. They ordered their investment advisers, Allen & Co., to proceed with the offering that had been put on hold. On December 12, 1978, MCI made its third public stock offering. It sold out within hours. Late the same afternoon, check number 53456 drawn on Allen & Co.'s account at Chemical Bank was in English's hands. It was for $28,575,412.50 to be exact. For the first time since 1975, MCI had a positive net worth.

The talks continued for three months. In the end, the parties came up with a two-year interim settlement that would peg rates well below AT&T's request, but higher than MCI and other services were then paying. Under the agreed formula, MCI would initially pay one-third as much for the interconnections as AT&T, which, after all, was shifting funds from one pocket to the other because it owned most of the local phone companies that were directly responsible for the hookups. Initially, services like MCI would have to put up with lower-quality connections that, for instance, would not allow MCI's customers to access the network from rotary-dial phones. Over the next three years, however, the charges would rise to 45 percent, then 55 percent of what AT&T was paying for hookups to its local operating companies for higher-quality connections.

Nineteen seventy-nine started off well for MCI in other ways, too. Although Bill McGowan had privately talked about breaking up Ma Bell, the talk was hardly taken seriously in Washington. But by early January the Justice Department had embarked on an internal inquiry into AT&T's role in the telecommunications market. As a result, investigators asked McGowan to hand over documents uncovered during discovery proceedings for MCI's pending antitrust suit against Bell. McGowan gladly obliged, but only after the cooperative effort was approved by a Washington court, which reasoned that the pooling of information would shorten the usually lengthy pretrial period in the event of a Justice Department antitrust suit against Bell.

At the same time, AT&T came under attack on Capitol Hill, and for the first time Washington began to explore seriously the option of forcing AT&T to divest some of its businesses as part of an antitrust settlement. South Carolina senator Ernest (Fritz) Hollings introduced a rewrite of the 1934 Communications Act, which still governed telecommunications policy in the United States. In the new version, Hollings proposed the breakup of Ma Bell into distinct and unrelated companies.

McGowan pounced. Hollings would be holding hearings in Washington shortly, and MCI's five-year-old antitrust suit against AT&T would soon be going to court. So to keep the heat on Bell, McGowan filed a second antitrust suit against the behemoth. MCI's new suit updated allegations that Bell had engaged in illegal and unethical attempts to stop MCI dead in its tracks. The suit asked for unspecified damages to exceed $1 billion, but it went further. McGowan again asked, this time as a formal component of MCI's suit, that AT&T be broken up. McGowan even provided a blueprint, one that was not unlike that put forth by Hollings. He proposed that Ma Bell spin off its local phone companies into separate units and transfer all intercity telephone facilities to AT&T, its long-distance operation. In turn, the core company would be divided into three or more separate, independent companies. McGowan was especially concerned that Bell's manufacturing arm, Western Electric, be prevented from remaining the sole supplier of equipment to the spun-off Bell companies, a sop to MCI's allies in the battle against Ma Bell. McGowan was already getting support from equipment suppliers who had been shut out of AT&T's market because of Bell's insistence on purchasing most of what it needed in-house, and the attack on Western Electric would solidify the alliance.

AT&T countered the new charges in a prepared statement, calling MCI's action a "transparently frivolous lawsuit" and a "contrived media event." Either way, McGowan and Senator Hollings had separately managed to thrust the possible breakup of AT&T into the spotlight, and the timing was perfect. One day after filing, McGowan testified on many of the same topics in front of a congressional panel holding hearings on the Hollings legislation. Two weeks later, a Chicago federal district judge announced that MCI's original lawsuit against AT&T would finally go to trial on December 3, 1979, more than five years after it was filed.

With a trial pending and MCI's second antitrust suit initiated, Bill McGowan turned his attention to the other battle. So far, the company's services were available only to corporations, and most of the new business was generated by individual sales representatives calling on major corporate accounts. MCI was spending tens of millions of dollars each year to expand its nationwide microwave network, but a lot of the capacity went unused during off-peak hours. It was essential, McGowan knew, to boost usage during those hours. In June MCI introduced discounted evening and weekend rates for MCI's Execunet customers to encourage off-peak calling, but as McGowan had suspected, most of his business customers were reluctant to use the service at night just because of lower rates. To beef up off-peak business, therefore, MCI would have to target a new type of customer: people at home. When Ed Gallagher's letter landed on his desk, MCI's chief executive officer decided it was time to start exploring the home market further.

McGowan was interested in the residential market for two reasons: first, to expand usage on the microwave network MCI had already developed, and second, to rally popular support for MCI's fight against Ma Bell. To that point McGowan's lobbying efforts had been focused strictly on the FCC and the Justice Department. Though the FCC was clearly in AT&T's camp, Justice appeared to be on MCI's side — or at least it wasn't on Ma Bell's.

With legislation pending in Congress, it was essential that MCI broaden its base of support, to bring public opinion to bear on legislators in its uneven battle with the Bell System. By bringing in tens of thousands of home users and helping them to save money on their long-distance calls, MCI would be able to count on a new constituency, and an influential one where Congress was concerned. McGowan knew the strategy was risky. AT&T would try to

> *A victorious army wins its victories before seeking battle.*
> —Sun Tzu

stymie MCI's move. The giant could get a court injunction stopping MCI's expansion into the residential market, in which case any major advertising campaign could turn out to be a waste of money, money that MCI could put to better use building more microwave towers to expand its existing system for business customers.

If MCI wanted to go after the home market, though, advertising would be essential. So without committing the company to any major advertising dollars, McGowan chose one of MCI's original employees to work closely with Ed Gallagher on the project. Soft-spoken and a technician by training, Gerry Taylor had joined MCI ten years earlier and was instrumental in expanding the Execunet service. Taylor and Gallagher went to work on the consumer research. They organized focus-group meetings in Ridgewood, New Jersey, and Daly City, California. Each session included a group of men and women who regularly called long distance, and MCI's researchers, who proceeded to grill them on their phone habits. How often did they call long distance? Where did they call most frequently? How important was cost in determining the frequency or length of their long-distance calls? Would they ever consider using a service other than AT&T? Had they heard of MCI? Would they be willing to pay a monthly fee for access to the network? Would they be willing to dial the extra digits needed to place a call on the MCI network?

Out of that profile came a strategy for reaching "target" customers, most of whom had never had to make a decision about telephone service other than the color of their phones. As Gallagher outlined the program to McGowan, MCI would first have to establish its credibility. The research showed that people were impressed with the fact that several hundred of the Fortune 500 companies were MCI customers. If General Motors was willing to spurn AT&T, they figured, why not I? Research also indicated widespread distrust of AT&T, which would allow MCI to jab and poke fun at the leviathan in its TV commercials without the risk of setting off a backlash of support in favor of Bell.

At 9:30 in the morning on the last day of 1979, Ed Gallagher and Gerry Taylor presented an advertising strategy to a roomful of MCI executives, including Bill McGowan and Wayne English. According to the plan, MCI would test public acceptance of its residential phone service in three cities, Denver, Cincinnati, and Kansas City. Beginning in Denver the following March, the main vehicle would be local TV, using frequent spots over a short period of time — what Gallagher liked to call a high-penetration strategy. The targeted customer was anyone who spent more than $25 a month on long-distance calls with AT&T. To reach them, Ally & Gargano was proposing two basic commercials. The first one, titled "Big Business," would show how various big-name companies were saving millions on their phone bills. The second would zero in on the residential user. It would open with a woman talking on the phone; sharing the screen would be two video displays, one marked Bell, the other MCI. As the woman talked, the cost of the call began adding up, at a more rapid rate for Bell than for MCI. When the woman finished her call, the cost of the Bell call totaled $6.05, the MCI just $3.07. "You haven't been talking too much," went the voice-over at the end of the commercial, "you've just been *paying* too much." The concept was simple and to the point, a graphic way of telling Americans that they could save money on long-distance calls by using MCI.

In both commercials the announcer referred to MCI as "the nation's long-distance phone company," even though Gerry Taylor worried that the statement was a bit too presumptuous, even for MCI. Ally & Gargano was also insistent that MCI drop the name Execunet for its long-distance service; it was too "corporate."

McGowan agreed. "Eddie," he asked Gallagher, while the rest of the Ally & Gargano team waited with baited breath for a sign of whether MCI liked the campaign enough to proceed, "how much is all this going to cost?"

"Including production costs and a strong push in Denver, Cincinnati, and Kansas City," Gallagher replied, trying to make the sum seem less than it was, "about $1.1 million."

There was a brief silence in the room after Gallagher put his price tag on the project. For MCI the amount was phenomenal.

Until then the company had spent virtually nothing on advertising, and the figure Gallagher was talking about accounted for almost a third of its net profits the previous year. Despite McGowan's reputation as a gambler, this wasn't Las Vegas. Would he willingly gamble that much on a six-month advertising test?

Almost as an afterthought, and with no further discussion, McGowan decided yes.

As Ed Gallagher and Gerry Taylor got to work on the marketing push, Bill McGowan went back to court. After a two-month delay, opening arguments in MCI's first antitrust case were to begin on February 5. MCI's Chicago counsel, Jenner & Block, had spared no expense in readying its case. The rigorous preparation ended on three successive nights in late January, when Jenner & Block attorneys tested their case in front of mock juries. A different "jury" came in every evening, each made up of eight Chicagoans hired for $20 to listen, deliberate, and render a verdict. Using evidence but no witnesses, MCI's lawyers delivered two forty-five-minute presentations, one covering MCI's case, the other the case they expected AT&T to make. As the surrogate jurors deliberated, Jenner & Block attorneys watched and listened behind a one-way mirror, picking up valuable tips on the points they would want to emphasize — or ignore — during the actual trial.

The real trial got under way in early February 1980 with few surprises. In his opening statement for MCI, Jenner & Block partner Chester Kamin walked the jury through a litany of complaints against AT&T. "They decided to choke off MCI," he said, referring to the Key Largo meeting of top Bell officers. AT&T had decided, Kamin declared, to institute predatory, below-cost pricing on some long-distance services to stop MCI from making further inroads into AT&T's market. Kamin's colleague and MCI's in-house counsel, Robert Hanley, also told the jury of five men and seven women that AT&T had refused to provide MCI with many necessary connections and had overcharged for others. It was, Hanley asserted, an "obstructionist" strategy that culminated in April 1974, when AT&T "ripped out" numerous interconnections, disconnecting MCI customers without warning. As a result, Kamin and Hanley stated, AT&T had irreparably damaged the smaller company's reputation as a reliable supplier of long-distance phone service, thus forcing MCI to lay off hundreds of people. All told, Kamin claimed, MCI had lost $900 million in revenues between 1972 and 1975 because of AT&T's abuse of its powerful position. If the jury agreed, AT&T could have been liable for three times that amount in damages, the trebling based on a standard provision of the Sherman Antitrust Act.

AT&T opened its case the next day with a stinging attack on MCI. George Saunders, a partner in the Chicago firm of Sidley & Austin, told jurors that MCI had filed the case in desperation to mask its financial problems. Speaking for an hour and forty minutes, Saunders said MCI's case was built on "fabrications." Trying to portray Ma Bell as the victim in the case, even at the risk of seeming to contradict himself, Saunders called MCI's bid to enter the long-distance business the "most profitable scam in the history of American business."

Bill McGowan turned out to be the star witness for both sides. He was questioned for two hours and forty minutes by Kamin and Hanley, then, under cross-examination, for a day and a half by Saunders. He denied AT&T's charges, countering that any financial problems at MCI were the direct result of AT&T's intransigence and stonewalling. More important, McGowan immediately won converts among the jury with his self-effacing style and occasional flashes of humor, both in sharp contrast to the dour Saunders.

The highlight of MCI's case came two weeks into the trial. On February 19 Kamin introduced, over strenuous objections from AT&T's counsel, handwritten notes taken at Bell's 1972 Presidents' Conference. The notes were barely legible, attributing shorthand sentiments to key Bell officers. "Large amounts of revenues vulnerable which we can preserve if we choke [MCI] off now," read one snippet, attributed to Charles Brown. Later in the discussions, though, as the notes revealed, Brown seemed less convinced. "How badly would we be hurt," he had asked, "if we wait to see the whites of their eyes?" "I would meet 'em or beat 'em," another Bell chief executive, Thomas Nornberg of Northwestern Bell, was quoted as saying. "You bastards are not going to take away my business."

Because of the case's complexity, Judge John Grady gave jurors five weeks to digest MCI's charges before allowing AT&T to proceed with its defense. The break couldn't have come at a better time for MCI. The first advertising test was due to start a few days later in Denver. Ed Gallagher and Gerry Taylor had set up a battery of school desks in a small office rented especially for the occasion. At each desk sat a phone operator. Some were long-time MCI salesmen, but most were reservation clerks from Continental Airlines who had gone on strike the previous week. Gallagher also set up a TV monitor in the already crowded room and, finally, there was "Big Business" flashing across the screen.

"Last year we saved the big automakers almost $2 million in long-distance bills," the narrator boasted as the sixty-second commercial began. "We saved a band $75,000. An oil company $1 million. A computer company $600,000. All told, 40,000 companies used us to cut their long-distance bills up to 50 percent.

"We're MCI," the commercial went on. "The nation's long-distance phone company. And starting now, *you* can be saving on long distance with your own home phone. This year, MCI will save Nancy Bryant, who calls her son a lot, $400. We'll save Mr. and Mrs. Sadler, whose son is in college, $500. We'll save Mrs. Payne $300. If your long-distance bills are running $25 a month or more, call MCI and find out how to start cutting them down to size." With that, a number flashed onto the screen: 842-5731.

In their makeshift Denver office, Taylor and Gallagher sat with the operators in anxious silence. Nothing. Then one phone rang, and another, and another. As each call came in, the operator filled out a customer questionnaire, then handed it to another person who entered the data into a computer. The response went beyond MCI's wildest expectations: the Denver test brought in between three hundred and four hundred new customers that first day.

The next day, however, something happened. The phones stopped working. At first one of MCI's corporate customers in Denver began having trouble with its private-line service. Then many of MCI's Execunet customers in the area reported being unable to make calls on the service. Next, Taylor and Gallagher's own phone bank inexplicably went out of service for six hours. During that time, some people who saw MCI's commercials and called the number displayed on their TV screens got a recorded message telling them that the number was no longer in service. Immediately, McGowan suspected foul play, probably on the part of AT&T's Denver subsidiary, Mountain States Telephone & Telegraph Co. "I thought somebody was pulling my leg," McGowan told a reporter. The MCI chief promptly dispatched the company's attorneys to Denver to take depositions, just in case the affair ended up in court. For its part, Mountain Bell apologized for what it called a "human error in reprogramming." "There wasn't any intentional misconduct on the part of Mountain Bell," declared one company spokesman. "MCI is a customer and we want to give them good service." By the end of the week, service was back to normal. But the incident wouldn't be forgotten. McGowan would see to that.

Given the disruption in phone service, the high volume of calls in the Denver test seemed all the more impressive. And residential users weren't the only ones responding, although they were the target. An added bonus came from the corporate sector. Impressed by how much MCI said it was saving "big" businesses, a lot of small companies were eager to sign up. Even Prudential Insurance's Denver office, which had repeatedly turned away MCI's salesmen, signed up almost immediately after the commercials went on the air. The success of the test was apparent within days, and it shocked a lot of people inside MCI. Until Denver, MCI's entire sales strategy had been based on direct sales to major corporate customers. All of a sudden, mass marketing seemed to be bringing in new customers, at a much lower cost per subscriber. Rather than supporting a national sales force to solicit new customers, MCI saw that it could make the pitch through advertising, then sit back and take orders over the phone. The cost of booking new customers could be kept to a bare minimum. Only a small sales staff would be

needed to handle large corporate accounts when the personal
touch was necessary.

A week after the Denver test started, MCI added Cincinnati
to the list and again the response was overwhelming. The tests
were supposed to last six months before a final decision on
whether to take the residential service public, but for all intents
and purposes the test was over the day it began. Given the ex-
traordinary results, McGowan knew he couldn't waste any time
rolling out home service in MCI's major markets. And after the
run-in with Mountain Bell, he knew that AT&T's subsidiaries
in other markets would be too scared to pull similar stunts lest
they backfire on the parent company in court.

There was no mention of the Denver incident when the antitrust trial resumed in Chicago on April 8. AT&T had originally
notified Judge Grady that its defense presentation could take up
to eighteen months. At Grady's insistence, AT&T's attorneys
scaled back their request to five weeks. Even so, Grady continually admonished Bell's defenders for burdening the jury with
thousands of pages of exhibits and, in some cases, patently
needless documents. At one point Judge Grady even refused to
allow certain papers to be introduced at all. AT&T's lead attorney, George Saunders, spent much of his court time arguing
that MCI had stretched the limits of the ambiguous 1971 FCC
decision that granted it entry into the field. When AT&T denied MCI access to certain interconnections, Saunders argued, it
was because the smaller company had gone well beyond the
original FCC judgment allowing it into the private-line business
between corporate offices. MCI had acted unfairly, Saunders
continued, not AT&T.

The defense rested its case on May 23, and Judge Grady dismissed the jury for a week. Then, on June 11, after rebuttal testimony from several MCI witnesses, Grady read his two-hour
charge to the jury. There was a great deal for them to consider.
During 54 days of testimony, some 70 witnesses had taken the
stand, filling 12,000 transcript pages, not including the thousands of documents entered into the record as exhibits and evidence.

Three days later twelve jurors walked back into the wood-paneled courtroom of the Dirksen Federal Building in Chicago. It was 8:45 on a stormy, muggy June evening — Friday the thirteenth, to be exact — when Judge Grady asked the jury foreman, an engineer who worked for International Harvester, to read the verdict. Twenty-five-year-old James G. Barone complied. AT&T, the jury had agreed after two days of deliberation, was guilty on ten of the fifteen counts brought against it by MCI. The award, reached after less than twelve hours of discussion, a whopping $600 million, one-third less than MCI had requested. Grady immediately dismissed the jury and left the courtroom for several minutes. When he returned, the judge huddled with attorneys from both sides. "Well," he told them, "let's just do it." He ordered the clerk to enter a trebled award. The final damages: $1.8 billion, the largest amount in U.S. antitrust history.

Bill McGowan was ecstatic over the verdict. "The case was clear and we had good evidence," he told reporters in Washington. As a result, he added, "Smaller companies that get stepped on by larger corporations will come to realize that it is not true that nothing can be done. Big companies can no longer beat them by 'deep-pocketing' them." Also jubilant was Jenner & Block, and for good reason. The law firm stood to gain 5

> *If a general wins a battle, it cancels all other errors and miscarriages.*
>
> —Niccolò Machiavelli

percent of all damages in excess of $20 million, on top of a basic $3.5 million fee for handling the case. If the full award was upheld despite appeals through the courts, the Chicago law firm could end up with an astonishing $93 million.

At AT&T a spokesman immediately branded the verdict and award "inconceivable," and George Saunders blamed the verdict on the backgrounds of the jurors. Only three of them were college graduates, and, Saunders stated, they were the only ones "who could understand accounting and economics." Back at 195 Broadway, however, a lot of the blame was being pinned on Saunders himself. Since graduating from law school in 1959, he had never faced a jury. He had made a name for himself in a series of staff positions, including clerking for Supreme Court justice Hugo Black. Saunders refused to take the blame, and the Chicago attorney persuaded Bell executives not to accept defeat. On AT&T's behalf, he filed a written motion to vacate the jury's verdict, but in late July Judge Grady refused. Saunders then took the case to the Seventh Circuit Court of Appeals in Chicago, attempting to get the verdict and award overturned. No one expected AT&T to pay up at any time soon. Its appeal would take years.

The jury's verdict grabbed headlines across the country. All of a sudden, people had heard of MCI. At the time, MCI was available in seven cities, and in a few days, on July 12, the company would take its biggest step yet, offering the service to consumers in the biggest market of all, New York. MCI used the same commercials in New York that it had in Denver, but this time it had credibility. TV viewers knew it had gone up against AT&T and won.

The verdict also gave MCI a shot in the arm on Wall Street. During 1980, the company's stock rose from a low of $5.00 to just under $14 a share by the end of the year. Fortunately for McGowan, investors weren't just pinning their hopes on the outcome of the court case. In fact, MCI was starting to show just how profitable long-distance service could be. For the first six months of 1980, the company made a $9.2 million net profit, more than double what it earned during the same period a year earlier. And overall revenues were up by nearly two-thirds, to $90 million.

As 1980 drew to a close, Bill McGowan was a happy man. MCI was positioned to somersault into the ranks of the Forbes 500. Personally, McGowan was making nearly half a million dollars a year in salary. And the surge in the company's stock price was a windfall. With nearly three million shares, the fifty-two-year-old entrepreneur's estimated net worth on paper had soared to more than $40 million. For the first time in years, the debonair, lifelong bachelor was taking off more time, squiring a series of beautiful women around the social circuit in Washington and

New York. He had also begun to toy with other pastimes, purchasing a series of ramshackle buildings in the fashionable Georgetown section of Washington and undertaking the ambitious task of restoring the nineteenth-century edifices.

At the company's annual meeting in early 1981, McGowan was visibly buoyant about MCI's future. The company's acronym, he told shareholders, no longer stood for Microwave Communications, Inc. From now on, he avowed, MCI would stand for Money Coming In. Those three letters could also stand for More Changes Inside. Even as the company was spending $100 million a year to beef up its microwave network and the executive staff grew, McGowan was slow to change his occasionally autocratic style of management. Often accused of surrounding himself with yes men, the MCI boss good-naturedly denied it. "It's not true," he would joke. "When I tell them to say no, they say no."

McGowan was well aware that MCI was poised for a period of major growth in customers and revenues, however, and it would require more than just yes men to manage the company's rapid expansion. So he brought in a number of key managers from the outside, including Orville Wright (no relation to the pioneers of flight) as president and McGowan's number two. After stints in senior positions at IBM, Amdahl, RCA, and Xerox, Wright was the consummate administrator. In contrast to the street-smart Irish entrepreneur who was his boss, Wright was low-key, affable, and patrician, MCI's careful planner to McGowan's seat-of-the-pants visionary. Unlike McGowan, Wright became worried about a very basic element of the business, customer satisfaction.

In 1981 MCI was signing up residential customers at the phenomenal rate of ten thousand a month. But subscribers were also canceling at an alarming rate, eight out of a hundred each month. The reasons for the high rate of attrition were obvious. Home users didn't take easily to dialing twenty-two digits to get a long-distance number, compared with eleven for using AT&T. Other users discovered that they had signed up for a service that didn't yet reach towns the customers wanted to call frequently. Still others were dissatisfied with the poor audio quality of MCI's connections, which usually resulted from the inferior interconnection equipment supplied by Bell. There were also frequent billing errors because MCI hadn't invested in computerized data banks to speed up the process of sorting out the payments process. Finally, many subscribers signed up for MCI and agreed to pay the $5 or $10 monthly charge, but then didn't use the service. In mid 1981 MCI reckoned that just over 11 percent of its "subscribers" weren't making a single call on the system. Over time, they, too, would cancel.

The defections weren't apparent from the steady flow of revenue and profit reports emanating from the company to shareholders and the financial community. After all, new customers were signing up in droves, quickly replacing the lost accounts. Inside MCI, though, the cancellations were a source of disagreement. Some executives, notably Martha Hiney, a former secretary to McGowan who later took charge of customer service administration, said that MCI had to put more emphasis on keeping existing customers rather than earmarking most of the marketing dollars to generating new business. Ed Gallagher at Ally & Gargano agreed. Once consumers tried the product and found it wanting, he postulated, it would be extremely difficult to win them back. Negative word-of-mouth about the long-distance service would, in turn, undercut the message in future TV commercials. But the company's top sales manager, senior vice president Carl Vorder Bruegge, claimed that it was easier to sign up two new customers than to keep one and sign up one new one. McGowan sided with Vorder Bruegge. While admitting that MCI should be spending more money on customer service and new computer systems, especially to sort out the billing problems, McGowan was reluctant to emphasize painstaking service at the expense of aggressive sales. He feared such a shift would be tantamount to forsaking growth. "I'm open to new ideas [on customer service]," McGowan wrote in a confidential memo to Vorder Bruegge, Hiney, and other senior managers in late 1981. "But I also see other priorities. During the next year, for example, we will spend more than $200 million expanding our network, and may well face a capacity problem before we have to deal with a levelling off of the growth rate of our customer base."

What McGowan didn't put into that memo was his principal reason for stressing sales over service. The potential market for long-distance phone service generated $40 billion annually, and AT&T still had more than 90 percent of the market. McGowan wanted to position his network as the only full-scale alternative to Ma Bell at a time when such other rivals as ITT, Sprint, and Western Union were coming on strong as well. But McGowan felt there was plenty of room for the newcomers, who would also help MCI chip away at AT&T's dominance in the field. Besides, he knew that MCI had a major competitive advantage over the likes of ITT and Sprint. The new rivals had lagged behind MCI in building microwave facilities and in many cases were actually leasing lines from AT&T to transmit their own calls. It would take years for them to catch up to MCI in terms of the "reach" that their networks provided to customers.

The major exception was Satellite Business Systems (SBS), which was gearing up to offer long-distance service via satellite rather than microwave transmission. SBS was in fact McGowan's own brainchild. MCI created the company in 1972, just as the microwave business was getting started. SBS was initially a joint venture among MCI, Lockheed, and Comsat. Later MCI sold its one-third stake in the venture to IBM, and Lockheed sold out to Aetna Life and Casualty. With new backing from such large corporations, SBS had the financial clout to challenge MCI in the major metropolitan markets it would serve.

MCI never let up on its aggressive construction strategy. The top thirty cities were on line by late 1981, and McGowan was determined that every phone in America have access to the MCI network within two years. MCI was positioning itself as a leader among alternative long-distance services, and it had to solidify that position quickly to take advantage of a rapidly changing telecommunications industry that McGowan was certain would eventually lead to the breakup of Ma Bell. What McGowan didn't anticipate was how quickly the breakup would occur.

* * *

Bill McGowan was also starting to see that MCI had to control its own destiny in other ways. He figured that with big names like IBM entering the long-distance phone business, MCI would soon become a prime target for a takeover. In late summer the MCI boss attended an industry conference in Los Angeles sponsored by Drexel Burnham Lambert, a co-underwriter of MCI's various public offerings. Also attending the conference were some of the savviest takeover "artists" around — men like David Mahoney, who built up the Norton Simon conglomerate, and Saul Steinberg of the Reliance Group, who had made aborted passes at Paine Webber while succeeding in a series of smaller hostile bids. MCI's shares were trading at around $10 apiece, more than double the level six months earlier.

But McGowan knew his company was still undervalued, given the fast clip at which MCI's revenues and profits were growing. And he knew it would be only a matter of time before corporate raiders figured it out, too. The specter of any of these high-powered investors taking over the company, then selling it off to the highest bidder among MCI's rivals, galvanized McGowan into action. Once back in Washington, he asked general counsel John Worthington to work up a series of amendments to the company's by-laws that would make a hostile takeover virtually impossible, provisions that would provide shark repellent, as the antitakeover technique would soon come to be called.

The concept didn't originate with McGowan. But with his close links to Wall Street, the MCI chairman was among the first corporate leaders to use the simple but revolutionary technique. Boiled to the essentials, the new statutes meant that any takeover attempt had to be approved by the holders of 80 percent of all MCI stock. In addition, they gave MCI's board of directors the authority to issue new preferred stock in the event of a takeover attempt, which meant that management could dilute the number of outstanding shares and make it even harder for a bidder to reach the required 80 percent. McGowan demanded, however, that MCI refuse to include "golden parachute" provisions in the new amendments. Senior executives at a few companies had begun awarding themselves huge severance payments in the event of a corporate takeover. The parachutes were ostensibly supposed to scare off hostile bidders, but in practice they simply made a takeover a bit more expensive — and the ousted executives a whole lot richer. McGowan considered such provisions offensive and not in the best interests of shareholders, although his concern wasn't entirely unselfish. After all, McGowan was also the biggest individual shareholder in MCI.

The shark repellent provisions became more and more necessary as MCI moved into 1981. The company was signing up twenty thousand new residential customers each month despite increasing competition from rival services. MCI's expansion plans were also bearing fruit, with the service accessible from more than 60 percent of all phones in the country. In January 1981, MCI pulled off a marketing coup of sorts. American Express agreed to offer to its upscale cardholders, on an experimental basis, an MCI Expressphone service at a 20 percent discount off the basic rate. Fliers were mailed out to 120,000 cardholders, nearly 4 percent of whom immediately signed up. For MCI the test represented a sweet victory. MasterCard, VISA, and Sears had all rebuffed McGowan's original offer to go into a similar venture before he approached American Express, the company he thought was least likely to take the gamble. Now, given the results of the dry run, American Express was eager for more. The following October the two firms announced a long-term, full-scale, and exclusive arrangement for offering MCI to American Express cardholders.

Even without the American Express deal, MCI was starting to show just how much money it could make in the long-distance arena. Profits after tax were up nearly 60 percent for fiscal 1981, to $21 million. In the following three months MCI did even better, making a profit of more than $10 million in a single quarter. Not surprisingly, Wall Street sat up and took notice. MCI shares had doubled in value in 1980 to close at $13.25; then, by June 1, just five months later, MCI's stock was trading at a lofty $23.75, and it was regularly the most actively traded company in the over-the-counter market.

Against that backdrop Bill McGowan convened the company's 1981 annual meeting on July 30 in Washington. The stock price, however, wasn't the only thing to cheer about. With profits growing by leaps and bounds, MCI had recently paid off the last $15 million it owed to its bank creditors. Most of the company's debt was in longer-term, less-onerous corporate paper — bonds and debentures — and McGowan knew he could get any new funds MCI needed from other bond investors now that Wall Street had decided MCI would be a permanent member in the long-distance game. Shareholders thus obliged when McGowan asked them to approve the by-law amendments to thwart an unwanted takeover. He also announced that the U.S. General Services Administration had awarded MCI a $10.9 million contract, the largest federal communications contract ever awarded to a Bell System competitor. The federal government, too, seemed to have acknowledged the strength of MCI's position as a stable number two to AT&T.

There were other reasons for McGowan's manifest optimism. Before the annual meeting, MCI had reached an unprecedented agreement with a small, non–Bell phone company in Iowa. The Northern Iowa Telephone Company had only twenty-one hundred customers, most of them farmers in the western part of the state. Without any reason to curry AT&T's favor, the tiny utility offered its customers a choice: they could tap into the AT&T network by dialing a "1" and then the area code and telephone number, or they could go through MCI by dialing a "5" and following it with the same seven-digit number. For the first time, it was just as easy for a caller to use MCI as AT&T, and MCI quickly signed up over 20 percent of Northern Iowa's customers, more than five times its national market share. McGowan was under no uncertainty about the potential impact of the Iowa experiment. "History will show this agreement as a watershed in our relationship with the telephone industry," he told a press conference in Washington. "The whole industry knows this is possible." The Iowa test had shown that local phone companies could easily figure out a way to give customers a choice when they dialed long distance.

After that success it was clear that MCI was around for good. It was a heady realization even for perennial optimists like

McGowan, and it provided the company with a respite from the day-to-day legal and financial scrambling that had characterized its workings in the 1970s, allowing its top man to step back and focus on the future. For the first time since 1968, money wasn't really a problem. MCI could go on building microwave towers without worrying about how to pay for the expansion. But within two years the service would reach every phone in America, and what then?

Bill McGowan and Orville Wright wanted to expand the company's service overseas, but regulated telephone monopolies in most countries didn't allow it. What's more, AT&T maintained an absolute stranglehold over international phone lines out of the United States. On at least two occasions, McGowan had seriously considered starting up an international data service but decided against it. But now that money was no longer a major issue, MCI could look around for an existing network to buy, and Wright took the lead. In early September he picked up the phone and called an old friend and colleague from his Xerox days, David Kearns, the company president. Wright asked Kearns whether Xerox was interested in selling its Western Union International (WUI) subsidiary. The major international transmitter of data via telex and cable had been spun off in 1963 by Western Union, which continued to operate domestically. WUI operated independently until 1979, when Xerox bought it in the hope of challenging the two biggest companies in the international market, ITT and RCA. WUI operated in more than one hundred countries worldwide. Initially MCI would be able to use the service only for data transmission, but eventually WUI could become the basis of an international version of MCI.

Barely one week after Wright's phone call, Kearns called back to say that Xerox *was* interested in selling WUI, with one caveat: other companies were vying to acquire the unit as well. Among them were GTE, Tymshare, and Western Union Corporation, which had expressed interest in regaining its old subsidiary after receiving early word from the Justice Department that it would no longer consider the combined operation in breach of antitrust law. Still, Xerox, having had a change of heart about its push into the suddenly crowded communications business, was willing to sell to the highest bidder. Almost immediately, investment advisers for the two companies, Goldman, Sachs for Xerox and Salomon Brothers for MCI, entered negotiations to put a price tag on the deal. And on December 15, MCI announced that it was buying WUI, subject to FCC approval, for $185 million in cash, roughly $25 million less than Xerox had paid for the company just two years earlier.

The WUI deal was another feather in MCI's cap. As 1981 drew to a close the company's stock was trading at $35 a share, nearly triple the level of a year earlier. Between October and December MCI showed a profit of $26.5 million, more than five times the amount it had earned in the same quarter of 1980. The earlier fears that MCI wouldn't be able to generate the profits necessary to keep expanding the network were erased, at least inside the company. Ironically, AT&T was losing business to MCI while making money on the long-distance carrier. For every dollar it took in, MCI was paying out twenty-one cents to Bell System companies for hookups between home phones and the MCI network. In late 1981, AT&T asked federal authorities for permission to double those charges, a move that would have eradicated MCI's profits overnight. But without warning, AT&T was on the defensive.

On the morning of Friday, January 8, 1982, news began to spread around Washington that something was stirring at the Justice Department. By noon it was official: the U.S. government was dropping the two largest antitrust cases in history. In a ten-year-old case against IBM, which involved charges that the computer giant had used its size and power to run rough-shod over smaller companies in the industry, the suit was simply dropped for lack of clear evidence that IBM had breached antitrust law.

As for AT&T, antitrust authorities weren't so lenient, negotiating a tough consent agreement. Behind closed doors, Justice Department officials and AT&T representatives worked on a plan that would resolve Justice's desire to see Bell divest its regional operating companies without crippling the remaining

AT&T operations — and without crippling the nation's telephone system itself. The pact was complex and would require months of further refinement, but it meant that AT&T would ultimately be chopped up into little pieces as of January 1, 1984, two years away.

By settling the case out of court, AT&T averted any formal finding of guilt in the government's litany of antitrust allegations. And since September, when Judge Harold Greene had denied AT&T's motion to dismiss the Justice Department case altogether, it looked very much as if Ma Bell would be found guilty. Greene, after all, publicly stated that the government's case against AT&T had demonstrated "that the Bell System has violated antitrust laws in a number of ways over a lengthy period of time." If a jury agreed, Judge Greene would almost certainly have meted out a sentence that involved a drastic divestiture program which might have crippled AT&T. Instead, AT&T opted for a Justice Department plan that seemed somewhat more lenient. However, the consent agreement was contingent on Greene's approval, which wouldn't be final until both Justice and AT&T agreed to toughen some of the terms considerably, including provisions to phase out the preferential treatment AT&T wanted to continue receiving from the divested local phone companies.

The decision to break up Ma Bell changed the environment in the telecommunications industry in MCI's favor, and predictably, the first real evidence of that change occurred in a court of law. AT&T had appealed the earlier $1.8 billion judgment in favor of MCI, and after frequent delays, a federal appeals court was ready to render its verdict. When it did, it was a bombshell for both plaintiff and defendant. In a 2 to 1 ruling, the court upheld eight of the ten counts on which the earlier court had found AT&T guilty. As a result, Judge Richard Cudahy ordered a new trial, not to determine guilt, but to reassess how much AT&T should pay in damages. AT&T promptly responded to the appeal decision by claiming victory. The federal appeals court had overturned one of the earlier decisions that AT&T had engaged in "predatory pricing" to damage MCI. After the decision a Bell spokesman called that charge "the heart of MCI's case," adding, "What remains are only minor matters," and insinuating in no uncertain terms that the earlier $1.8 billion would be drastically reduced on retrial.

McGowan got word of the appellate court decision late in the day at MCI's Washington headquarters. Ordering two six-packs of beer and pizza, he and his senior staff stayed for hours to discuss the case's implications. Once again, they knew, MCI would have to wait months, and probably years, for a final decision in the case. But essentially, the court had agreed that the law was on MCI's side. And if AT&T was now expecting a new jury to put a much lower figure on Ma Bell's guilt, McGowan saw at least a chance that the final sum could actually be higher than $1.8 billion. The rapid growth in MCI's revenues and profits since AT&T stopped refusing to provide the crucial interconnections, McGowan reckoned, meant that MCI had been denied substantially more than the company had calculated in its original 1974 petition — as much as ten times more. If AT&T wanted to prolong the fight by appealing the $1.8 billion judgment, McGowan and his colleagues agreed, MCI would simply up the ante. The court battle would be costly, but McGowan was convinced that any final judgment would more than make up for it. Meanwhile, AT&T would remain on the defensive, diverted from the day-to-day task of competing with MCI.

MCI could afford to up the ante. For years, there had been doubts that it could survive in its battle with Ma Bell. Now the company was not only surviving, it was prospering. For the fiscal year that ended in March 1983, MCI's revenues topped $1 billion for the first time ever. Profits more than doubled, to $171 million. And by mid 1983, Wall Street was putting a price of $50 on each share of MCI stock, despite two stock splits in the previous twelve months. Anyone who invested $20 in MCI shares in 1977 would, only six years later, own $1,000 worth of MCI stock, and the future was reassuring. In the short run, MCI knew that the breakup of AT&T would lead to higher interconnection rates because local phone companies would probably start charging MCI and other rivals the same fees for local hookups as they did AT&T. As a result, the gap in long-distance fees between AT&T and the "alternative" carriers would narrow. An August 1983 ruling to that effect by the FCC sparked a sell-off in MCI stock, sending its share price down nearly $5.00 in a single session. But McGowan had estimated that hookup rates would increase anyway. The only question that remained was, By how much? MCI also expected AT&T to become a stronger competitor after the breakup, if only because it could no longer sit back and let its monopoly do the talking. The giant bureaucratic organization that had thrived under regulation would have to become more marketing oriented, competing for customers rather than simply servicing them.

On the other hand, MCI was positioned strongly for the long haul. In its consent agreement with AT&T, the Justice Department ordered complete and equal access for all long-distance services. In other words, the spun-off Bell regional operating companies would have to give AT&T, the long-distance subsidiary after the breakup, as well as MCI and other carriers absolutely equal treatment when it came to hooking up local phone users to the long-distance service of their choice. The equal-access rule would apply to most of the country by late 1985, and it was mandatory nationwide by September 1, 1986. The delay was permitted by the Justice Department only to allow the regional phone companies to invest in the necessary equipment and systems.

For MCI, equal access would be the ultimate test of its mettle. "Under these new ground rules we are very confident of our ability to compete head-to-head against AT&T because of our greater efficiency in use of capital and greater productivity on the part of our people," MCI's financial officer Wayne English wrote in an internal report soon after the Justice Department announcement. "We believe there is no question that we can construct, maintain and operate a system considerably more efficiently than can AT&T." MCI was saying that if all else was equal, it could operate more cheaply, and therefore charge customers less, than AT&T.

But when customers were offered the chance to route their long-distance calls via AT&T or MCI, which would they choose? It wasn't long before MCI would find out. On January

1, 1984, the Bell System was formally disbanded, and MCI's world changed overnight. The ties that bound most of the country's local phone companies to AT&T were severed. The battle that had begun and dragged on in the courts would continue. But with the prospect of absolutely equal access within two years and a more competitive climate in the long-distance business, MCI would have to redouble its marketing efforts.

MCI fired the first major salvo the following spring. On April 12, Bill McGowan flew to Charleston, South Carolina, then made his way to the Marriott Hotel downtown. There, in front of two dozen reporters, he offered a brief description of MCI and quickly segued into his pitch. "Charleston is right now," McGowan said, "for this point of time, the center of the communications world." Charleston, after all, would be the first local phone company of the now-defunct Bell System to offer equal access, and everyone was vying for a piece of the $10 million pie that local residents spent each year on long-distance calls. AT&T was operating a round-the-clock phone solicitation service; Sprint, recently taken over by GTE, was there; Satellite Business Systems was touting its new Skyline service for home phones; and several much smaller rivals were making similar pitches. The previous night MCI had dropped more than thirty thousand letters in the mail, one to every family in town. Said McGowan, with characteristic bluntness, "We want your business."

And business he got. Within months MCI quadrupled its number of customers in Charleston, taking a full 15 percent of the market despite competition from AT&T and nearly a dozen other rivals. The proportion would have been even higher, except for one last vestige of preference for AT&T despite the equal access rule. If customers had no preference, the Charleston phone company would continue to route long-distance calls via AT&T.

It was the last major vestige of *un*equal access, and McGowan began to pressure the FCC for a change in the rules. At the beginning, the federal agency balked. The local phone companies were not obliged to provide equal access until the end of 1986. But in March 1985, the FCC began its own internal review of the system that allowed AT&T to keep long-distance customers by default if they didn't specifically choose an alternative carrier. AT&T executives objected, charging that any attempt to "divert" customers to other carriers "would usurp customers' rights to make their own decisions and coerce them into a process not of their own making."

In late May the FCC handed down its verdict. It ordered local phone companies to end the practice of assigning customers to AT&T by default. The decision was unanimous and in sharp contrast with the federal agency's earlier penchant for siding with the former Ma Bell. Under the FCC order, those customers who did not specifically sign up for a long-distance carrier would be assigned to AT&T, MCI, and alternative carriers according to the same percentages of the market that each company garnered among phone users who *did* sign up. It was a clear victory for MCI and a defeat for AT&T, although the full extent of the victory wouldn't be clear until equal access was in place throughout the country in 1987.

The FCC decision provided a welcome boost to spirits at MCI headquarters. Forty-eight hours earlier, on Tuesday, May 28, a federal jury in Chicago had shattered MCI's hopes of winning an even larger award than the overturned $1.8 billion antitrust verdict. The jury had been asked to review earlier testimony and assess the proper amount of damages AT&T owed to MCI. McGowan was asking for triple the earlier award, and AT&T wanted to pay nothing. In the end the jury agreed that AT&T had tried to disrupt MCI's operations in the early 1970s, but it refused to go along with McGowan's argument that the disruptions had postponed MCI's entrance into the residential long-distance market, thereby costing the company billions of dollars in forgone revenues. Instead the jury awarded MCI $37.8 million, an amount that was tripled to $113.4 million under antitrust statute.

Rather than appeal the decision, McGowan decided to accept the defeat, although the defeat did leave MCI more than a hundred million dollars richer. Besides, MCI's second antitrust suit against AT&T was still pending. The first suit had involved only Bell's actions before 1973; the second asked for more than

$1 billion in damages that McGowan claimed resulted from anticompetitive practices in the mid seventies as MCI began to market Execunet.

On the day of the verdict the price of MCI stock fell more than 20 percent. But Bill McGowan did not panic, for reasons that outside investors would have been hard pressed to understand at the time. A surprise was in the works, a deal that would dramatically change the shape of the long-distance business while solidifying MCI's claim to the number two spot behind AT&T.

Surprise lies at the foundation of all military undertakings.
—Karl von Clausewitz

The deal began to take shape over lunch at IBM headquarters in Armonk, New York, in late 1984. At McGowan's request, IBM vice chairman Paul Rizzo hosted a session to explore future business links between IBM and MCI. With AT&T moving quickly into the computer world, IBM was keen to expand its own presence on AT&T's turf, telecommunications. It had recently bought a sizable minority stake in Rolm Corporation, a Silicon Valley manufacturer of advanced phone-switching equipment. But its entry in the long-distance market was flagging. Despite its 60 percent stake in Satellite Business Systems, IBM had been unable to coax the satellite long-distance network into profitability, and it looked as though the losses would continue well into the future.

For months into 1985, the discussions went on, McGowan himself frequently making the trek to Armonk. Less than a month after the jury's verdict in Chicago, McGowan and Rizzo jointly dropped their bombshell. On June 25, 1985, they announced a marriage of convenience. IBM bought out the 40 percent of SBS owned by Aetna Life and Casualty and, in turn, agreed to fold the satellite service into MCI. In addition, IBM would pay $400 million, in exchange for MCI debentures. The deal was complicated but not the result: IBM would henceforth own 18 percent of MCI, with an option to acquire up to 30 percent of the company's shares.

For its part, MCI got to keep its independence; it added a

major new vehicle to expand its long-distance service through SBS's satellite network; and the long-distance carrier now had the financial backing that only a $45 billion company like IBM could provide. For McGowan, the merger with IBM was pure vindication. The entrepreneur was relinquishing his position as MCI's largest shareholder, but as part of the deal, IBM had insisted that McGowan continue running the combined operation. "After all," he told reporters on June 25, only half in jest, "IBM has admitted that it doesn't know as much about running a long-distance business as I do."

If the claim seemed like a boast, it was well deserved. Once and for all, McGowan had dispelled any lingering doubts that MCI was a viable, long-term competitor for AT&T in the long-distance telephone business. By late 1986 most long-distance customers across the country had cast their ballots for AT&T, and more than one out of ten picked MCI, despite the declining cost differential of under ten cents on the dollar between the two carriers. At the same time, with equal access votes out of the way, McGowan would no longer have to spend heavily on attracting residential customers. The focus of MCI's battle with AT&T would shift back to where it started: big business, the 1 percent of customers who accounted for almost half of all the dollars spent on long-distance phone bills each year.

To do that, McGowan knew, required a wholesale shift in the way MCI sold its service. The irreverent Joan Rivers commercials touting MCI's lower rates were no longer relevant. From then on, the company would have to push the reliability of the MCI network and its ability to service large accounts. To show he meant business, McGowan ordered a complete review of MCI's advertising strategy. This time Ally & Gargano had to compete against stiff competition for MCI's future business. Its principal competitor was Benton & Bowles, the agency that had handled MCI's business-to-business advertising during the long, lean years when Ally & Gargano was earning most of MCI's advertising dollars with campaigns aimed at individual subscribers.

It came as a shock to Madison Avenue when MCI announced in early 1976 that, from then on, Benton & Bowles (later merged into D'Arcy Masius Benton & Bowles) would handle all of the company's advertising needs. Ally & Gargano, the company that played a critical role in turning MCI into a household acronym, was out of the picture. MCI, McGowan was signaling, would no longer have the residential customer in its marketing sights.

On June 1, 1986, MCI pulled its Joan Rivers commercials off the air. The company's new battle cry, "Because we compete, you win," went up the same day. The TV spots featured what one advertising columnist called "killer-instinct." MCI representatives engaged in feverish, sweaty duels of fencing, judo, and racquetball. One by one, they vanquished their adversaries before MCI's new tag line appeared in a voice-over: "Communications for the next hundred years." And just to make sure the analogy wasn't lost on anyone, the conquered rival in each commercial subtly sported the label AT&T.

Bibliography

Clausewitz, Karl von. *On War*. Translated by Michael Howard and Peter Paret. Princeton: Princeton University Press, 1976.

Foch, Ferdinand. *The Principles of War*. Translated by J. de Morinni. New York: H. K. Fly Co., 1918.

Liddell Hart, Basil Henry. *Strategy*. Second revised edition. New York: Praeger, 1972.

Macchiavelli, Niccolò. *Discourses*. Translated by Leslie J. Walker. London: Routledge and Kegan Paul, 1950.

Mahan, Alfred Thayer. *Naval Strategy*. Boston: Little, Brown, 1911.

Moltke, H. Karl von. *Strategy: Theory and Application*. Westport, Conn.: Greenwood Press, 1971.

Musashi, Miyamoto. *The Book of Five Rings*. Translated by Nihon Services Corporation. New York: Bantam Books, 1982.

Sun Tzu. *The Art of War*. Translated by Samuel B. Griffith. London: Oxford University Press, 1972.

For a summary in English of works by Alfred von Schlieffen, Henri de Jomini, C. P. Ardant du Picq, and others, see Earle, Edward Mead, ed. *Makers of Modern Strategy*. Princeton: Princeton University Press, 1971.

Doug Ramsey, based at various times in Brussels, London, Tokyo, and New York, has written about business and the international economy for fifteen years. He began writing for the *Washington Post*, later joining the staffs of *The Economist* and *Newsweek* magazine. In 1982 he left his position as business editor of *Newsweek* to become editor and executive producer of *Business Times*, winner of the 1984 Award for Cable Excellence (ACE) as the best news program on cable television.

Mr. Ramsey lives in New York, where he is a correspondent for NBC News, covering business for *NBC Nightly News* and the *Today* show.